Religion long forgotten

Religion long forgotten

The importance of religion
in education towards civil society

edited by
Dariusz Stępkowski
Andrzej Murzyn

impuls

Cracow 2014

Reviewers:
Almazbek Beishenaliev, visiting professor
at Johns Hopkins University in Baltimore
Tadeusz J. Zieliński, associate professor
at Christian Theological Academy in Warsaw

Proofread:
Agnieszka Boniatowska
Tomasz Piast-Szlubowski

Desktop publisher:
Katarzyna Kerschner

Cover design:
Ewa Beniak-Haremska

ISBN 978-83-7850-682-9

Oficyna Wydawnicza 'Impuls'
30-619 Kraków, ul. Turniejowa 59/5
phone/fax: (12) 422 41 80, 422 59 47, 506 624 220
www.impulsoficyna.com.pl, e-mail: impuls@impulsoficyna.com.pl
Edition I, Cracow 2014

Table of Contents

Part II
Practical Approach

Introduction

End of religion?

The prophesied epoch of the end of religion did not come, and it is doubtful that it will ever happen. During a ceremony on 14 October 2001 in which the Peace Prize of the German Book Trade was awarded at the Paulskirche in Frankfurt am Main, Jürgen Habermas delivered a speech in which he focused attention on the need for shaping a new attitude towards religion in contemporary culture. By the way, it was shortly after the terrorist attacks by Islamic fundamentalists on the World Trade Center in New York. He described the new attitude as 'secularization in postsecular society'.[1] It would be erroneous to understand this as RESECULARISATION consisting on the coming back to the separation of state and church or, in broader terms, the public and religious spheres. It seems that what Habermas meant was to draw a conclusion from a substantial conditionality of 'a postsecular society which adapts to the fact that religious communities continue to exist in a context of ongoing secularization'.[2] Therefore, the new kind of secularisation is neither an antidote to religion nor a tool used for marginalising it from social, political, economic or cultural spheres. Habermas argues that it is quite to the contrary, as beliefs based on faith have the same right to exist in the public space as those referring to the secular worldview.

Habermas in his speech put forward an interesting view of the dialogue between the religious and non-religious (secular) spheres from the perspective of observers who consciously distance themselves from religion. Paradoxically, from this perspective they can see damage, if not a gap, threatening secular society.

> But only if the secular side, too, remains sensitive to the force of articulation inherent in religious languages will the search for reasons that aim at universal acceptability not lead to an unfair exclusion of religions from the public sphere, nor ever secular society from important resources of meaning.[3]

---

1 J. Habermas, *Faith and Knowledge*, [in:] *The Future of Human Nature*, trans. from German W. Rehg, M. Pensky, H. Beister, Polity Press, Cambridge 2003, p. 103.

2 *Ibid.*, p. 104.

3 *Ibid.*, p. 109.

Suggesting a dialogue, he demands from non-religious members of society not only an attempt to regard those who have different religious beliefs as equal, but to also understand the arguments presented by them in typically religious language. Furthermore, in order to enable dialogue, the latter should be capable of presenting their opinion in secular language. Only if the rule of reciprocity is kept can the 'cooperative translation of religious content' (translation based on Polish)[4] be possible.

The dialogue between the religious and non-religious spheres has always been polemical and full of tensions. Thus, Habermas defines the pivotal role of democracy in this way: 'the neutral state [...] abstains from prejudging political decisions in favour of one side or the other'.[5] In this light, religious impartiality cannot be confused with the state's inactivity in matters concerning faith; just the opposite – involvement that does not favour one side or the other.

The situation presented above provokes reflections on the significance of religion in education for secular civil society. This raises a number of questions. What is the role of religion in the upbringing and education of the young generation? Should interference in religious beliefs be allowed? Is the inheritance of religious traditions needed, and who is responsible for that? Do the church and other religious communities have the right to participate in creating public education?

The above list could be extended to infinity. The aim of the editors and authors who submitted their papers for publication was not to provide full characteristics of religion's contributions to social, political and cultural life. The main concern was to highlight the topicality of the existence of religious questions in broadly understood contemporary discourse on education, culture and politics. In this context it is necessary to reconsider the concept of 'forgetting' as it is applied to the presence of religion in individual and social life.

Forgetting of religion towards the culture of remembering

In order to explain the phenomenon of forgetting and its specific dialectics, it is necessary to refer to a book by Paul Ricoeur entitled *Memory, History, Forgetting* (*La memoire, l'histoire, l'oubli*). The three parts unfold along a course of mnemonic phenomena. On this basis Ricoeur examines the development of mnemonic traces and methods of recording them as well as fading memories and the loss of memories. This course crosses with another one created by Ricoeur that uses the concept of forgetting. He distinguishes in it the steps that form a certain

---

4   J. Habermas, *Wierzyć i wiedzieć*, trans. from German M. Łukasiewicz, 'Znak' 2002, 9, p. 15.
5   *Id., Faith and Knowledge, op. cit.*, p. 105.

A dozen authors expressed their willingness to present a critical consideration in this field. Most of them come from Poland. However, several authors come
from the following countries: Canada, Czech Republic, Germany, Sweden and
Japan (one from each county).

The monograph consists of two parts. The first part, titled *Basic Concepts*,
contains six chapters. In the first one, Dariusz Stępkowski addresses the subject
of Non scholae sed vitae: Bildung, *Religion and Society in Herbart's & Schleiermacher's Pedagogical Theories*. Despite the fact that both mentioned in the title
authors lived a long time ago – at the turn of the 18th and 19th centuries – their
observations are still valid. In addition, they were both protagonists of general
pedagogy as an independent scientific field. The article is divided into three parts.
In the first one, the term *Bildung* is explained by using the metaphor of a ship.
Bildung is the individual process as well as the social process of becoming an individual, in which the combination of teaching-learning plays the key role. In the
second, Herbart's views on the 'place' of religion in *Bildung*, as well as in school
education, are presented. The third part of the article revolves around Schleiermacher's theory of *Bildung*. According to this theory, the environment for becoming a human being is social reality divided into four major communities: country
(German: *Staat*), science (German: *Wissenschaft*), church (German: *Kirche*), and
independent social organizations (German: *freie Gesellichkeit*). Becoming aware
of the similarities and differences between them induces the re-evaluation of the
current attitude toward religion that is unjustly eliminated from widely understood social discourse.

The author of the second chapter, titled *The Personalistic Ethics as a Support
for the Civil Society*, is Andrzej Murzyn. Referring to some outstanding representatives of contemporary Personalism, the author aims to prove the thesis that the
personalistic ethics can be very conducive to the development of a civil society. It
is only through making people sensitive to the needs of human person that each
of us can protect contemporary societies from many dangerous ideologies such
as the ideology of happiness and the ideology of eliminative materialism. These
ideologies separate man as a citizen from a man as a person.

The author of the third chapter is Mirosław Patalon who focuses on the question expressed in the title *Is Process of Theological Education Useful For the Civil
Society*. The article deals with the possible application of process theology for
interreligious dialogue and building the atmosphere of respect for other cultures
and ways of living. The focus on the thought of John B. Cobb, Jr. results with the
idea of the pedagogy of ecumenism understood as the way to protect the society
from the domination of any specific religion. This approach is meant to support
the idea of civil and free society.

The next chapter contains a comprehensive study by Uto Meier *Why Democracy Cannot Work without Unconditional Values: On Moral Boundaries and*

Ethical Guideposts for a Post-secular Generation. The Professor of religious education at the Catholic University of Eichstätt-Ingolstadt (Germany) intends to show
why democracy runs the risk of losing its very essence without being grounded
on unconditional, i.e. non-relativisable ethical norms, and why a vital democracy
thus requires a religiously founded 'commitment to unconditional values', even
though a plethora of decisions may be made by weighing up competing interests
by means of a 'trade-off' ethics.

   *Partnership in Innovation for the Good of Civil Society: A New Conceptual
Framework* is the title of a chapter by Dariusz Góra-Szopiński of Nicolaus Copernicus University in Toruń (Poland). The author addresses the perspective of future
development of the social doctrine of the Catholic Church. After the experience
of excessively separating the Church from the wicked world outside, and then
equally excessively reopening the Church to the outside without much care for
keeping their own identity, Catholic Christians have come to the age of developing a balanced and mutually fruitful relation with the outside world. If any
good initiative arises in the outside world, Christians should feel motivated to
get interested in promoting the good purpose. If the task of innovation currently
won the prime time of the debates within the global civil society, Christians shall
recognise their part in bettering the world, yet without forgetting their distinctive
role of apostles of the Gospel.

   The last chapter of this part of the monograph is authored by Mariusz Sztaba,
an lecturer from John Paul II Catholic University of Lublin (Poland). Titled *Postmodernism and Neoliberalism as Modern Ideologies Threatening Today's Civic
Society: An Educator's Afterthought in Terms of Catholic Church Social Doctrine*,
the article raises the idea of civic society. Among the many aspects of social life
undertaken by the Catholic Church in its social doctrine, there is the problem of
civic society. The Church focuses on this reality not from an organisational, or
legal point of view, but rather focusing on its ontological and ethical/moral foundation and meaning. That's why this problem is subject to profound analysis, in
terms of the phenomena and situation which affect the foundation and meaning
of civic society. They are, among others, postmodernism, which negates the legitimacy of all principles, propagating cognitive, axiological and theological relativism, and neoliberalism, which strives for social life marketisation, by submitting it
to the logic of supply and demand, and by the degradation of a citizen to the level
of a consumer. These are today's dominating ideologies, related to globalisation
processes. The author of this paper indicates the abovementioned threats in terms
of the Church's social doctrine concerning civic society.

   The second part of the monograph, *Practical Approach*, consists of more
practical papers outlining the problems of religious education in educational institutions and family, as well as in the broadly understood public sphere. The part
consists of six chapters. In the first one, Toshiko Ito, Professor of pedagogy at Mie

University in Japan, addresses the relation between the *Nuclear Disaster and the Quest for Meaning in the Civil Society: Religion in Japanese Educational Institutions Today*, in the article of the given title. According to the author, the Japanese tend to take an increasing interest in religion today, despite their self-description as non-religious. Public education has also laid increasing stress on religion for the last decade. This change was promoted by both policy makers and scholars. While policy makers increasingly seek to foster civil virtues by putting religious sentiment and religious knowledge on the curriculum, scholars increasingly try to foreground the benefits to civil society which they claim to accrue from the academic study of religion. The common ground lies in the assertion that the value of religious sentiment must be recognized by the public. This article examines the changes made to the 'Government Guidelines for Teaching' for primary education and secondary education, and the new systems to qualify the religious literacy for undergraduate or graduate school. This tendency is viewed in light of Niklas Luhmann's prediction of a flourishing of non-institutional religion, which, however, stands no chance of realisation unless the policy makers and scholars' curtailment of the free exercise of religion is overcome.

The author of the second chapter is a Polish specialist on the issue of Islam, Eugeniusz Sakowicz. His article titled *The Resolution of Conflicts and Building Unity* addresses the Muhammed Fethullah Gülen's Pedagogical Proposition. According to the author, interreligious dialogue plays a major role in the process of communication between people of various world views. This dialogue is a form of getting to know each other, which helps to overcome stereotypes and resentments that always create a mistaken, untrue reality. The fate of the world depends on dialogue which cannot exist without responsibility. Gülen's pedagogy of dialogue relies on responsibility. Built on the basis of his philosophy, words and actions, this pedagogy is not a utopian vision. Nor does it constitute a new trend or direction within pedagogical sciences. It is founded on a profound belief in God, fidelity to the Islamic creed, openness to the world and its challenges, and deeds conforming to God's will. Gülen's pedagogy of dialogue is aimed at the intellectual and spiritual renewal of Muslims. Without this renewal, any changes in the life of society will be a mere illusion.

In the third chapter, Nazila Isgandarova of Wilfrid Laurier University (Canada) provides the *Critical Analysis of Feminist Movements of Azerbaijani Muslim Women during Russian Colonialism*. The article presents a brief historical narrative of the secular Muslim feminist movements in Azerbaijan in order to examine the effects of patriarchy and colonization on the status of women and the emergence of Muslim feminist movements in Azerbaijan. Resources have been taken from the writings of the Muslim men and women in Azerbaijan. The paper provides a general background on the secular feminist movements of the Muslim women and their struggle for equality in Azerbaijan in order to answer the question: 'What role did the struggles of particular women (e.g. the struggles against colonialism and patriarchy) play in the emergence of the feminist movements in Azerbaijan?'. The paper also deals with the emergence of the feminist movements and provides examples of the achievements and struggles of the Azerbaijani feminists, especially in terms of women's right to education.

In the next chapter, Ewa Teodorowicz-Hellman of Stockholm University (Sweden) analyses the *The Place of Christianity in Swedish Primary Schools. Historical Outline and Contemporary Social Discourse*. The author shows how the place for Christianity in Swedish elementary school curricula has changed over time. The presented analysis reveals that religious education classes have evolved from lessons devoted to Luther's teachings to lessons about world religions and ethical issues. It appears that religious education classes in their present form, including their teaching content, are the result of Sweden's advanced laicisation and secularisation, but also, to a large extent, the result of Swedish society's shift towards multiculturalism and relativism of values. Faith is becoming more and more an individual and private issue in Sweden. The social discourse on religious traditions as an element of the activity of contemporary Swedish schools presented in the paper indicates how certain organisations are attempting to eliminate Christian elements from the education of the young generation, often without realising that they constitute an inherent element of Swedish culture.

The second last chapter is authored by a Czech lecturer Zuzana Svobodová of Charles University in Prague (Czech Republic), and titled Paideia *as Care of the Soul – the Potentials of Contemporary School*. In her article, Zuzana Svobodová focuses on the concept of *paideia* and its transformations in the history of education. She compares the objectives of education in the works of Plato, Aristotle and other prominent personalities in the development of the theory of education as well as the objectives of education in the current official EU documents on education. Tensions between civil education and religious education are shown with the help of specific historic examples with the aim of demonstrating the necessity of a philosophical approach towards the theory of education and the need of philosophical education itself. As an example taken from practice, the Ethics and Religious Education in European Schools (*Schola Europaea*) project is analysed. The author is convinced that the concept of *paideia* is based on radical openness, which may be twofold: on the one hand, an openness of the educator/teacher (educator) and the one who is educated, while on the other hand, their ability to dialogically listen to what enables the very fact of dialogue. This is why she considers it crucial that educators and teachers be led to the essence of philosophy of education as part of their professional training.

The last chapter of the second part of the monograph has been written by Katarzyna Wrońska of Jagiellonian University in Cracow (Poland). The author addresses the phenomenon of *The Polish Family in View of the Idea of a Civil Society*.

The text is an attempt to describe the relationship between the family and civil society in the Polish reality. It asks about the reasons for the low level of public trust and describes the related Polish familism. It analyses the role of the Catholic Church as an institution permanently present in the lives of the majority of Polish families and still the authoritative institution. For this reason it indicates the possibility and the need to build a Christian civil society in Poland. A new formula of the parish as the community of communities is its exemplification. The activities of the Church in the area of civil society is an attempt to strengthen the bridging capital in Poland that enables new social ties and commitments based on a mutual trust, benevolence and a cooperation with others to be built.

Acknowledgements

The editors would like to thank all the authors who have contributed to the preparation of this monograph. We extend our thanks to the reviewers: Almazbek Beishenaliev, visiting professor at Johns Hopkins University in Baltimore (U.S.) and Tadeusz J. Zieliński, associate professor at Christian Theological Academy in Warsaw (Poland). Their critical remarks contributed to the increase of the professional quality of our work.

14 June 2014
Dariusz Stępkowski
Andrzej Murzyn

Bibliography

Assmann J., *Cultural Memory and Early Civilization: Writing, Remembrance, and Political Imagination*, trans. from German D.H. Wilson, Cambridge University Press, New York 2011.

Habermas J., *Faith and Knowledge*, [in:] *The Future of Human Nature*, trans. from German. W. Rehg, M. Pensky, H. Beister, Polity Press, Cambridge 2003.

Habermas J., *Wierzyć i wiedzieć*, trans. from German M. Łukasiewicz, 'Znak' 2002, 9.

Michalski J., *Edukacja i religia jako źródła rozwoju egzystencjalno-kognitywnego. Studium hermeneutyczno-krytyczne*, Nicolaus Copernicus University Press, Toruń 2004.

Ricoeur P., *Memory, History, Forgetting*, trans. from French K. Blamey, D. Pellauer, University of Chicago Press, Chicago 2004.

PART I
BASIC CONCEPTS

Dariusz Stępkowski
Cardinal Stefan Wyszyński University
Warsaw (Poland)

Non Scholae Sed Vitae:
Bildung, Religion and Society
in Herbart's & Schleiermacher's Pedagogical Theories

A popular Latin adage, which states that one does not learn for school but for life, is used in the title of this paper. It reflects the common and current belief that a school education is not an end in itself, but is supposed to serve the needs of life. Though the adage had been known for a long time, it was written down in 1806 by Johann F. Herbart in the publication *Allgemeine Pädagogik aus dem Zweck der Erziehung abgeleitet* (translation of the title based on Polish: *General Pedagogy Deriving from Educational Purposes*).[1] The author transformed the words of the ancient writer Seneca the Younger, who, in one of his letters, wrote something completely opposite: *non vitae, sed scholae discendum*[2] – we do not learn for life, but for the school.

Providing the final answer to which of the two above versions is right is not the aim of this article. Instead, the purpose is to think about the relation that unites education (German: *Bildung*[3]), religion, and society in both school (*schola*) and life (*vita*). The foundation of this analysis will be the pedagogical theories of J.F. Herbart and F.D.E. Schleiermacher. The latter was a German pedagogue and

---

1 J.F. Herbart, *Pedagogika ogólna wywiedziona z celu wychowania*, trans. from German T. Stera, Żak, Warsaw 2007, p. 122.

2 Seneca Minor, *Epistula CVI*, [in:] *id.*, *Epistulae morales ad Lucilium*, lib. XVII, ep. CVI, available at: http://www.thelatinlibrary.com/sen/seneca.ep17-18.shtml (accessed: 21.02.2014).

3 Due to terminological specificity of the notion 'education', German term *Bildung* will be used. D. Benner, *Pedagogika filozoficzna a badania edukacyjne. Próba zrekonstruowania ich powiązań w kontekście aktualnych tendencji rozwojowych*, trans. from German D. Stępkowski, 'Kultura i Wychowanie' 2014, 1.

theologian as well as a philosopher. Despite the fact that they both lived a long time ago – at the turn of the 18th and 19th centuries – their observations are still valid. In addition, they were both protagonists of general pedagogy as an independent scientific field.[4] Its birth is closely related with the emergence of a new social group, the post-feudal (republican) society, which not only chronologically preceded modern democracy, but also anticipated its ideological side.[5] This state of affairs is not accidental, and it is reflected in the concept of *Bildung* developed by both authors. Analysing this concept opens the path to a new outlook on the presence of religion in education and public life.

In the first part of this paper, the term *Bildung* will be explained by using the metaphor of a ship. This notion should not be considered as the equivalent of English terms 'education', 'learning' or 'instruction', which are the names for different types of actions referring to the education system and its institutions.[6] *Bildung* is the individual process as well as the social process of becoming an individual, in which the combination of teaching-learning plays the key role. In the second part of this paper, Herbart's views on the 'place' of religion in *Bildung*, as well as in school education, will be presented. The third part of the article will revolve around Schleiermacher's theory of *Bildung*. According to this theory, the environment for becoming a human being is social reality divided into four major communities: country (German: *Staat*), science (German: *Wissenschaft*), church (German: *Kirche*), and independent social organisations (German: *freie Gesellichkeit*). Becoming aware of the similarities and differences between them induces the re-evaluation of the current attitude toward religion that is unjustly eliminated from widely understood social discourse.

Bildung – education of lifelong learning?

The term 'lifelong learning' is commonly used in the English language. The word 'learning' indicates that modern society, which eagerly calls itself 'a knowledge society', is interested in learning or instruction, rather than in *Bildung*.[7] It seems that the difference is insignificant, but this is not true. The term *Bildung* is

---

4   J. Oelkers, *Die große Aspiration: zur Herausbildung der Erziehungswissenschaft im 19. Jahrhundert*, Wissenschaftliche Buchgesellschaft, Darmstadt 1989.

5   S. Filipowicz, N. Gładziuk, S. Józefowicz, *Republika: rozważania o przemianach archetypu*, Institute of Political Studies of the Polish Academy of Sciences, Warsaw 1995.

6   P. Hogan, *Recent Trends in Anglophone Philosophy of Education*, [in:] S. Sztobryn, E. Łatacz, J. Bochomulska (eds.), *Filozofia wychowania w XX wieku. Zarys problematyki*, University of Łódź Press, Łódź 2010, pp. 9–14.

7   *Knowledge society*, available at: http://en.wikipedia.org/wiki/Knowledge_society (accessed: 20.02.2014).

not only reserved for the German language. It refers to an entirely different way of looking at learning and school education, as well as to the relation between the individual and society. That is why modern times (the presence belongs to them!) differ greatly from the former eras of development in Western civilization. The most apparent factor is the role of the process of *Bildung* and, consequently, the importance of school education. By using the ship metaphor, Herbart presents a new view on this state of affairs in *Allgemeine Pädagogik*.

In the introduction to the fourth chapter of the second part of *Allgemeine Pädagogik*, Herbart compares the student to the ship, 'whose exquisitely masterful and fine construction is designed to obey the waves and the wind in the best possible way' (translation based on Polish).[8] However, this ship 'waits a helmsman, who will steer it to the destination and will give it direction' (translation based on Polish).[9] Those influenced by the stereotypical interpretations of Herbartian pedagogy will be wrong when thinking that the person meant in the quote is a tutor who will control the students. The awaited helmsman is not a tutor, but the students themselves, who – whether they like it or not – must at some point steer their lives by themselves. In order to not be surprised by this, they should be prepared for that moment by a proper school education. It cannot be mere 'instruction' or one-way 'teaching', but it must be educative instruction (German: *erziehender Unterricht*). What is the idea behind it?

The main purpose of educative instruction is achieving student autonomy both in thinking and in actions. Herbart uses another metaphor to describe the way to make it happen. The students, similar to a magnificent sailing ship, are constantly influenced by two external (i.e. outside-of-school) factors: 'the current' (translation based on Polish)[10] and 'the wave of life' (translation based on Polish).[11] They push them, frequently against their will, 'to the arena of life' (translation based on Polish).[12] Student helmsmen must, in order not to lose direction, under the burden of these factors, learn to lie at anchor from time to time and reflect on themselves and their aspirations. The meaning of the term *Bildung* and the function of learning life autonomy, which Herbart attributes to school, will now be analysed. It was pointed out in the introduction that Herbart starts with the postulate made during his times towards school: *non scholae, sed vitae*! However, he distances himself entirely from this statement, as he holds a completely opposing view. Herbart remarks:

---

8 J.F. Herbart, *Pedagogika ogólna…, op. cit.*, p. 71.
9 *Ibid.*
10 *Ibid.*, p. 127.
11 *Ibid.*
12 *Ibid.*

School is leisure, and leisure is the right kingdom of speculation, taste and RE-
LIGION. Life – it is the surrender of the sympathetic observer to the external wave of
active and passive living [translation based on Polish, highlighted by D.S.].[13]

It is clear that, in Herbart's view, school has nothing to do – at least in the
foreground – with the building or educational institution; it is a state of soothing
the thoughts which enables reflection. A human being has to

[...] go from one [...] to another and regard transitioning from active and passive surrender [to the wave of life] to leisure [school], and the other way round: from leisure
to action [...], as the breath of human soul, the necessity and the sign of health [trans-
lation based on Polish].[14]

'Life should constantly create school' (translation based on Polish),[15] which
is understood as the time to stop and to reflect. Acquiring the ability to think is
probably the most important purpose of a school education. In order to serve the
needs of life (in accordance with the maxim: *non scholae, sed vitae*), a school must
paradoxically train to some passivity – to giving consideration. This is school's
most important input in the process of *Bildung*, understood as the lifelong shaping of a person. Therefore, *Bildung* is neither identified with school education nor
does it end after leaving the institution's building.

Another German word, *Bildsamkeit*,[16] is worth paying attention to, as it is
closely related to *Bildung*. It is commonly believed that *Bildsamkeit* is a strictly
Herbart notion. However, the analysis that has been recently presented by Diet-
rich Benner and Friedhelm Brüggen reveals something entirely different. Modern
German researchers proved that the phenomenon of *Bildsamkeit* is much older
than its notion and it might be traced back to the beginnings of Western European culture.[17] The term did not appear in Europe until the second half of the
18th century.[18] At that time, Jean Jacques Rousseau transformed the French noun
perfectibilité, which had already been used in pedagogy for a certain period of
time. The word derives from the verb *se perfectionner*, which means 'perfecting
oneself, seeking wholeness'.[19] A little later, the term *Bildsamkeit* was coined and

---

13   J.F. Herbart, *Pedagogika ogólna...*, op. cit., p. 125.
14   *Ibid.*
15   *Ibid.*
16   Translates into English as 'flexibility', 'plasticity'.
17   D. Benner, F. Brüggen, *Bildsamkeit/Bildung*, [in:] D. Benner, J. Oelkers (eds.), *Historisches
     Wörterbuch der Pädagogik*, Beltz Verlag, Weinheim – Basel 2004.
18   *Ibid.*, p. 174.
19   D. Benner, F. Brüggen, *Das Konzept der perfectibilité bei Jean-Jacques Rousseau. Ein Versuch,
     Rousseaus Programm theoretischer und praktischer Urteilsbildung problemgeschichtlich und
     systematisch zu lesen*, [in:] O. Hansmann (ed.), *Seminar. Der pädagogische Rousseau*, vol. 2,
     Dt. Studien-Verlag, Weinheim 1996.

Figure 1. Herbart's Tasks of Educative Instruction

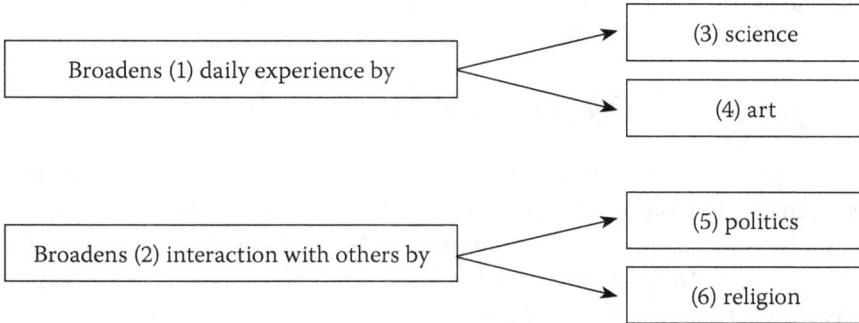

From: D. Benner, *Nieprzemijające znaczenie herbartowskiej koncepcji nauczania wychowującego*, 'Horyzonty Wychowania' 2008, 13, p. 130 (translation based on Polish).

Herbart's famous 'theory of interest' relates closely to educative instruction. According to Herbart, cognition resulting from daily experiences needs to be supplemented with the emphasis on its empirical correctness in the first place, and secondly, with the analysis of its aesthetic relationships.[26] He believes that modern science develops a student's speculation skills,[27] which are helpful in the first case, whereas in the second case art will be useful.[28] The second layer of educative instruction encompasses 'only some aspect of humanity' (translation based on Polish).[29] Apart from initial interaction with others two elements belongs here: first, problems resulting from 'living together' (translation based on Polish),[30] and second, 'their attitude toward The Highest Being' (translation based on Polish).[31] It is noticeable that Herbart meant politics and religion respectively. In the first one,

the student's p... ould 'make an attempt to combine [...] contradictions [between at anchor from time rested in the well-being of the whole' (translation based tion of religion will be dis the purpose of the second one and the way in which it chors – is motivated by the da discussed in this paper.[33] aspect of *Bildung* is determining the mentioned above, it becomes clear that Herbeing). However, determining it requir lates directly to religion. Both functions accordance with the old art of sailing, and (e.g. the North Star), in relation to which it wo coordinates. It is striking that in *Kurze Enzyklop* of the title based on Polish: *Concise Encyclopaea*.

20   D. Stępkowski, *Ukształcalność jako zasada działania edukacyjn...nianego wątku na pod- nej kategorii J.F. Herbarta i jej współczesnej reinterpretacji*, [in:] ...rancis de Sales Scien- A. Famuła-Jurczak (eds.), *Przestrzeń edukacyjna – dylematy, doświa* społeczne, Impuls, Cracow 2010.

of religion – showing the transcendental purpose in the process of *Bildung* and being one of the school subjects – create a homogenous whole.

Bildung – social life – religion

One theme from Schleiermacher's prolific literary legacy will now be discussed: the idea of four major communities. Schleiermacher creates a vision of the ideal social community in *Grundzüge der Erziehungskunst* (translation of the title based on Polish: *An Outline of the Art of Education*) written in 1826. This community is the background of his pedagogical discussion and it is describes as follows:

> The more perfect social life becomes, the less purposeful and methodological [pedagogical] support it requires, since four major life communities are morally perfect, [that is], there exists harmony between THE COUNTRY, THE CHURCH, THE SOCIAL LIFE AND KNOWLEDGE AREA. They have all become ONE AND THE SAME CUSTOM [translation based on Polish, highlighted by D.S.].[34]

Unfortunately, the reality of everyday life contradicts the existence of such unity and harmony. The elements of the public sphere that were mentioned before – the country, the church, science, and independent social organizations (nowadays called non-governmental organizations) – not only compete with each other, but frequently they eliminate each other. This tendency is particularly evident in reference to the Church or – in a broad sense – to the religious sphere. According to Schleiermacher, lack of harmony between individual spheres poses a danger of developing 'a caste system'.[35] Such system is not a primary threat to the political systems of developing countries, but to the post-feudal (republican) societies, which Schleiermacher calls civil societies (German: *Bürgergesellschaft*). In *Grundzüge der Erziehungskunst*, Schleiermacher claims that the disharmony in civil society lies in 'rationing the participation of individuals in the entirety of the country cooperation' (translation based on Polish).[36] Nowadays, this phenomenon is known as social exclusion, and it presents itself as hindering or preventing some social groups or their individual representatives from participation in public life. Schleiermacher observes this with special concern in reference to the younger generation, which is reflected in the common saying 'the son will not make a step further than the father'[37] (translation based on Polish). As a result of

---

34   F.D.E. Schleiermacher, *Grundzüge der Erziehungskunst (Vorlesungen 1826)*, [in:] *id.*, *Texte zur Pädagogik*, vol. 2, Suhrkamp, Frankfurt am Main 2000, p. 58.

35   *Id.*, *Vorlesungen zur Pädagogik (1813-1814)*, [in:] *id.*, *Texte zur Pädagogik*, vol. 1, Suhrkamp, Frankfurt am Main 2000, p. 241.

36   *Id.*, *Grundzüge der Erziehungskunst...*, *op. cit.*, p. 149.

37   *Ibid.*

social exclusion, instead of developing, the son reproduces and petrifies the existing social and political relations,[38] without leaving any 'room for communicating the thoughts and their impact' (translation based on Polish).[39]

The caste system presented above distorts the understanding of *Bildung*, as it brings it down to squeezing an individual into the prearranged social framework of life. According to Schleiermacher, the purpose of the modern interpretation of the process of *Bildung* is entirely different. In order to present this issue properly 'the relation between what is universal and what is individual'[40] (translation based on Polish) needs to be analysed. In this context, *Bildung* has a twofold task: 'perfecting for community'[41] and 'developing personal "separateness"'.[42] Therefore, a clash of these two tendencies occurs in *Bildung*. The first one is socialization, which is the preparation to live in four communities mentioned above. The second one is individuation, whose priority is personal development ('separateness'). On this basis, Schleiermacher makes a distinction between UNIVERSAL (social) and INDIVIDUAL (separate) aspects of the process of *Bildung*. The agreement between these aspects is to be reached through education. In spite of appearances, this is not an easy task.

In *Grundzüge der Erziehungskunst*, Schleiermacher states

> Education [...] has to lead people, as a work of art, to full participation in the life of four major communities: the country, the church, independent organizations and science. [...] The point is to eliminate the contradictions between them. Yet, it is not uncommon to come across the real or ostensible DISHARMONY. [...] What shall we say, then? What attitude should we have when conflicts occur between major communities? [translation based on Polish, highlighted by D.S.].[43]

When analysing this issue, Schleiermacher begins with considering two solutions. He describes the first one as follows:

> Let us say that education should instruct teenagers in order to improve them, so that they are suitable for the country as it is. This would lead to nothing but immortalising the imperfection and no PERFECTING would occur. The generation of adolescents would enter this imperfection with their whole being and with full consent; we would find ourselves in a new contradiction [translation based on Polish, highlighted by D.S.].[44]

---

38 *Ibid.*, p. 174.
39 *Ibid.*, p. 257.
40 *Ibid.*, p. 72.
41 *Ibid.*
42 *Ibid.*
43 *Ibid.*
44 *Ibid.*, p. 33.

The alternative possibility is equally fatal:

> Since if it [education] was mostly about educating the reformers, then it [the task] is in striking contradiction with the idea that they should first be familiarised with what exists, before they proceed to a dangerous attempt to interfere with or change the existing state of affairs.[45]

Finally, the author suggests the following solution:

> Finding the right solution forces us to integrate two extreme views. [...] It might seem that RETAINING AND PERFECTING lead to contradictions, but that only happens when we stop at dead letter. [...] Education should be organized in a way that would enable the youth to become more skilful at entering what already exists, as well as to be prepared for active involvement in the occurring possibilities of perfecting things. The more perfect the manner in which it happens, the more contradictions disappear [translation based on Polish, highlighted by D.S.].[46]

The proposed dialectics of retaining-perfecting is central to Schleiermacher's discussion on modern education.[47] However, the reader might ask: 'What does these dialectics have in common with religion?'.

The explanation of this final issue requires a short introduction. Schleiermacher's peculiar deconstruction of social life into four spheres establishes that the unifying force which integrates society is the concept of Good. Despite the fact that 'good' is a classical term in practical philosophy (ethics), Schleiermacher reinterprets it in a modern way.[48] The category that becomes the most important is 'attitude' (German: *Gessinung*). In Schleiermacher's view, attitudes are what makes people different and they should become the main subject of pedagogical impact. The point is not to standardise the attitudes, which is characteristic of both old and modern ideologies, but to shape ETHICAL ATTITUDES that are orientated toward the common good. This orientation is what sets the process of *Bildung* apart both in individual and social dimensions. Schleiermacher is convinced that *Bildung* will lead to the progress of humanity only when each one of four forms of social life offers its input to the formation of ethical attitudes. In this context, religion plays a significant role that is worth considering.

In the oft-quoted *Grundzüge der Erziehungskunst*, Schleiermacher explains the idea of the common life. Among other examples, he writes:

---

45   F.D.E. Schleiermacher, *Grundzüge der Erziehungskunst...*, *op. cit.*, pp. 33–34.
46   *Ibid.*, 34.
47   W. Schmied-Kowarzik, *Schleiermachers dialektische Grundlegung der Pädagogik als praktischer Wissenschaft*, [in:] K.-V. Selge (ed.), *Internationaler Schleiermacher-Kongress Berlin 1984*, Verlag de Gruyter, Berlin 1985, pp. 778–781; D. Benner, H. Kemper, *Theorie und Geschichte der Reformpädagogik*, vol. 1, *Die pädagogische Bewegung von der Aufklärung bis zum Neuhumanismus*, Beltz Verlag, Weinheim – Basel 2003, pp. 276–280.
48   D. Stępkowski, *Pedagogika ogólna...*, *op. cit.*, pp. 211–219.

We must say that, there is no single action of an individual that is not simulta-neously an action of all people, and there is no action of the whole society that is not an action of an individual human being. What refers to the action is also meaningful for experience, and reciprocal relation in which they [action and experience] occur. If in such community we think about some individual, than this individual's rela-tion to it [the community] is already a certain *continuum*. Even if the individual's action does not enter the whole, [...] it will always places this individual in relation to the community; through active engagement, the activity of all participants will be harmonised in this individual in a manner that will make them practically identical [translation based on Polish].[49]

Undoubtedly, the picture of permeating individual and collective actions has clear 'utopian features'.[50] This might have been the reason why some of the researchers did not notice religion in it. The reason for that is because religion is frequently treated as one of the spheres of common life.[51] Yet in Herbart's view, religion permeates through whole human existence. It is reflected in a famous maxim: 'EVERYTHING WITH RELIGION, NOTHING BECAUSE OF RELIGION' (*alles mit der Religion, nichts aus der Religion*) (translation based on Polish).[52] In ac-cordance with this maxim, religion, 'like holy music',[53] is supposed to accompany all human actions, but it cannot initiate them. It should be sufficient to men-tion military conflicts caused by religious differences, regardless of whether they happened in the past or in modern times. Therefore, 'the competence of religion encompasses the whole area of finiteness and it refers to the relation of a human being to what is infinite [the Absolute]' (translation based on Polish).[54] Yet,

[...] wherever religion goes beyond this perspective and demands the status of the only representative of the whole human *praxis*, different areas of thinking and action are not only deprived of their right to existence, but also religion loses its *proprium*[55]

and contradicts itself.

---

49 F.D.E. Schleiermacher, *Grundzüge der Erziehungskunst...*, op. cit., pp. 157–158.
50 F. Brüggen, *Die Pädagogik F.D. Schleiermachers*, Kurseinheit IV–VI, Fernuniversität–Ge-samthochschule, Hagen 1990, p. 102.
51 *Ibid.*, p. 103.
52 F.D.E. Schleiermacher, *Mowy o religii do wykształconych spośród tych, którzy nią gardzą*, trans. from German J. Prokopiuk, Znak, Cracow 1995, p. 83.
53 *Ibid.*
54 D. Benner, *Kształcenie a religia. Rozważania o ich problematycznym stosunku oraz współczes-nych zadaniach nauczania religii w szkole*, trans. from German D. Stępkowski, [in:] *id., Edu-kacja jako kształcenie i kształtowanie. Moralność – kultura – demokracja – religia*, UKSW Press, Warsaw 2008, p. 131.
55 *Ibid.*

The above statement leads to the following conclusion:

> Religious community must care about developing religious attitudes in younger generations within families, and about supplementing [in school] what was overlooked at homes. Also, everyone should be granted the possibility to understand what appears in the cult, and to participate in [...] religious life' [translation based on Polish].[56]

The ultimate situation will be when 'a Christian attitude spreads everywhere at an even pace' (translation based on Polish).[57] It is by no means about the dominance of the Christian religion, but about Schleiermacher's belief that religion is an indispensible and irreplaceable component of individual and collective life.

Conclusion

Both authors – Schleiermacher and Herbart – present religion (Latin: *religio*) with reference to the etymological meaning of the Latin verb *religare*, that is, 'to bind', 'to bond'. It was in ancient times when 'Lactantius [...] defined religion as the bond of a human being with God'.[58] It should be strongly emphasised that for both authors religion lost the privilege of dominating over other areas of life like politics, economy, art, science or morality. It does not stand in opposition to the need for religion in both school education (Herbart) and in social life (Schleiermacher). Religion is a crucial determinant of the individual and social process of *Bildung*. Bringing this to attention might incline people to reconsider the interdependence between *Bildung*, religion and society, which all blend in modern times.

Bibliography

Benner D., *Kształcenie a religia. Rozważania o ich problematycznym stosunku oraz współczesnych zadaniach nauczania religii w szkole*, trans. from German D. Stępkowski, [in:] *id., Edukacja jako kształcenie i kształtowanie. Moralność – kultura – demokracja – religia*, UKSW Press, Warsaw 2008.

Benner D., *Nieprzemijające znaczenie herbartowskiej koncepcji nauczania wychowującego*, trans. from German D. Stępkowski, 'Horyzonty Wychowania' 2008, 13.

Benner D., *Pedagogika filozoficzna a badania edukacyjne. Próba zrekonstruowania ich powiązań w kontekście aktualnych tendencji rozwojowych*, trans. from German D. Stępkowski, 'Kultura i Wychowanie' 2014, 1.

---

56 F.D.E. Schleiermacher, *Grundzüge der Erziehungskunst...*, *op. cit.*, pp. 129–130.
57 *Ibid.*, p. 30.
58 Z.J. Zdybicka, *Religia*, [in:] Z. Pawlak (ed.), *Katolicyzm A–Z*, Księgarnia św. Wojciecha, Poznań 1982, p. 326.

Benner D., Brüggen F., *Bildsamkeit/Bildung*, [in:] D. Benner, J. Oelkers (eds.), *Historisches Wörterbuch der Pädagogik*, Beltz Verlag, Weinheim – Basel 2004.

Benner D., Brüggen F., *Das Konzept der perfectibilité bei Jean-Jacques Rousseau. Ein Versuch, Rousseaus Programm theoretischer und praktischer Urteilsbildung problemgeschichtlich und systematisch zu lesen*, [in:] O. Hansmann (ed.), *Seminar. Der pädagogische Rousseau*, vol. 2, Dt. Studien-Verlag, Weinheim 1996.

Benner D., Kemper H., *Theorie und Geschichte der Reformpädagogik*, vol. 1, *Die pädagogische Bewegung von der Aufklärung bis zum Neuhumanismus*, Beltz Verlag, Weinheim – Basel 2003.

Brüggen F., *Die Pädagogik F.D. Schleiermachers*, Kurseinheit IV–VI, Fernuniversität––Gesamthochschule, Hagen 1990.

Filipowicz S., Gładziuk N., Józefowicz S., *Republika: rozważania o przemianach archetypu*, Institute of Political Studies of the Polish Academy of Sciences, Warsaw 1995.

Herbart J.F., *Kurze Enzyklopädie der Philosophie aus praktischen Gesichtspunkten*, Schetschke und Sohn, Halle 1841.

Herbart J.F., *Pedagogika ogólna wywiedziona z celu wychowania*, trans. from German. T. Stera, Żak, Warsaw 2007.

Hogan P., *Recent Trends in Anglophone Philosophy of Education*, [in:] S. Sztobryn, E. Łatacz, J. Bochomulska (eds.), *Filozofia wychowania w XX wieku. Zarys problematyki*, University of Łódź Press, Łódź 2010.

Knowledge society, available at: http://en.wikipedia.org/wiki/Knowledge_society (accessed: 20.02.2014).

Oelkers J., *Die große Aspiration: zur Herausbildung der Erziehungswissenschaft im 19. Jahrhundert*, Wissenschaftliche Buchgesellschaft, Darmstadt 1989.

Schleiermacher F.D.E., *Grundzüge der Erziehungskunst (Vorlesungen 1826)*, [in:] *id.*, *Texte zur Pädagogik*, vol. 2, Suhrkamp, Frankfurt am Main 2000.

Schleiermacher F.D.E., *Mowy o religii do wykształconych spośród tych, którzy nią gardzą*, trans. from German J. Prokopiuk, Znak, Cracow 1995.

Schleiermacher F.D.E., *Vorlesungen zur Pädagogik (1813–1814)*, [in:] *id.*, *Texte zur Pädagogik*, vol. 1, Suhrkamp, Frankfurt am Main 2000.

Schmied-Kowarzik W., *Schleiermachers dialektische Grundlegung der Pädagogik als praktischer Wissenschaft*, [in:] K.-V. Selge (ed.), *Internationaler Schleiermacher-Kongress Berlin 1984*, Verlag de Gruyter, Berlin 1985.

Seneca Minor, *Epistula CVI*, [in:] *id.*, *Epistulae morales ad Lucilium*, lib. XVII, ep. CVI, available at: http://www.thelatinlibrary.com/sen/seneca.ep17-18.shtml (accessed: 21.02.2014).

Stępkowski D., *Pedagogika ogólna i religia. (Re)konstrukcja zapomnianego wątku na podstawie teorii Johanna F. Herbarta i Friedricha D.E. Schleiermachera*, Francis de Sales Scientific Society, Warsaw 2010.

Stępkowski D., *Ukształcalność jako zasada działania edukacyjnego. W sprawie zapomnianej kategorii J.F. Herbarta i jej współczesnej reinterpretacji*, [in:] M. Kowalski, A. Pawlak, A. Famuła-Jurczak (eds.), *Przestrzeń edukacyjna – dylematy, doświadczenia i oczekiwania społeczne*, Impuls, Cracow 2010.

Zdybicka Z.J., *Religia* [in:] Z. Pawlak (ed.), *Katolicyzm A–Z*, Księgarnia św. Wojciecha, Poznań 1982.

Andrzej Murzyn
University of Silesia
Cieszyn (Poland)

The Personalistic Ethics as a Support for the Civil Society

One of the representatives of Polish Personalism Karol Górski held the view that every pedagogue[1] should do everything possible to stay in dialogic relationship with his/her pupils and students.[2] Luisa Santelli would say, I believe, that the very essence of the dialogue consists in BEING RESTRAINED IN CONTACTS with others. In other words, the point is that we stay on the outskirts of the OTHER and we do not demand participation in the existence of the OTHER.[3] If the pedagogue moves away from the dialogical relationship with pupils, the belief that 'the truth always finds the way to people's spirit even if they do not want to admit it'[4] will be replaced by all forms of violence and abuse. Personalistic attitude towards education means that pupils and students are allowed to develop their spirituality by themselves. Spirituality must not be regarded as something that can be taught or trained. Karol Górski would say that spirituality is embedded in every person even if he/she does not want to admit it. If you think in terms of personalism, you do not demand any declaration and you do not apply any coercive measures. The point is that the dialogue is not deprived of its religious dimension and does not change into ideological fight in which human person is the main victim. Annihilation of a person means annihilation of culture that is conceived of as 'a peculiar kind of personalization of reality.'[5] When the person ceases to be the deepest meaning

---

1 A pedagogue is much more than a teacher.
2 K. Jodłowska, *Karola Górskiego 'wychowanie personalistyczne'*, [in:] F. Adamski (ed.), *Wychowanie na rozdrożu. Personalistyczna filozofia wychowania*, Jagiellonian University Press, Cracow 1999.
3 G.F. d'Arcais, *Pedagogia della Persona*, Milan 1994.
4 K. Jodłowska, *Karola Górskiego...*, *op. cit.*, p. 213.
5 '[S]zczególny rodzaj personalizacji rzeczywistości' (Cz. Bartnik, *Personalizm*, Czas, Lublin 1995, p. 401).

of human culture – as Czesław Bartnik says – religion and culture split up.[6] Religion then, instead of harmonizing with culture in order to foster its spiritual dimension, becomes its arch-enemy and consolidates dark sides of culture such as intolerance or nationalism. In Bartnik's opinion religion and culture are mutually dependent on each other. Religion without culture is not able to come into bloom and exposes itself to irrationalism and backwardness. Culture without religion is not able to ascend to spiritual heights and becomes hollow. It is the person that is able to prevent the conflict between culture and religion. The religion that respects a person is able to support culture constructively and creatively in order to protect it from becoming the totalitarian one. Such a religion, as I believe, is sure to sustain liberal virtues. If the culture is supported by religion, it will never reduce the human being to a citizen and it will always conceive of him/her as the person which means that it will never deprive them of religious dimension.

There is much to be said for the thesis that the culture open to religious values supports the development of a liberal society rather than hinders it. According to Galston, religion and liberal order can support each other on condition that they do not go to extremes.[7] Religion should defend against thinking in terms of fundamentalism which is conceived of as politicisation of religion. The fundamentalism does undercut the essence of a liberal society. Religion should go beyond INHERENT TRADITIONALISM that uses terms such as GODLESS or SINFUL and states that – as Galston puts it – everything that is not accepted on the basis of such criteria can be outlawed. Religion should lean toward FUNCTIONAL TRADITIONALISM that recognizes the relationship between certain moral principles and public virtues or institutions on which liberal society is based.[8] It is also very important that liberal theorists are not extremely skeptical about the possibility of state intervention in such areas as moral education or family stability, otherwise they contribute to the undermining of values they themselves would like to support. In my opinion it is mainly the respect for the mystery of person and its spirituality that does unite religion and liberal view of man. What is more, if you have respect for the mystery of person, you have respect for the mystery of social life. Czesław Bartnik is right in saying that one should not forget that there are many things in social life that happen spontaneously and one cannot influence them or they largely get out of our observation. The social life – as Bartnik puts it – has never ceased to be a mystery just like a person.[9] According to American writer Henry Thoreau, there should not be any interpreter between the person and his/her consciousness because it is the principle of divinity that is embedded in every

---

6 Cz. Bartnik, *Personalizm, op. cit.*, p. 401.
7 W. Galston, *Cele liberalizmu*, trans. from English A. Pawelec, Znak, Cracow 1999.
8 *Ibid.*, p. 302.
9 Cz. Bartnik, *Kiedy myślę: naród*, Polwen, Radom 2003, p. 39.

human being.[10] This principle makes it possible for us to be in a personal relationship with God. Unfortunately – as Thoreau concluded – most of the people had been educated, as had been his neighbour who was a wood-cutter:

> He has been instructed only in that innocent and ineffectual way in which the Catholic priests teach the aborigines, by which the pupil is never educated to the degree of consciousness, but only to the degree of trust and reverence, and a child is not made a man, but kept a child.[11]

If you conceive of society in terms of personalism, you will never forget about the difference between individual and person. According to Maritain and Mounier, man as the individual is subordinate to community but man as the person is an end in itself because no value is higher than human person. The community of individuals, all institutions, including the state, should serve person.[12] Bartnik is right in saying that every man exists both in individual dimension and in collective one. Neither of these dimensions may be diminished:

> 'For there would exist neither a genuinely human community without persons nor genuine persons without the community of 'the others', fellow human beings.[13]

It is the personalism that promotes the THIRD WAY that is between radical individualism and extreme collectivism. Bartnik says:

> Community is a co-humanity, co-quest, co-existence of people, co-operation. And it is much more than the accidental reference to some future and uncertain COMMON GOOD.[14]

If you go back to the disruptions of the 1960s in the United States, you may not overlook one of the greatest puzzles of that time: Why did many young people coming from upper classes characterize themselves as 'niggers'? Why were they not satisfied with living in flourishing American capitalism? Why did they become hostile to America? In trying to answer the above mentioned questions, Norman Podhoretz[15] writes that there were three related elements of the culture critique shared by many young people from prosperous American families. First of all – according to Podhoretz –

---

10 J. Cramer, *The Portable Thoreau*, Penguin Books, London 2012.
11 *Ibid.*, p. XXIV.
12 Cz. Bartnik, *Personalism*, 'OK' Tomasz Wiater, Lublin 2000, p. 196.
13 Original text: 'Nie byłoby bowiem zbiorowości prawdziwie ludzkiej bez osób, jak i nie byłoby osób prawdziwie ludzkich bez społeczności "drugich", bliźnich.' *Ibid.*, p. 196.
14 Original text: 'Społeczność jest współ-człowieczeństwem, współ-byciem ludzi, współ-istnieniem, współ-życiem, współ-dążeniem, współ-działaniem. A to jest więcej niż tylko przypadkowe odniesienie do jakiegoś przyszłego i niepewnego "dobra wspólnego"'. *Ibid.*, p. 197.
15 N. Podhoretz, *The Bloody Crossroads. Where Literature and Politics Meet*, Simon and Schuster, New York 1986.

> [...] it was said that a society in which business was the leading species of enterprise put a premium on selfishness while doing everything it could to dampen the altruistic potentialities of human nature. People were rewarded for being selfish and penalized for caring about others; they were encouraged to compete instead of to cooperate.[16]

The society was considered to become more and more brutal and heartless. It was not a society of persons but a society of isolated individuals connected one to the other only by a 'cash nexus.'[17] Secondly, a business civilisation – as Podhoretz says – stimulated material greed which is one of the basest of human passions: 'People grew narrow and gross, incapable of appreciating anything whose value could not be counted in dollars.'[18] The only religion of the individuals living under such circumstances was worship of success. Podhoretz emphasises that these attacks on the individualism and materialism that were characteristic features of a business civilization were rooted in Christianity. He adds that there was the third element of the critique which came from people belonging to secular milieu. They protested against the society that rewarded the lust for money and penalized all the healthier appetites. Podhoretz writes:

> The only pleasure it sanctioned were whatever pleasure might be connected with work, ambition, the sense of having ‹made it› or won out in a brutal competitive struggle.[19]

But the belief in individualism and the other features of liberalism had been weakened very long before the events of the Sixties took place. At the end of the 19th century the belief in the inevitability of liberalism and its sociological validity underwent a serious crisis. Bracher writes:

> This applied not only to economic *laisser-faire* liberalism itself but also to the belief in the political priority of liberty over equality, of the individual over the group. The pressing social problem, the expansion of imperialism, and finally a nationalism that was leading to war were all challenges to political ideas which far exceeded the basic individualist and rational axioms of liberalism.[20]

Bracher adds that it turned out that liberalism and humanism, personal rights and human rights were indissolubly intertwined. It also turned out that the self-interest, happiness and freedom of the individual are as important as caring relations between the individual and his social milieu. Friedrich Naumann stressed

---

16 N. Podhoretz, *The Bloody Crossroads...*, *op. cit.*, p. 118.
17 *Ibid.*
18 *Ibid.*
19 *Ibid.*, p. 119.
20 K.D. Bracher, *The Age of Ideologies. A History of Political Thought in the Twentieth Century*, Methuen, London 1984, p. 62.

the importance of education that should – according to him – be conceived of as not only the enlightenment in the broad sense but also as developing religious sensitiveness to social affairs.[21] At the end of the 19th century many researchers wondered why the belief in man and his potential, the political and moral perfectibility of human systems and the idea of freedom and human rights were significantly undermined. The weaker that belief was, the more realistic became the vision of a totalitarian society.

There is much to be said for the thesis that in the history of Western civilisation there have not been many persons courageous enough to show that third way that personalism promotes – the way between radical individualism and extreme collectivism. Maybe it is because not many persons can tell the difference between community and society. For Personalism, in contrast to socialists and marxists, the community is considered to be 'a social entitativity, complete and general one.'[22] The society is perceived of as the phenomenal, secondary and cultural shaping or embodiment of population element.[23] A society is the subject of research for social science but a community is investigated by social philosophy and social theology. Referring to Pope John Paul II's teachings, Bartnik says that it is the community of persons and not some abstract unity or community in general. It is the communion and more or less advanced communication that is the soul of community.[24] One should never forget that belonging to a community does not arise from the necessity, as for example, in the case of belonging to the state. Belonging to a community – as Bartnik stresses – is based on some choice, freedom, on the spiritual and emotional bond. It is the thinking in terms of personalism that can help people become more and more independent of THE COLD SOCIETY and turn to the WARM COMMUNITY.[25]

Adolf Szołtysek holds the view that the education of man as a person cannot be achieved simultaneously with the education of man as a citizen. He adds that the education of I – MAN AS A PERSON is needed before the education of I – MAN AS A SOCIAL BEING and the education of I – MAN AS A CITIZEN.[26] Referring to St. Augustine's theory, Szołtysek stresses that the human person constitutes THE INNER MAN, the citizen constitutes THE OUTER MAN but the social being bonds THE INNER MAN and THE OUTER MAN together. It means that man as a social being is to realize established ethical norms that are always perceived of as the complement to natural moral values dictated by conscience.

---

21 *Ibid.*, p. 64.
22 '[B]ytowość społeczną, pełną i ogólną' (Cz. Bartnik, *Personalizm, op. cit.*, p. 199).
23 *Ibid.*
24 *Ibid*, p. 200.
25 *Ibid.*
26 A. Szołtysek, *Nieokreślony podmiot wychowania: pytanie o filozofię człowieka*, [in:] F. Adamski (ed.), *Wychowanie na rozdrożu..., op. cit.*, p. 20.

The personalistic ethics is needed in order to protect contemporary societies from many dangerous ideologies, which include the ideology of happiness and the ideology of eliminative materialism. According to the author of an article entitled *On happiness*, Siobhan Lyons,[27] contemporary culture is obsessed with happiness which is very unhealthy in many ways. What happiness does she have in mind? Lyons writes:

> By 'happiness' I mean an ongoing state of contentment and joy in life, or more basically, an experience of pleasure and absence of pain.[28]

She stresses that the message and doctrine of happiness is present in the most spheres of social activities. Referring to Baudrillard, Lyons writes that people are BOMBARDIED by the images that compel them to believe that they are obliged to be happy:

> In advertisements, and not only for skin creams, the key message is if we only purchase the these products or these foods, we will achieve what we dutifully must: contentment.[29]

The new industry described by Lyons as *Happiness Industry* has been invading the societies and made more and more people believe that every unpleasant aspect of life should be dismissed as AN UNNECESSARY SOCIAL EVIL. Lyons shares the opinion of dr. Russ Harris who is the author of the book entitled *The Happiness Trap*. Harris holds a view that

> [...] the growing influence of happiness ideologies and institutions has created a generation of people unable to cope with or even understand the dynamics of grief, suffering and despair.[30]

What is more, the one who is dominated by happiness obsession is not able to understand and manage his/her self and becomes more and more dependent on self-help books that are produced by *Happiness Industry*. The worst of it – if we look at the issue from the educational point of view – is that more and more young people fall into the HAPPINESS TRAP and instead of learning to cope with existential aspects of human life such as fear, sadness, loneliness or boredom, they avoid them and lose their ability to put up with the most mundane problems of life. There is much to be said for the thesis that – as Lyons writes at the end of her article – 'unhappiness is in fact the antidote to existence purely because it opens facets of human psychology and thought otherwise neglected as unnecessary.'[31]

---

27   S. Lyons, *On Happiness*, 'Philosophy Now' 2014, 100.
28   *Ibid.*, p. 28.
29   *Ibid.*
30   *Ibid.*
31   *Ibid.*, p. 31.

What is more, as I believe, unhappiness is needed to open facets of human spirituality. If one wants to avoid being condemned to conventionality, one should realise – Lyons concludes – that 'misery, or at least unhappiness, is an invaluable element of life, and must be embraced as a catalyst of human triumph, insight and critical self-reflection.'[32] It is the personalistic ethics that is able to be a counterbalance to the contentment ideology that seems to be typical of our times.

The ideology of eliminative materialism has been aimed at – as Kevin Roddy says – 'our common-sense psychological theory about ourselves.'[33] This theory is often called FOLK PSYCHOLOGY. The eliminative materialists shared the view that FOLK PSYCHOLOGY should be ultimately reduced or replaced by the matured neurosciences.[34] According to Roddy, there is one major reason for which FOLK PSYCHOLOGY is exceptional regardless of the developments in the field of neurosciences. Roddy says:

> The primary reason I will give for folk psychology's special status is that a quite legitimate interpretation of it and its domain can be made which makes it irreplaceable as long as we wish to treat ourselves and others as intelligent and moral human beings.[35]

Roddy is referring to Daniel Dennett's book entitled *The Intentional Stance*. In Dennett's opinion even if one has a complete physical description of a human being, one will still not have as complete a description of it as one could or would wish to have. Roddy says:

> What would make this description as complete as we could hope possibly for is one which would include, *inter alia*, what can be 'seen' from what Dennett refers to as 'the intentional stance.' This stance refers to such states as 'believing that p,' 'fearing that p,' broadly speaking, all the other states commonly referred to by folk psychology.[36]

One should always have in mind that – as Roddy and Dennett point out – the intentional stance is not reducible to any sort of physical description. It means that it cannot be revised or replaced by neurosciences. Another researcher to whom Roddy refers is Thomas Nagel. Nagel says:

> There are things about the world and life and ourselves that cannot be adequately understood from a maximally objective standpoint, however, much it may extend our understanding beyond the point from which we started. A great deal

---

32 *Ibid.*
33 K. Roddy, *Folk Psychology and the Non-Scientific Reality of Its Domain*, 'Irish Philosophical Journal' 1990, 7, 1 & 2, p. 119.
34 *Ibid.*
35 *Ibid*, p. 122.
36 *Ibid.*

is essentially connected to a particular point of view, or type of point of view, and the attempt to give a complete account of the world in objective terms detached from these perspectives inevitably leads to false reductions or to outright denial that certain patently real phenomena exist at all.[37]

There is one very important remark made by Roddy. The point is that folk psychological concepts are not treated in purely instrumental way. These concepts – as he points out referring to Dennett – refer to real objective patterns in human behaviour, but they are describable only from the intentional stance and not from the point of view of the neurosciences or any other physical science.[38] Roddy is right to say that

[...] if future neuroscientist wishes to treat someone as intelligent and moral, they cannot simply refer to their brain activity. To treat them as a person, the use of folk psychology is unavoidable.[39]

There are some real patterns of human behaviour that can be described only by means of folk psychological terms such as 'belief' and 'desire.' Any attempt to reduce human behaviour to neurosciences, no matter how much progress they have made in understanding of human brain, poses a great threat to human person.

Conclusion

I hope to have proved – at least partly – that one could hardly imagine the development of a civil society without the support of the personalistic ethics. The society – as Ortega y Gasset puts it – is not a kind of association that results from an agreement because every agreement does assume the existence of a society conceived of as the coexistence of people within the certain system of customs.[40] The society can not be programmed or made the subject of a political program because it is based on what Roger Scruton would call a quasi-religious human need for belongingness.[41]

---

37 K. Roddy, *Folk Psychology...*, *op. cit.*, p. 125.
38 *Ibid.*
39 *Ibid.*
40 A. Murzyn, *Edukacja filozoficzna a rozwój społeczeństwa obywatelskiego*, [in:] *id.* (ed.), *Samo-rządność wczoraj i dziś. Wychowanie do społeczeństwa obywatelskiego*, Impuls, Cracow 2011, p. 74.
41 R. Scruton, *Zachód i cała reszta*, trans. from German T. Bieroń, Zysk i S-ka, Poznań 2003.

Bibliography

Arcais G.F. d', *Pedagogia della Persona*, Milan 1994.

Bartnik Cz., *Kiedy myślę: naród*, Polwen, Radom 2003.

Bartnik Cz., *Personalism*, 'OK' Tomasz Wiater, Lublin 2000.

Bartnik Cz., *Personalizm*, Czas, Lublin 1995.

Bracher K.D., *The Age of Ideologies. A History of Political Thought in the Twentieth Century*, Methuen, London 1984.

Cramer J., *The Portable Thoreau*, Penguin Books, London 2012.

Galston W., *Cele liberalizmu*, trans. from English A. Pawelec, Znak, Cracow 1999.

Jodłowska K., *Karola Górskiego 'wychowanie personalistyczne'*, [in:] F. Adamski (ed.), *Wychowanie na rozdrożu. Personalistyczna filozofia wychowania*, Jagiellonian University Press, Cracow 1999.

Lyons S., *On Happiness*, 'Philosophy Now' 2014, 100.

Murzyn A., *Edukacja filozoficzna a rozwój społeczeństwa obywatelskiego*, [in:] A. Murzyn (ed.), *Samorządność wczoraj i dziś. Wychowanie do społeczeństwa obywatelskiego*, Impuls, Cracow 2011.

Podhoretz N., *The Bloody Crossroads. Where Literature and Politics Meet*, Simon and Schuster, New York 1986.

Roddy K., *Folk Psychology and the Non-Scientific Reality of Its Domain*, 'Irish Philosophical Journal' 1990, 7, 1 & 2.

Scruton R., *Zachód i cała reszta*, trans. from German T. Bieroń, Zysk i S-ka, Poznań 2003.

Szołtysek A., *Nieokreślony podmiot wychowania: pytanie o filozofię człowieka*, [in:] F. Adamski (ed.), *Wychowanie na rozdrożu. Personalistyczna filozofia wychowania*, Jagiellonian University Press, Cracow 1999.

Mirosław Patalon
Pomeranian University
Słupsk (Poland)

Is Process of Theological Education Useful for the Civil Society?

The connection between religious paradigms and forms of social life is well described and grounded in both classical scientific works and new research. Also, from a historical point of view, it is beyond doubt that theological concepts caused links between theological concepts and, for example, the sphere of politics. As far as civil society is concerned, we may point out the fundamental change that occurred in Europe during the Reformation. The appearance of Protestant Churches broke the paradigm of epistemological singularity in theology and grounded the path of pluralism and individualism. Later on, Baptist ideas opened the way for the separation of church and state exercised fully for the first time by Roger Williams in Rhode Island. Today, the role of religion and its institutions, along with theological instruction, seems to be very important as a potential factor for creating a positive atmosphere for multilateral respect. Nowadays, even more than in the past, the Western world is a complicated mixture of cultures. Among many other projects that try to harmonize these powers and thus enable the peaceful coexistence of different cultures and religions, there is a concept named the pedagogy of ecumenism based on the process theology of John B. Cobb.

In this paper, I will focus on religious education, which I have been dealing with both as a Protestant pastor and university teacher. In particular, I would like to refer to the summary of my book, *A Pedagogy of Ecumenism. Processuality as a Paradigm for Interconfessional and Interreligious Hermeneutics According to John B. Cobb.*[1] The philosophical and sociological background of the researched

---

1 M. Patalon, *Pedagogika ekumenizmu. Procesualność jako paradygmat interkonfesyjnej i interreligijnej hermeneutyki w ujęciu Johna B. Cobba, Jr.*, University of Gdańsk Press, Gdańsk 2007, pp. 240–243.

problem here is posed in the question concerning the relationship between one-ness and fragmentation in the context of process theology. A historical survey of possible solutions to this problem leads one to consider it as one of the leitmotifs of human reflection across the ages. It also seems central to the philosophy of Alfred North Whitehead, which then became the starting point for the thought of John B. Cobb.[2]

Theological reflection should be preceded by the mention of the major ele-ments of Whitehead's metaphysics (the oneness of reality as well as its dynamism and variability, the integration of apparent antagonisms and contradictions into a single whole). According to Whitehead:

> Turning now to the examination of an occupied event the electron has a deter-minate individuality. It can be traced throughout its life history through a variety of events. A collection of electrons, together with the analogous atomic charges of positive electricity, forms a body such as we ordinarily perceive. The simplest body of this kind is a molecule, and a set of molecules forms a lump of ordinary matter, such as a chair, or a stone. Thus a charge of electricity is the mark of individuality of content, as additional to the individuality of an event in itself. This individual-ity of content is the strong point of the materialistic doctrine. It can, however, be equally well explained on the theory of organism. When we look into the function of the electric charge, we note that its role is to mark the origination of a pattern that is transmitted through space and time. It is the key of some particular pattern. For example, the field of force in any event is to be constructed by attention to the adventures of electrons and protons, and so also are the streams and distributions of energy. Further, the electric waves find their origin in the vibratory adventures of these charges. Thus the transmitted pattern is to be conceived as the flux of aspects throughout space and time derived from the life history of the atomic charge. The individualisation of the charge arises by a conjunction of two characters, in the first place by the continued identity of its mode of functioning as a key for the determina-tion of a diffusion of pattern; and, in the second place, by the unity and continuity of its life history.[3]

It is only against this background that the chief tenets of process theology (pragmatism, panexperimentalism, the relationality of God and other beings and their correspondence to the nature of the world, the atomistic concept of time) may be presented and discussed topically with reference to questions about reli-gious doctrine, the concept of God and man, the nature of the world, the problem of theodicy and the idea of the Holy Trinity.

Doctrinal formulations are not perceived here as an absolute determinant of faith but rather as a socially construed result of its connection with a given

---

2   J.B. Cobb, D.R. Griffin, *Process Theology. An Introductory Exposition*, Westminster Press, Phi-ladelphia 1976, p. 21.

3   A.N. Whitehead, *Science and the Modern World*, New American Library, New York 1948, p. 155.

culture.[4] Process theologians see the justification of this conviction not only in philosophical analyses but also in the Biblical text, particularly in the Old Testament differentiation between priests (preserving the social and theological *status quo*) and prophets (who demanded a change). Therefore, the role of a theologian is about a responsible (i.e. non-revolutionary) transformation of reality through a re-interpretation of the functioning religious symbols in the context of the changing culture. This is how the activity of Moses and Jesus is viewed; this is also the task of their followers, as 'where there is no prophecy, the people cast off restraint'.[5] God is seen as the source of love and the exemplification of metaphysical principles; in Him the a-temporal eternals become facts, which means that reality is not created by Him *ex nihilo* but rather conditioned by Him (*creatio ex Deo*). Cobb, after Whitehead, depicts God as a relational being constantly participating in complementation processes.[6] His creative activity is an example to all other beings. Man's humanity, therefore, should not be considered as a 'given' but as a 'task', because freedom is linked to the responsibility for co-creating history through active multiplication of an individual experience. Significantly, process theologians stress the necessity of the dialogue between religion and science, hence their approval of the evolutionary model of the origins of the world.[7]

The next topic under possible discussion is the pantheistic view of reality, resulting in the concern for nature and, in theology, a shift of the emphasis from theo- and anthropocentrism toward the sacredness of Life and the ecological awareness.[8] This leads to certain repercussions in Cobb's ethical thought: in the idea of ecojustice and the paradigm of adventure and joy of life as a starting point in the quest for specific ethical assertions.[9] In the processual perspective, however, these assertions are always local and temporal because of the freedom and activity of the relationally situated ethical subjects. In this system, God is no longer an omnipotent decision-maker responsible for the condition of the world but rather a co-creator of history who offers His help, which in the opinion of process theologians is the only solution to the theodicy problem. Thus, the sense of life lies in the very existence on this earth and not in the anticipation of the ephemeral heavenly reality; consequently, the paradigm of certainty of salvation, typical of Evangelical Christianity, is replaced by the paradigm of the hope of

---

4 M.H. Suchocki, *God, Christ, Church. A Practical Guide to Process Theology*, Crossroad, New York 1989, pp. 3–11.

5 *Proverbs* 29:18, NRSV.

6 See A.N. Whitehead, *Process and Reality*, Macmillan, New York 1929, pp. 225–257.

7 J.B. Cobb, *Christ in a Pluralistic Age*, Westminster Press, Philadelphia 1975, pp. 220–227.

8 Ch. Birch, J.B. Cobb, *The Liberation of Life. From the Cell to the Community*, Cambridge University Press, Cambridge 1981, pp. 199–200.

9 J.B. Cobb, *Sustainability. Economics, Ecology, and Justice*, Orbis Books, Maryknoll 1992, p. 21.

salvation, which in Cobb's opinion stimulates Christians to get actively and crea-tively involved in the socio-cultural life of the contemporary world.[10]

The theological buttressing of such an attitude is the person of Jesus Christ as described in the creed of the Chalcedonian Council – the true God and concur-rently true man, with the two natures not confused but united in one person and one hypostasis:

> We, then, following the holy Fathers, all with one consent, teach men to con-fess one and the same Son, our Lord Jesus Christ, the same perfect in Godhead and also perfect in manhood; truly God and truly man, of a reasonable [rational] soul and body; consubstantial [coessential] with the Father according to the God-head, and consubstantial with us according to the Manhood; in all things like unto us, without sin; begotten before all ages of the Father according to the Godhead, and in these latter days, for us and for our salvation, born of the Virgin Mary, the Mother of God, according to the Manhood; one and the same Christ, Son, Lord, On-ly-begotten, to be acknowledged in two natures, INCONFUSEDLY, UNCHANGEABLY, INDIVISIBLY, INSEPARABLY; the distinction of natures being by no means taken away by the union, but rather the property of each nature being preserved, and concurring in one Person and one Subsistence, not parted or divided into two persons, but one and the same Son, and only begotten, God the Word, the Lord Jesus Christ, as the prophets from the beginning [have declared] concerning him, and the Lord Jesus Christ himself has taught us, and the Creed of the holy Fathers has handed down to us' [highlighted by M.P.].[11]

This ideal harmony of the reality in Jesus is a complete exemplification of process principles.

Process theology – conceiving of God and the world in a permanent organic relationship – implies an active participation of believers in the social life. Cobb argues:

> [...] because all that I am and do is taken up into the divine life along with all the consequences of my acts in the lives of others, I cannot escape the seriousness, the importance, of how I use my freedom. I see the truth of the idea that everything I do to my neighbour I do also to God. I can experience God's acceptance of my efforts, even when they fail. Because the Consequent Nature of God takes up into itself all that I am and do and all the consequences of my life, I must also recognize that my failure to respond forever forecloses some possibilities, and that the injuries I inflict on others cannot be undone. Whitehead was sensitive to an objection that might be raised at this point. What would it really mean for God to include forever all the suffering and sin of human history? Would it mean that even in God there is no redemption? Whitehead's response was to consider how in human experience there could be a kind of redemption of past suffering and sin. The consequences of

10   J.B. Cobb, *Liberal Christianity at the Crossroads*, Westminster Press, Philadelphia 1973, p. 107.
11   *Christian Classic Eternal Library*, available at: http://www.ccel.org/ccel/schaff/creeds2.iv.i.iii.html (accessed: 14.08.2013).

my past suffering and sin remain in my experience now, but it is possible that they have been so transmuted through my growth and repentance as to enrich rather than degrade my present life. Whitehead envisions that in the divine life, far more than in the human, there is a redemption of the evil of the world, a redemption which does not remove its evil, but which includes it within a whole to which even human evil can make some positive contribution, however limited. God suffers with us, but the suffering does not destroy God as it can destroy us. The relevance of Whitehead's thought for eschatology needs further exposition. In the first place, his position provides no grounds for doubting the possibility, even the likelihood, that we human beings will destroy ourselves. For this reason it cannot assure us of the meaningfulness of our actions by pointing toward a future Kingdom of God on this planet. On the other hand, Whitehead by no means precludes the possibility of drastic changes for the better taking place in the future. There is no inevitability about our imminent extinction. There is no special likelihood that the patterns of future events will continue those of the recent past. The course of life on this planet has involved many drastic changes, and there is no reason to suppose that it has now arrived at permanent stability.[12]

This issue should be discussed against the background of the changes in the contemporary culture largely affecting the internal structure of the Church as well as its message and social status. In particular, this refers to the complementariness as the gnoseological principle as well as catholicity understood as a partnership of the dialoguing traditions. The calling of the Church is to initiate changes in the world; these, for the most part, are generated in dialogue with other religions and philosophical systems. In this respect, theology fulfils a role similar to that of art: constantly looking for new means of expression, it liberates and transforms human reality.[13] The calling of a Christian, then, is not religious activity; Christ must not be a character absolutising the culture but instead a power transforming the actual world with the whole array of its problems. Among the most urgent ones are those related to the progressive degradation of the natural environment and the atomization of social life. Cobb attempts to present a solution through his idea of Christian communitarianism in which health, work, education, safety, and other earthly needs are integral parts of the salvation project carried out by religions. In light of this, the Church should be THE VANGUARD OF THE NEW AGE, as well as in the field of economy. Cobb criticises what he views as the neo-colonial politics of the West (particularly the United States) toward the rest of the world. Social relationships, so far regulated by the interests of a small group

---

12 J.B. Cobb, *Process Theology as Political Theology*, available at: http://www.religion-online.org/showchapter.asp?title=3035&C=2540 (accessed: 14.08.2013).
13 J.B. Cobb, *Christ in a Pluralistic Age, op. cit.*, p. 40.

of decision-makers, should be based on neighbour solidarity, the model of which may be found in the Old Testament community of Israel.[14]

The subject of process pedagogy should begin with a presentation of the chief principles of American Pragmatism because of its direct connection with the idea of the interpenetration of religious traditions and theological concepts, regarded by Cobb as a necessary catalyst of development, both in the dimension of a single human being and the whole society. The concepts of reality as a dynamic collection of interactions occurring between the participants, the open (non-determined) world, the relational character of the awareness (soul) and the being (body), the complementariness of apparently mutually exclusive notions and phenomena, and viewing truth in terms of everyday life seem common to both pragmatism and post-Whiteheadian processualism.[15] So the vision of education is based on the idea of intertwining perspectives and a maximally broad spectrum of worldviews; in addition, the legitimacy of the Enlightenment purpose of social progress is questioned. Cobb demonstrates that the replacement of process with progress brings to the contemporary world a growing chaotic fragmentation of social life and alienates man from nature, which has its own pace of development. A solution to this problem is seen in the remarriage of science and religion, i.e. the harmony of rational and irrational factors, as postulated by processists.[16] This theory, thus enabling a simultaneous perception of reality in terms of the general (God) and the specific (fact), should be reflected both in education concepts and in school curricula; here, the school is considered as a natural point of encounter (of students, teachers, books, histories, present and potential problems, spaces, etc.) while the role of the teacher is not to pass on 'ready' knowledge but to creatively coordinate the mutual influences occurring among the participants of such encounters.[17] The methodological and content-related dynamics of theological education may be demonstrated with the example of gender socialisation as the discourse-shaped masculinised image of God and should be analysed critically.[18]

Following the discussion of the chief principles of process philosophy and theology along with their social implications, we may deal with the subject of interreligious dialogue and the idea of the development of religion viewed as a result of the dialogue occurring between representatives of particular traditions and

---

14   J.B. Cobb, *Sustaining the Common Good. A Christian Perspective on the Global Economy*, Pilgrim Press, Cleveland 1994, pp. 7–11.

15   See for example J. Dewey, *Logic. The Theory of Inquiry*, H. Holt and Company, New York 1938, pp. 66–67.

16   D.W. Oliver, *Education, Modernity and Fractured Meaning – Toward a Process Theory of Teaching and Learning*, State University of New York Press, Albany 1989, pp. 19–20.

17   A.N. Whitehead, *The Aims of Education & other Essays*, Macmillan, New York 1929, p. 39.

18   J.C. Hough, J.B. Cobb, *Christian Identity and Theological Education*, Scholars Press, Chico 1985.

theological trends.[19] This idea, far from being confined to the changing doctrines, is vital for the development of man in the whole cycle of life and to the harmonious coexistence of various human communities in the contemporary world; hence, here it is referred to as pedagogy of ecumenism. A survey of the basic formulations of the twentieth-century theology of religions (the simultaneous complementariness and completeness of the economy of salvation of the individual persons of the Holy Trinity, the progressive character of God's Epiphany) provides a background against which examples of the interpenetration of religious ideas may be presented. Of significance is Cobb's belief in the existence of more than one irreducible sphere: apart from God, he isolates the category of CREATIVENESS as equivalent to notions like SUNYATA or DHARMAKAYA but different from specific exemplifications of the Supreme Being, such as ISHVARA, JAHVEH or CHRIST.[20] This distinction is to enable a dialogical development of particular theologies while at the same time preventing them from ideological homogenisation.

The fact that theology is construed socially leads one to consider not the dogmatic essence of Christianity but rather the Christian structure of existence, rooted in the awareness of God's presence in the world and realised in the human responsibility for the experienced reality. The same is true of other religions; so we may also discuss their structures in the context of the processuality of reality by reference to the examples of Judaism, Buddhism and Islam. Jewish thinkers combine the concept of God's processuality with His immanent presence in the constantly created world and with the problem of theodicy. This leads to a reinterpretation of the Old Testament idea of a covenant, here extended to the whole world according to the promise given to Noah.[21] The common elements of Buddhism and process theology refer to the coherence of notions such as CONCRESCENCE and PRATITYASAMUTPADA as well as the DHARMAKAYA and the KENOSIS OF GOD; furthermore, the convergence of the Chinese tradition with Pragmatism and Marxism, underlying the interest in process philosophy in China, may be also demonstrated. Finally, Islam's openness to the dialogue with other religions should be considered in light of the original teaching of Mohammed and the views of Muslim scholars inspired by processual ideas.[22]

19   N. Pittenger, *The Christian Church as Social Process*, Westminster Press, Philadelphia 1972, p. 131.

20   L. Swidler *et al.*, *Death or Dialogue. From the Age of Monologue to the Age of Dialogue*, Trinity Press International, London – Philadelphia 1990, pp. 5–14.

21   See S.B. Lubarsky, D.R. Griffin (eds.), *Jewish Theology and Process Thought*, State University of New York Press, Albany 1996.

22   See M. Abduh, *The Theology of Unity*, Allen & Unwin, London 1966.

In his essay *Beyond 'Pluralism'* (1990), John B. Cobb states:

> In many traditions there is an internal emphasis on the difficulty, if not the impossibility, of grasping the truth and expressing it in language. Laying out the conflicting doctrines and developing arguments for and against each is a questionable preoccupation. Instead, it is best to listen to the deep, even ultimate, concerns that are being expressed in these diverse statements. My goal is to transform contradictory statements into different but noncontradictory ones. My assumption is that what is positively intended by those who have lived, thought, and felt deeply is likely to be true, whereas their formulations are likely to exclude other truths that should not be excluded. [...] Of course, there are many grossly erroneous statements that have been affirmed with great seriousness by adherents of the great religious traditions. It is not true that the world is flat. There is no point in seeking some deeper meaning behind such statements, since we know how they arose from a literalistic reading of certain passages of scripture. There are similar ideas in all the traditions. There are also far more damaging ideas, such as misogynist ones, in most of the religious traditions. These, too, should be condemned as false. [...] My claim is simply that all this is not truly faithful to Jesus Christ, and that the true meaning of faith HAS expressed itself, imperfectly but authentically, in other features of our past history. I believe it is expressing itself today in movements of liberation and also in enthusiastic efforts to encounter other religious traditions at a deep level. Roman Catholics have appropriated many of the meditational methods of the East, and the experience generated by these methods cannot but be transforming. Both Catholics and Protestants are struggling with new ideas and ways of thinking. The Christianity that emerges will be different from anything we have known before, but that does not mean that it will be less Christian. On the contrary, it will be one more step toward that fullness that is represented by the coming of the Realm of God. All traditions are unique. The role of each in history has been unique for good and ill. Each responds uniquely to our pluralistic situation. The potential of each for becoming more inclusive is unique. Let us celebrate the uniqueness of all of our religious traditions [highlighted by M.P.].[23]

Mutual respect and readiness to learn from other traditions to build the common good of civil society may be supported by the framework proposed by process theology. So many examples of serious social turmoil in the history of mankind were caused by religious prejudice. Keeping religion far from the public sphere or fighting its institutions was never a good solution to this problem. On the one hand, the liberal approach includes faith into private domain of every man, but on the other hand, the approach allows its growth and change by the mutual impact of one on another. Both globalisations as a general process and specific examples of interreligious tensions (e.g. in Northern Ireland) demand responsible solutions. Open theology that is not narrowed into apologetic or persuasive type approach seems to be a good proposition to be considered in states based on the idea of civil citizenship.

---

23 J.B. Cobb, *Beyond Pluralism*, available at: http://www.religion-online.org/showarticle.asp?title=3347 (accessed: 15.08.2013).

Bibliography

Abduh M., *The Theology of Unity*, Allen & Unwin, London 1966.

Birch Ch., Cobb J.B., *The Liberation of Life. From the Cell to the Community*, Cambridge University Press, Cambridge 1981.

Christian Classic Eternal Library, available at: http://www.ccel.org/ccel/schaff/creeds2. iv.i.iii.html (accessed: 14.08.2013).

Cobb J.B., *Beyond Pluralism*, available at: http://www.religion-online.org/showarticle. asp?title=3347 (accessed: 15.08.2013).

Cobb J.B., *Christ in a Pluralistic Age*, Westminster Press, Philadelphia 1975.

Cobb J.B., *Liberal Christianity at the Crossroads*, Westminster Press, Philadelphia 1973.

Cobb J.B., *Process Theology as Political Theology*, available at: http://www.religion-on-line.org/showchapter.asp?title=3035&C=2540 (accessed: 14.08.2013).

Cobb J.B., *Sustainability. Economics, Ecology, and Justice*, Orbis Books, Maryknoll 1992.

Cobb J.B., *Sustaining the Common Good. A Christian Perspective on the Global Economy*, Pilgrim Press, Cleveland 1994.

Cobb J.B., Griffin D.R., *Process Theology. An Introductory Exposition*, Westminster Press, Philadelphia 1976.

Dewey J., *Logic. The Theory of Inquiry*, H. Holt and Company, New York 1938.

Hough J.C., Cobb J.B., *Christian Identity and Theological Education*, Scholars Press, Chico 1985.

Lubarsky S.B., Griffin D.R. (eds.), *Jewish Theology and Process Thought*, State University of New York Press, Albany 1996.

Oliver D.W., *Education, Modernity and Fractured Meaning – Toward a Process Theory of Teaching and Learning*, State University of New York Press, Albany 1989.

Patalon M., *Pedagogika ekumenizmu. Procesualność jako paradygmat interkonfesyjnej i interreligijnej hermeneutyki w ujęciu Johna B. Cobba, Jr.*, University of Gdańsk Press, Gdańsk 2007.

Pittenger N., *The Christian Church as Social Process*, Westminster Press, Philadelphia 1972.

Suchocki M.H., *God, Christ, Church. A Practical Guide to Process Theology*, Crossroad, New York 1989.

Swidler L. *et al.*, *Death or Dialogue. From the Age of Monologue to the Age of Dialogue*, Trinity Press International, London – Philadelphia 1990.

Whitehead A.N., *Process and Reality*, Macmillan, New York 1929.

Whitehead A.N., *Science and the Modern World*, New American Library, New York 1948.

Whitehead A.N., *The Aims of Education & other Essays*, Macmillan, New York 1929.

Uto Meier
Catholic University of Eichstätt-Ingolstadt
Eichstätt (Germany)

Why Democracy Cannot Work without Unconditional Values: On Moral Boundaries and Ethical Guideposts for a Post-secular Generation

Let us begin by taking a closer look at a contemporary poem. Interestingly enough, its quintessential meaning harks back to an ancient view on moral philosophy which this essay on fundamental ethics shall develop a little further.

Die gute Sache	The Greater Good
wenn ich sehe	when I see
was alles	everything
um der guten Sache willen	that is done
getan wird	for the greater good
dann denke ich	then sometimes
manchmal	I think
es wäre	it might be
vielleicht eine gute Sache	for the greater good
wenn es überhaupt	if there
keine	was no
gute Sache	greater good
mehr gäbe	at all

Taken from: E. Fried, *Lebensschatten. Gedichte*, Wagenbach, Berlin 1981.

In this poetic play on words, Erich Fried addresses a central issue of contemporary theories on responsibility, which essentially deals with the question of whether that which we perceive as legitimate and strive towards, i.e. our free as well as purposeful actions, should be determined by 'ultimate greater goals' or whether it is not precisely this orientation towards an external purpose as an ultimate guideline – in practical philosophy, this is known as consequentialism – which poses a serious philosophical problem.

The author of this essay is part of the philosophical tradition which views definitions of goodness as deriving from an external purpose as problematic, regardless of what this purpose is called: classless society, race, progress, or rate of return. All of us know the price that has historically been paid – and is still being paid – for these and similar figures of thought. The Gulag, the concentration camps, but also the child labour of millions of children producing, for our own sake, the rugs, paving stones and all the other ever-so-nice bargain goods which warm our hearts when shopping at the big discount stores (such as *Tchibo* and *Aldi* in Germany). This attitude of submitting to the greater good is hidden behind the numerous immediate ethical decisions that constitute our life.

The following considerations intend to show why democracy runs the risk of losing its very essence without being grounded on unconditional, i.e. non-relativizable ethical norms, and why a vital democracy thus requires a religiously founded 'commitment to unconditional values', even though a plethora of decisions may be made by weighing up competing interests by means of a 'trade-off' ethics.

Therefore, as a work on the conception of responsibility based on moral boundaries, this essay will explore a question of moral philosophy, namely the question of an anchor point for an ethical approach sustainable enough not to fall prey to the human habit of expediently weighing up and shifting between various hegemonic conceptions of values.

In short: What are the guidelines (i.e. the ethical principles) by which we should orient ourselves? What are the limits (i.e. the concrete normative postulations) we should categorically acknowledge if we do not want to dispense with our human nature in favour of the goal of a 'Beyond Good and Evil', as Nietzsche put it?

An empirical glimpse into the *status quo* on contemporary values and religious identity: Secularism in post-secular aspirations, or: Does democracy need religion?

To begin with, international insight on the topic shall be given by means of the International Social Survey Program's survey on 'Beliefs about God across Time and Countries', which concerns itself with people's 'religious status' and has been conducted biannually since 1991.[1] The surveys register a decline in religious (i.e. mainly ecclesiastical) affiliations between 1991 and 2008 in Europe. In the

1 H. Meier, *Politik, Religion und Philosophie*, [in:] W. Graf, H. Meier (eds.), *Politik und Religion. Zur Diagnose der Gegenwart*, C.H. Beck, München 2013, p. 301.

western federal states of Germany, 54.2% of the population believe in any kind of god, in the Eastern states of Germany only 13.2%. When asked whether they believe in a personal god, a mere 23% of Western Germans replied with 'Yes', compared to 8.2% in Eastern Germany. In the United States, the figures amount to 80.8% and 67.5%, respectively.

This is mirrored by the empirical findings of the most significant study on German youth, the 16th 'Shell Jugendstudie' bearing the title 'Jugend 2010'.[2]

Whereas in 2002, 68% of Catholic youth considered any belief in God to play an important role in their lives, this figure amounts to 66% for 2010, thus it is particularly the share of 'highly religious' youth which has declined sharply. 'Religious insecurity', on the other hand, is on the rise: from 23% to 28% among Catholics, and from 28% to 33% among Protestants between 2006 and 2010.[3]

Another finding, which may seem counterintuitive at first, is the answer given by youth to the question of the general validity of moral standards, which 82% of youth acknowledge: 'There have to be moral standards which are valid for everybody to guarantee the functioning of our society.'[4] Does the decline of religious thinking thus coincide with a rise of moral consciousness? A counter-argument may be that some youth believe that 'we can no longer afford feeling pity or compassion for our fellow humans.'[5]

A result that may show what price a society pays if it exchanges religiously grounded solidarity, handed down for generations, with purely functionalist and utilitarian considerations. Morality thus becomes subordinate to considerations of 'affordability', while abandoning the traditional metacognitive conviction, deeply grounded in religious rites, that a suffering fellow human deserves empathy simply due to his or her belonging to the race of mankind.

When asking youth about their trust in democratic institutions, an interesting priority given to a 'justice vision' manifests itself, which may – in the context of a generally high appreciation for democracy as a form of government – hint to the fact that mere procedural justice is not the only thing which youth expect from democracy.

The police, courts, human rights and ecology groups (!), even the *Bundeswehr* (the German army), the EU, as well as unions and action groups, rank higher than churches in measures of the trust that youth invest in them; only banks, political parties, and corporations are viewed with more suspicion than the institutions run by religious believers.

---

2 Shell Deutschland Holding (ed.), *Jugend 2010. Eine pragmatische Generation behauptet sich*, Fischer-Taschenbuch Verlag, Frankfurt am Main 2011, here Chart 5.9 (p. 205) and Chart 5.10 (p. 207). The study questions youth between the age of 15 and 25 (survey period: 2010).

3 *Ibid.*, chart 5.10, p. 207.

4 *Ibid.*, chart 5.12, p. 214.

5 *Ibid.*, chart 5.12, p. 215.

Yet if one tries to interpret these findings in the context of the political consciousness of German youth, one also finds that the decline in ecclesiastical affiliation correlates with a decline in the interest in politics, as chart 3.1 of the 16th 'Shell Jugendstudie' demonstrates in the chapter on 'Youth and politics'[6]: interest in political questions has declined from 55% in 1984 to 40% in 2010.

Is there a connection between the abandonment of political consciousness and the abandonment of ecclesiasticism? If so, this would be a first piece of evidence demonstrating that democracy lives due to the practice of religion. It should, however, give food for thought that, despite all functionalist-secular demystifications, in most – and also in developed – societies a majority of people, especially of youth, partake in a metaphysically and thus religiously grounded worldview (according to a six-dimensional concept of religiousness)[7] as the international study 'Religionsmonitor 2008' shows.[8]

The assumption that religions would lose their efficacy as a side effect of the technological and scientific advancement of modern societies, and humans would come up with their own personal and intrawordly answers to the great questions of life with the help of science or ideologies[9], this assumption, which has been in circulation since Auguste Comte and Max Weber, is obviously mistaken, as the 'Religionsmonitor' of 2008 convincingly demonstrates. Religious as well as highly religious people (in theory and in *praxis*) are in a great majority worldwide, even though there are segments of life (and thus also societies) which operate more strongly with non-religious semantics.[10]

The data for German youth (between 18 and 29) still point to a comparatively high percentage of religious self-conceptions: 14% of youth within this age group can be considered 'highly religious', 52% 'religious'. Thus, two-thirds of German youth conceive of themselves, both intellectually and practically, as religious peo-

---

6   Shell Deutschland Holding (ed.), *Jugend 2010...*, *op. cit.*, p. 131.

7   The so-called 'Religionsmonitor' operates with six core dimensions in order to define and measure its understanding of religiousness: 'intellect' (interest in religious topics), 'ideology' (religious stance concerning the belief in god or a divine force), 'public practice' (church attendance, spiritual rituals), 'private practice' (prayer or meditation), 'experience' ('you'-experience, experience of unity), and 'consequences' (everyday relevance in one's personal life). S. Huber, *Der Religionsmonitor 2008: Strukturelle Prinzipien, operationale Konstrukte, Auswertungsstrategien*, [in:] Bertelsmann Stiftung (ed.), *Woran glaubt die Welt*, Verlag Bertelsmann Stiftung, Gütersloh 2009, p. 19.

8   Bertelsmann Stiftung (ed.), *Woran glaubt...*, *op. cit.*

9   P.L. Berger, *The Heretical Imperative*, Doubleday, Garden City, NY 1979, p. 102.

10 H. Meulemann, *Säkularisierung oder religiöse Erneuerung? Weltanschauung in 22 Gesellschaften: Befunde und Hinweise einer Querschnittsbefragung*, [in:] Bertelsmann Stiftung (ed.), *Woran glaubt...*, *op. cit.*, pp. 691–723.

ple. It may be mere coincidence that it is also two-thirds of (Western!) German youth who are fairly or very content with Germany's democratic system.[11]

Thus, several leading Western intellectuals speak of a 'post-secular' process,[12] as particularly in the context of an all-encompassing liberalization and adaptation to the rules imposed by 'the market', religious interpretations give room for the

> [...] prospect for a justice [...] which goes beyond a generalizable procedural justice. [...] In the resurgence of religious orthodoxies as well as the free-floating longings of Western intellectuals for a renewed commitment to unconditional values, for 'the other', or for the disruption of a process which is perceived as bringing humanity closer to its doom, we may encounter manifestations of a discontent with modernity. By studying these, we may be able to get an idea of what it is that our society lacks.[13]

Even Jürgen Habermas ('religiously unmusical' according to his own famous dictum) has recently been calling for a mutual reconciliation between the necessarily secular self-conception of the state and the ultimate groundings of self-conceptions and conceptions of reality in religious 'language games', inaccessible to majority decisions:

> The liberal state must welcome religious voices in the political public life, as far as these can be seen as contributions to the democratic processes of opinion-forming and decision-making.[14]

In this context, Habermas speaks of the 'socially integrative role of the sacral complex'[15] and calls for philosophy not to

> [...] sever the thread of dialogical interchange with religion. For we cannot know whether the [...] ongoing process of translating unredeemed religious meaning potentials into the terminology of post-metaphysical thought has already come to an end.[16]

Concerning the justification of claims for moral universals, the great discourse ethicist sceptically resumes that we do not know

> [...] whether the resources of an INALIENABLE (!) but only weakly motivating rational morality, on which also the constitutional integration of widely secularized societies must be grounded in the end, will suffice [highlighted by U.M.][17].

---

11   Shell Deutschland Holding (ed.), *Jugend 2010...*, *op. cit.*, chart 3.4, p. 137.

12   Jürgen Habermas famously coined this idea of 'disclosure' in his speech on the occasion of being awarded the peace prize of the German book trade in 2001 in St. Paul's Cathedral in Frankfurt, quite unambiguously as a response to the terrorist attacks of September the 11th.

13   H. Meier, *Politik, Religion...*, *op. cit.*, p. 304.

14   J. Habermas, *Politik und Religion*, [in:] W. Graf, H. Meier (eds.), *Politik und Religion...*, *op. cit.*, p. 293.

15   *Ibid.*, p. 204.

16   *Ibid.*, p. 299.

17   *Ibid.*

The current president of Germany's parliament, Prof. Dr. Norbert Lammert, conceives of the interdependence between the truth claims of religions and the majority-based decision-making processes in democracy as follows:

> The hopelessness of answering the question for truth once and for all is also the prerequisite of democracy. Religious belief concerns itself with truths which are not open to debate, politics deals with interests which are not eligible to be recognized as truths.[18]

This is why democracy needs religious convictions:

> I would oppose the assumption that the price for living in modern democratic societies is a loss of religious values – or at least the voluntary [...] surrendering of religious orientations and values – by stating that neither the social fabric nor the coexistence of humans can be understood without reference to religious thought; and neither the political constitution of our society and certainly not our culture can be understood without reference to our Judeo-Christian heritage.[19]

But at the beginning of scientific thought was the postulate of constructing theories without normative appropriation.

A second glance, from a scholarly-ethical perspective: On the paradigm shift from a value-neutral to a value-bound conception of science

In his time, Aristotle propagated (in *Metaphysics* IV.3 and *Nicomachean Ethics* VI.3) an ideal of science without presuppositions, autonomous and value-free, whose search for the truth – and the purpose – of things and processes was for truth's sake alone, and conducted with methods free of contradiction, following a describable logic (syllogism and induction). Critical modernity, however, acknowledges, at least since the critical rationalism of Karl Popper (1902–1994), both the positive and negative influence of interest (be it of political or economic nature) on science: 'While we philosophers still discuss whether the world around us actually exists, this world is already about to perish.'

Differential geometry was famously brought forth by early ballistic technology used in early modern artillery; similarly, navigation, cartography, and (colonial) geodetics have helped develop and motivate mathematics, this allegedly strictly neutral field of science. At the beginning of the 20th century, value-free science

---

18   N. Lammert, *Glaube Politik und Demokratie*, [in:] U. Kropac, U. Meier, K. König (eds.), *Jugend, Religion und Religiosität. Resultate, Probleme und Perspektiven der aktuellen Religiositätsforschung*, Pustet, Regensburg 2012, pp. 237–239.

19   *Ibid.*, p. 239.

irretrievably lost its innocence when Germany's world-leading chemical industry subjected itself to the (pre-)wartime demands of militarist *Wilhelminism* like an eager schoolboy. Fritz Haber, the Nobel laureate in chemistry (1868–1934, Nobel Prize in 1919 for the synthesis of ammonia, revolutionizing both the production of fertilizers as well as the production of explosives), went down in history as the 'father of chemical warfare', which he invented perfectly in time for the German military to use in the war (his wife Clara Immerwahr, a chemist herself, may have committed suicide for that very reason).

The spring of 2012 saw commemorations of the 100th birthday of Wernher von Braun. Von Braun came to fame both as the 'father of space travel' and, having compliantly invented the V2 rockets for the NS regime, as the embodiment of the Janus-faced modern scientist, who cannot, and probably does not want to, accept ethical boundaries imposed on the free weighing of interests, which was already getting out of hand, even without him. After the war, Wernher von Braun and his *protégé*, General Dornberger, justified themselves – especially in regard to the thousands of dead people due to the V2 production in the concentration camp of Mittelbau-Dora – with the argument 'that we always regarded the development of missiles as a necessary detour. We knew that, all over the world, pioneers of flight always had to take this detour'.[20] 'Instrumental (or purposive) reason' is what Jürgen Habermas has called this way of thinking. Indeed, we can easily identify an instrumentalized morality in this unobstructed weighing of different ways of giving reasons to our actions, which pays homage to the principle of 'the end justifying the means'.

In Karl Popper's work, this loss of scientific innocence led to a necessarily value-bound conception of science; a rationale based purely on advancing knowledge is no longer acceptable. Instead, science should conceive of itself as the search for truth (though subject to the scepticism of theoretical falsifiability), in addition to being a means of problem-solving and the alleviation of suffering and affliction.

Robert Oppenheimer (1904–1967), who played a decisive role in developing the nuclear bomb in the U.S.-based Manhattan Project, was probably one of the most tragic (as well as one of the most alert) figures of modern science. He had to face the problem of scientific responsibility in his own lifetime. After the two nuclear bombs had been dropped on Hiroshima and Nagasaki (which killed 125,000 people instantly, all of them civilians, and about 100,000 indirectly due to severe radioactive contamination), Oppenheimer tried to stop the development of the hydrogen bomb because he no longer conceived his work in the project as ethically tenable.

---

20 B. Ruland, *Wernher von Braun. Mein Leben für die Raumfahrt*, Burda, Offenburg 1969, p. 71.

The traditional method of acquiring scientific knowledge, 'trial and error', had been perverted in this select assemblage of scientists to 'trial and terror' precisely because of the abandonment of unconditional boundaries.

In the literary world, Heinar Kipphardt famously inserted the aforementioned personality into his 1964 drama *In the Matter of J. Robert Oppenheimer*, in which he gave a lucid artistic rendering of theoretical questions of responsibility.

At the end of World War II, the political consciousness of the Western nations sacrificed − as the latter have belatedly begun to concede nowadays − the unconditional religious commandment 'thou shalt not kill' as an unconditional obligation to protect the innocent, on the altar of the demands of the daily events, i.e. setting an end to the war as soon as possible.

The organs of democratic decision-making should not have ignored the 'Stop!' sign imposed on them by the moral convictions deeply rooted in the Judeo--Christian tradition. Democracy needs religion!

Purposive rationality, part three: Moral obligations despite economics?

Another important area of society dominated by the principle of an unchecked weighing of interests is economics. According to Eugen Buss's expansive 2007 study on German economic elites, members of these elites show a surprising diversity with regard to their ethical sensibilities.[21] Exactly 13% of the top executives interviewed either attribute only minor significance to ethics or perceive it as a hindrance[22], while another 13% view ethics as the fundamental basis of any business activity. In total, 31% see ethical categories as playing an important part, while another 33% see them as an ambivalent factor.[23]

Clearly oriented towards ethical standards, the following statement by a chief executive officer (CEO) as cited in Buss may serve as a guiding example for ethically oriented economics:

> The role of ethics cannot be underestimated [...]. There are many business owners that act ethically as well. There are very few who consciously act unethically. Ethics is a subject taught at university, which really should be mandatory for everybody.

---

21   E. Buss, *Die deutschen Spitzenmanager. Wie sie wurden, was sie sind. Herkunft, Wertvorstellungen, Erfolgsregeln*, Oldenbourg Wissenschaftlicher Verlag, Oldenburg 2007, pp. 149–175.

22   *Ibid.*, p. 130.

23   Bucksteeg's more recent 2010 study shows an increasing acceptance of ethical values as tools for business management. M. Bucksteeg, K. Hattendorf, *Führungskräftebefragung 2010*, available at: http://www.wertekommission.de/content/pdf/kampagne/Fuehrungskraeftebefragung_2010.pdf (accessed: 17.08.2014).

You cannot talk enough about it [...]. In my opinion, people in business should always take a decisively humanist position.[24]

However, a statement from among those 13% who believe economic objectives and ethical orientations to be irreconcilable shows the incompatibility of ethical stances with business goals:

> In my opinion, this discussion about ethics is basically a fig leaf discussion. Discussions on leadership ethics [...] are nothing but a futile attempt to cover up ethical deficits on the management level; eventually, while they may preach water, they will drink wine [...]. I don't believe that top managers have internalized any form of ethical principles whatsoever, let alone that they would act upon them.[25]

So how exactly do these elites view the relationship between ethics and economics? A total of 25% of top managers (only?) deem it necessary to develop ethical guidelines.[26] An equal amount of those interviewed (again: only) believe ethics to be ingrained in the model character of the executives' personalities. One in five employers (19%) considers globalization to be an obstacle for ethical standards that would serve mankind; 17% think ethical principles collide with economic necessities.[27]

Many elites also share an uncertainty about the relativity of ethical positions:

> If it is the categorical imperative, well then of course this plays some sort of role [...]. Is the merging of companies, with all its consequences such as labour displacement, morally right or wrong? If you ask those affected and those doing it you get very different answers [...]. But morality is an elusive category. What would have been called 'right' ten years ago might not be 'right' today.[28]

By now, the phenomenon of morally relative positions characterizes German management thinking. Nevertheless, the difficulty of combining economic necessities with their wish for alternative ethical options is frequently lamented by top managers supposedly constrained by economic circumstances:

> [...] this feeling of utter impotence is almost inevitable. Often, the market's deterministic conditions simply force you to make decisions somebody else would call 'wrong' and unethical.[29]

---

24 E. Buss, *Die deutschen...*, *op. cit.*, p. 153.
25 *Ibid.*, p. 160.
26 Differently Bucksteeg's 2010 study: here, 71% of the top managers call for a public transparency of ethical guidelines (M. Bucksteeg, K. Hattendorf, *Führungskräftebefragung...*, *op. cit.*, p. 22).
27 E. Buss, *Die deutschen...*, *op. cit.*, p. 165. Differently Bucksteeg's 2010 study: here, over 50% favor ethical values when they collide with monetary interests (M. Bucksteeg, K. Hattendorf, *Führungskräftebefragung...*, *op. cit.*, p. 23).
28 E. Buss, *Die deutschen...*, *op. cit.*, p. 166.
29 *Ibid.*

Once again, we have to raise the question whether transcendental convictions do not promote a stronger resilience to resist the obviously destructive. It might be interesting to investigate the convictions of those investment bankers who did not join in the lottery game which spawned the financial crisis of 2008, and who refused to sell worthless shares to inexperienced investors.

We have now come to the point of this essay at which we have to try to resolve the question of what ethos, what ethical standards, could provide orientation in the face of such a pervasive relativism; ethical positions that, when needed to make a responsible decision, enable one neither to surrender to the perceived omnipresence of relativism nor to succumb to the hubris of believing one's one ethics to be the ultimate answer.

This leads us to the following question: To what or to whom do managers and scientists – and perhaps everybody who is forced to make decisions – answer? Do they answer, in an Aristotelian manner, to the search for truth only? Or do they eventually answer to profit? Maybe they answer to the more remote consequences of how their knowledge and their strategies to generate profit are used? Or is this the responsibility of the users of such strategies? Or maybe of the commissioning politicians or markets?

Even in our everyday lives, these questions press on our shoulders. Are we allowed to make this bargain at *Tchibo*, which, in all likelihood, has been produced under highly unfair conditions? Or do we answer to our family's low funds first? Can we still justify our weekend trip by plane when it affects global climate the way it does? Can we still listen to our financial consultant when he or she offers us an investment which may yield another percent more of interest? In short: Are not all of us enmeshed in unfair systems? Are not all of us (co-)responsible for the major and minor crises of this world, this environment, of posterity? Or is it enough to keep our immediate surroundings 'clean'? Might the 'greater good' even exempt one from a normative accountability which is independent of functional obligations in whatever form? Who can claim to live without contradictions? Even bishops drive Mercedes as their official cars – not exactly known to be an invention which preserves God's creation the best.

Or do these pervasive assignments of responsibilities rest on a problematic general accountability to which we cannot or even should not be bound, as responsibility would then be immediate and could not encompass all ends?

It seems helpful to me to search for a more nuanced definition of the term 'responsibility', which aims at initiating an 'ethics beyond instrumentality' and which can be articulated both as a general guidepost and as a normative-immediate boundary.

On the definition of the term 'responsibility'

Commonly[30], more recent discussions have seen the term 'responsibility' as relative to four positions:
- a SUBJECT TO RESPONSIBILITY (person/company/institution) – is responsible for;
- an OBJECT OF RESPONSIBILITY (an action or a speech act) – while answerable to;
- an AUTHORITY OF RESPONSIBILITY (court/conscience/public opinion) – against;
- a NORMATIVE BACKGROUND (sets of 'can', 'should', or 'must' rules, quality of a moral relationship, deontological versus teleological foundations of norms).

According to Höffe[31], this responsibility is
- RETROSPECTIVE (someone has to account for former actions) – as well as;
- PROSPECTIVE (for future actions) – as well as;
- RECONCILIATORY (reparative) – that is, liable.

This, however, still leaves open the question of the essential underlying conception of action. Even members of the Mafia have to answer for their actions: firstly, by being held personally responsible for any protection money exacted, and secondly, by being obliged to justify their actions in front of the 'honorary board' of their Honourable Society with regard to the set exaction goals. In terms of the national economy, the Mafia even creates several positive effects because it generates 'revenues' that fortify, without being taxed, the steady flow of goods (drugs and arms, that is). Without having first scrutinized the legitimacy of a normative background, we have not contributed anything towards a substantial ethical consideration. Such a consideration remains embedded in a problematic relativism as long as the normative background is not liberated from its functional rationale.

In his Jerusalem trial, Adolf Eichmann, organizer of the Holocaust, kept assuring to the judges that his role only consisted in providing trains, writing up lists of employees, and keeping the minutes at the Wannsee Conference. He insisted that he himself had never laid hands on any Jew. Nevertheless, his sentence was quite legitimate. Why?

For an act to be ethical or unethical, it has to be carried out with full knowledge of its consequences (and its legal or illegal nature) and also intentionally and out of free will; thus, an act's (long-term) consequences can still be ascribed to the subject. It is a known fact that when Adolf Hitler was a boy, his father used to beat him several times a week; does that mean that his father, Alois Schicklgruber, is responsible for World War II? No, he could not have foreseen the consequences of his pedagogy of corporal punishment (while it was reprehensible towards the child!). The function of trains to Auschwitz, however, could have easily been

---

30 M. Assländer, *Grundlagen der Wirtschafts- und Unternehmensethik*, Metropolis Verlag, Marburg 2011.
31 O. Höffe, *Einführung in die utilitaristische Ethik*, A. Francke Verlag, Tübingen 2003.

foreseen by Adolf Eichmann, who had directed them diligently since the Wannsee Conference.

Hegel, in his philosophy of law, has already warned that an arsonist could not claim his hand had only made a small dry blade of grass smoulder. For modern behavioural ethics, this fundamental insight is of especial relevance. In modern times, the scope of our actions have extended dramatically, with their abundant technological possibilities – both in temporal and in quantitative terms. Just think of research on nuclear fission driven both by military and by economic interests, or of genetic engineering, which does not act out of a pure search for truth, either. Faced with this increased scope, we have to realize the ever-growing velocity with which our decisions turn into irreversible facts (for example, with germ-line therapy), a velocity unthinkable in pre-modern times. The same holds true for the exponential increase in the number of side effects (who would have thought about endangering the ozone layer when those extremely useful refrigerators first utilised chlorofluorocarbons?) that current discussions on the 'sustainability' postulate have tried to encompass.[32]

These deliberations have hopefully shed some light both on the problematic issue of a 'normative background' that has to morally legitimate actions irrespective of their successful outcome as well as on the equally problematic question of the limits of responsibility, that is, how far we are responsible for the consequences of our actions and whether we can be made responsible for all of them. This brings forth the question of the precise meaning of 'assuming ethical and moral responsibility', if neither the realization of ultimate goals ('profitability is ethics!') nor the ignorance of possible consequences ('but I only charted some trains!') suffice as an ETHICAL legitimation.

Before we can delve into the concepts of moral obligation which European thought has to offer as alternatives to the principle of instrumentality, it may be useful to give some introductory thought to the question of whether there might not generally be different scopes of action.

Levels of responsibility as a theory of tiered (co-)responsibility

For these considerations, it is helpful to draw on a set of distinctions developed in economic ethics and consider a modified version of them in a discourse on general ethics, here using the example of science.

Levels of responsibility as graded scopes of responsibility can be described on:
– A MICRO-LEVEL OF AN ETHICS OF RESPONSIBILITY, which is concerned with immediate interpersonal interaction (individual accountability for a specific

---

32   H. Jonas, *Das Prinzip Verantwortung*, Suhrkamp, Frankfurt am Main 1984.

matter, such as methodological caution or performing one's duty according to role expectations, such as controlling hazards or performing a task) and therefore with the immediate responsibility towards the goals of professional as well as extra-professional obligations.

The cleaning lady that works for a microbiological institute possibly researching new viruses for use in biochemical warfare has to clean the rooms because her children are in need of the little money she can make. She is not responsible for the problematic issue of the institute's inhumane research.

— A MESO-LEVEL OF AN ETHICS OF RESPONSIBILITY, which pertains to an organization ('s goals) an individual answers to.

A medical doctor might, in research as well as in practice, 'do his job well' in taking care of the health of imprisoned torture victims – but he should not have been working or researching inside the structures of an inhumane system in the first place. If his research and his work are overtly geared towards being applied to unethical ends, his research and his work are unethical themselves. This responsibility can be understood as an institutional ethical guideline the individual is only partly accountable for, as individuals usually have to derive their own role identity from the objectives of their organization (an army general will eventually have to go to war, despite the fact that he might be a really nice guy in private – the head of an institute has to serve his research contract, while he must also constantly question its consistency with generally accepted research guidelines). Responsible parties continuously have to (co-)question such organization objectives critically.

— A MACRO-LEVEL OF AN ETHICS OF RESPONSIBILITY, which relates to general questions, such as how far science can serve other ends and the nature of such ends (science conceived as research without any specific purpose and indeed as blindly pursuing progress without considering the quality and the beneficiary of such progress); this macro-level is therefore to be understood as a reflection of the (financial as well as philosophical) conditions determining the form of scientific research (nuclear physics or the fight against poverty? economics as the science of profit maximization or the maximization of the public good? etc.). Eventually, this makes these considerations those of an ethics of resource allocation, since, in our modern world of scientific research, it is only those who are allocated resources that are successful – and the allocation of these resources has to be rationalized.

If this distinction of different LEVELS OF RESPONSIBILITY is valid, it follows that there are also different TIERS OF RESPONSIBILITY:

The PhD candidate should conduct the experiment his thesis adviser has told him to conduct – as, in general, he cannot know that his research results might be abused in the long run; the professor, on the other hand, would have to ask himself more acutely which research objectives he can follow, who his research serves and how; and finally, the minds behind science policies and the scientific community as a whole have to be able to explain what image of humanity and what values underlie their work when channelling or rerouting billions into particular directions.

The most obvious current example is economics. In economical sciences, vast financial and personnel resources are still allocated following a – hardly ever questioned – principle of economic profit maximization, which, as the recent financial crises have shown, can be highly counterproductive. The by-products created by such research on optimizing efficiency in economic activity, such as ecological by-products, are only eventually being recognized as economic objectives in themselves and treated accordingly. By now, balance sheets have been expanded to include criteria of sustainability; however, this has required economics to substantially rethink its academic self-conception.

Due to these changes, a scientific ethics of economy is increasingly becoming a public issue when discussing questions such as whether 'more' is always 'better' in regard to mankind and whether allegedly extra-economic categories such as 'justice' might not actually be indispensable in pursuing a meaningful approach to economics. This holds true for all sciences!

In the end, religious beliefs prove to be an essential part of the discussion once again, especially when tackling the fundamental question of what kind of 'human development' is desirable at all. The unleashed force of modernity has undoubtedly generated a degree of wealth which has opened up new horizons of freedom to human life. But, to take only one example, our current ecological crisis prompts metaphysical questions as well, such as whether we have not in fact only borrowed the earth which we exploit from our children. And this does not even touch upon the question of whether the plurality of life forms may not be an end in itself. A strictly economic approach to the world cannot, and does not want to, answer questions of this kind. This is where the wisdom teachings and the spiritual convictions to be found in the religions of mankind are called for, not a functionalist understanding of science with its instrumentalized rationality.

The idea that functionalist research has lost sight of any true meaning was laconically expressed by Heidegger in his famous dictum: 'Science does not think'.[33] In the end, this (also!) means that science does not have an ethical dimension *per se*. But this is exactly what we have to demand from it.

Concerning this demand, medical ethics is a step ahead, having shown foresight by imposing restrictions on itself, with an eye on other disciplines: Not simply with human experiments in mind, but also with regard to the philosophical question of what exactly constitutes a humane cure or therapy. In cases where this

---

33   M. Heidegger, *Was heißt denken?*, Kohlhammer, Stuttgart 1992, p. 8.

could allow for a (more) humane way of dying, sometimes this might even mean the discontinuation of a therapy.

Ethics as an elemental-essentialist reasoning

Thus, if we can state as a basic principle that we find ourselves on various levels of responsibility, we have to consider at what points we are still required to make decisions – despite all the different levels of ethical responsibilities – or whether the abovementioned problematic principle of 'the end justifies the means' reappears on these different levels of decision-making in the guise of different degrees of personal concernedness. For the ultimate rationale of these different degrees of responsibility would be that those above me on the scale would always liberate me from personal accountability. Always? In the vast and longstanding tradition of ethical considerations, there are many ways of legitimizing that which is to be done (and not to be done) and defining responsible behaviour.

Attempting to clarify this matter, let us take a closer look at two statements from the already cited German top managers:

> I highly doubt whether you can always start with directly throwing around the big words. Eventually, everybody has to set their own boundaries.[34]

And: 'If profitability demands it, you have to make use of ‹unethical› means as well'.[35]

The relativism proviso: Everybody has to decide on their own what is right?

The first objection, being quite representative of the current ethical mainstream, refers back to the basic axiom of relativism for answering questions of ethical responsibility: 'everybody has to set their own boundaries' is the answer we get here. This manifests an entire way of thinking, postulating the completely subjective nature of all ethical norms and clearly rendering homage to the conviction: 'the end justifies the means!'

One can quite quickly discard this first position as both contradictory and inhumane. It is evident that the postulate 'everybody has to define their own

---

34   E. Buss, *Die deutschen...*, *op. cit.*, p. 162.
35   *Ibid.*, p. 161.

values' is hardly conceivable.[36] Following this management dictum (coming from those 13% of the German economic elite critical of ethics), terrorists and sex offenders, stopping at nothing, might as well be ethical beings because one could not oppose such an idiosyncratic 'ethics' with any universally valid argument – since everybody can autonomously define the values they are bound to and that they deem 'right'.

It is, in fact, constitutional democracy that dismisses the arbitrariness of such a seemingly prevailing – individually as well as culturally relative – ethos. Additionally, Western constitutional history shows how parliamentary authority has been gradually stripped of the power to impinge upon fundamental personal rights of the individual as it is precisely their human nature that bestows these rights on them.[37]

Of course, different cultures believe very different actions to be morally justified: the Aztecs saw human sacrifice as a matter of course; a Roman father was granted the legal right to abandon his child; and Muslims practice polygamy, whereas European law prohibits all of the above. However, a discussion about diverging particular standards presupposes a norm (to be agreed upon) in the first place, which is impossible to interpret as proof for relativity.

In fact, the distinction between 'nature' and 'convention' or 'custom' marks the very beginning of philosophical thought.[38] In antiquity, the Greeks knew a norm which was accepted to stand above personal convenience: this was the *kata physin*, that is, the 'accordance with nature'. While, according to Herodotus, it was perfectly common among young Scythian women to amputate one of their breasts,[39] the Greeks opposed this tradition. They argued that it was not in the nature of the female breast to be amputated, but to be used for more life-affirming purposes. This idea of an 'accordance with nature' presupposes a fundamental nature of things, a teleological determination which can determine the essence of things and human actions (hence, the term 'essentialism' coined in this school of thought).[40]

---

36   The general contradiction that a relativist – *qua definitione* – cannot oppose someone with universalist claims has been set aside. Why should a universalist be excluded from the postulate of 'everyone according to their own fashion'? With this postulate, relativism has reduced itself *ad absurdum*.

37   H. Meier, *Politik, Religion...*, op. cit., p. 318.

38   L. Strauss, *Naturrecht und Geschichte*, Koehler, Stuttgart 1956, pp. 96 ff.

39   This example follows R. Spaemann, *Moralische Grundbegriffe*, C.H. Beck, München 2008, p. 14.

40   Casting a glance at the history of natural law, however, we have to note that often, the essence of things was prematurely detected in things only approximately essential; just think of the embarrassingly narrow views on women in which Thomas Aquinas was taken in by the prejudices of his time. The elemental essentialism proposed here confines itself to fundamental relationships and the internal directedness of institutions (such as jurisdiction, which is not

Even today, the 'relativity' of norms is apparent; one only has to think of traditional female circumcision in East Africa. Nonetheless, we can argue that it is the essence (and the right) of female sexuality not to be mutilated, even if – contrary to Habermas' postulate 'uncoerced and equal participation'[41] – the victims themselves have often accepted and still accept the tradition. There are, indeed, 'inhumane traditions and cultures' because they run counter to life (from slavery to anti-Semitism). Tolerance nullifies itself in the face of the inherently intolerant.

Elemental essentialism, or: the Good as memory of the 'nature of a thing'

In this essay, I would like to promote an approach to moral philosophy evocative of this nearly forgotten belief that 'good is that which is in accordance with reality'[42] – or, following the old terminology, that *agere sequitur esse* (the action follows the being). Ethics, then, would first and foremost be an 'attention to reality' (R. Spaemann), and not the fulfilment of a certain purpose or a utilitarian realization of objectives.

Recent ethnology has proven that all cultures and subcultures share a condemnation of intentional lies in relationships of trust, the disregard of something deemed legitimate, the theft of rightfully obtained property, the partiality of a judge, and especially the killing of the innocent (when affiliated with the in-group).[43]

---

supposed to be profitable but simply 'just' and impartial, to meet its responsibility (essence). On this concept of nature see R. Spaemann, *Philosophische Essays*, Klett-Cotta, Stuttgart 1994, pp. 19–40.

41 The original principle of discourse ethics reads somewhat more generally 'that only those norms can claim validity that can claim (or could claim) the approval of all those concerned, i.e. those participating in practical discourse', as in J. Habermas' *Moralbewusstsein und kommunikatives Handeln* (Suhrkamp, Frankfurt am Main 1983, p. 103).

42 Thus R. Spaemann, *Moralische Grundbegriffe, op. cit.*, p. 91.

43 J. Brantl, *Verbindende Moral. Theologische Ethik und kulturvergleichende Humanethologie*, Freiburg in Breisgau 2001, here: Kapitel 3.2: *Mögliche moralische Universalien im Licht kulturenvergleichender Verhaltensforschung*, pp. 126–142. Brantl lists four categorical universal-normative fields he believes to be common to all cultures:
  – obligations arising from kinship (prohibiting incest, proscribing exogamy, loyalty towards one's family, reciprocal care between parents and children),
  – in-group rules such as prohibiting violence or caring for the poor and disadvantaged,
  – strict rules about what to refrain from, such as condemning homicide – within the in-group (!) – respect for the dead, the binding nature of promises,
  – universal 'economic' demands, such as the right to own property, prohibiting theft.
From this point, Brantl develops an interesting 'ethological decalogue' (pp. 128–141), allowing for a well-founded proximity to the Biblical Decalogue. On the problem of the dichotomy between a normative religious cosmopolitanism and its institutional power to ostracise in an inverted form of fundamentalism, respectively, U. Beck, *Der eigene Gott. Friedensfähigkeit*

Elemental essentialism thus grounds norms not on the maximization of advantages, but on the binding nature of the essence of an entity or a relationship. For example, it is in the nature of a judge to administer justice impartially; it is in the nature of communication to always approximate truth; and it is in the nature of *oiko nomia* to secure the livelihood of those involved, and ALL those involved, while the accumulation of capital or even profit maximization as an end in itself are not within this nature.[44] Thus, coming up with an 'ethics' cannot be the objective of a couple of people involved in drafting a business policy; it is the norm to which business policy has to be adjusted. Ethics 'is nothing but arranging factual aspects in accordance with reality', Robert Spaemann writes.[45]

It is downright contradictory (at least in Western tradition) to conceive of ethics as one set of values *among* others, such as performance values, social values or communicative values, to be chosen or preferred for business guidelines.[46] To rate something as 'ethically good' has to be clearly distinguished from rating something as 'functionally good' (for health, for revenues, for business growth), as there may be circumstances detrimental to business that are ethically imperative; just think of rotten meat or child pornography, in whose cases a withdrawal from the market can quite definitely be called for.

In education politics, this thought has the potential of being highly explosive as well, such as if one should plan on quarantining all considerations on responsibility into subjects such as 'Ethics' or 'Religious Education'. No, ethics – i.e. 'reflected morality' – is part of a universal educational mandate to be dealt with in all subjects.

Before we can delve deeper into this complex, however, we will have to address what the second top manager stated. Dreaming of lashing down the 'greater good' as the ultimate norm for 'the good', we hear from this chairman that, for profitability's sake, one may act unethically.

---

und Gewaltpotential der Religionen, Verlag der Weltreligionen, Frankfurt am Main 2008, especially Kapitel VI: *Frieden statt Wahrheit*, pp. 207–249.

44 On Aristotle's *oiko nomia* and its criticism of purchases for the end of purchasing (chrematistics), M. Assländer, *Grundlagen der Wirtschafts...*, op. cit., pp. 28–31. As early as 1943, the American literary scholar C.S. Lewis presented a very interesting, albeit incomplete summary of essential intercultural ethical universals (C.S. Lewis, *Die Abschaffung des Menschen*, trans. from English M. Gisi, Johannes Verlag Einsiedeln, Freiburg 2003, pp. 91–103, English original: Oxford 1943). The fact that this essentialist approach may trigger fascinating developments in economic ethics is manifest in the recent criticism of the banking sectors having neglected 'essential' duties. *Cf.* H.-W. Sinn, *Kasino-Kapitalismus. Wie es zur Finanzkrise kam, und was jetzt zu tun ist*, Econ, Berlin 2010: Kapitel 4: *Warum Wall Street zum Spielkasino wurde*, pp. 108–138.

45 R. Spaemann, *Moralische Grundbegriffe*, op. cit., 89.

46 Josef Wieland partly tends towards this. J. Wieland, *Gesellschaftliche Verantwortung der Unternehmen*, [in:] J. Wieland et al. (eds.), *Unternehmensethik im Spannungsfeld der Kulturen und Religionen*, Kohlhammer, Stuttgart 2006, diagram p. 8.

Utilitarianism and the dehumanizing 'totalitarity of the greater good'

Having originated in macroeconomic theories (Jeremy Bentham and John Stuart Mill), this utilitarian approach to ethics still implies to originally be 'situated in real life'. It is all about optimizing, about achieving the greatest possible amount of happiness for the greatest possible amount of people, as the universally accepted ethical formula goes:

> That behavior or rule for behavior is ethically right whose effects on the well-being of those involved are the most beneficial ones.[47]

However, several objections have to be raised for humaneness' sake. Well-being, the common good, is an abstract authority of responsibility we believe to be answerable to. Thus, a concrete other (as found in centuries of religious tradition) has been substituted by an abstraction to which we only owe a general attempt to optimize it. Perhaps by now it has become clear that the optimization principle cannot prevent the objectification of people; on the contrary, it promotes this process by trade-offs that may often benefit a large number of people. Most likely, the current popularity of the responsibility concept rests on its clandestine connotation of morality as something personal; answerability implies the idea of 'face-to-face', irreconcilable with those anonymous powers (and 'markets') that would love to buy and win and adjust our convictions and our conscience. Answerability is a term of human belonging, of becoming aware while being in dialogue.

This metaphor of a dialogical responsibility has its roots in the understanding of final authority as a personal entity. God as the great 'other', the 'you': this is the heritage of the Judeo-Christian tradition, whose traditional legitimation may find its last refuge in the contemporary renaissance of the concept of responsibility. Without this image of having to 'respond' to someone, we would be left with being more or less well functioning parts of abstract systems, which could no longer be questioned whether they actually serve humanity. Humanity itself would be cancelled in this equation.

Similarly worth considering is the critical questioning of who believes what benefit to be worth striving for, and whether a category such as justice has its place when thoughts are governed by the principle of usefulness. Whose prerogative is the definition of usefulness, so to speak? This utilitarian way of thinking hands moral conscience over to an instrumental rationality. Or, to corroborate this by an example: if the costs of rescuing the three poor miners buried in a Chilean copper mine for three months had been higher (which they probably were) than

---

47 O. Höffe, *Einführung...*, *op. cit.*, p. 11.

the costs of creating the respective number of new beds in intensive care, why not simply cover the shaft with concrete?

If isolated from other principles, the utilitarian approach to ethics cannot – at least not by itself – break away from its *aporiae*.[48]

Elemental essentialism has an answer to the dilemma mentioned above: that we have an ethical relationship with these miners, which entails that we are not responsible for all of the world's problems, that we have a (professional) relationship with them, that we will not desert them as our business partners because they belong to us and costs are not the (first) priority.

Also, we have to scrutinize utilitarian ethics in regard to whether it might not actually nullify the essence of morality (when it only anonymously fulfils its optimizing function), since one of those 'greater goods' in favour of which a lesser evil may be accepted (usually that would be depriving the powerless of their rights[49]) is always conceivable (classless society, racially pure society,[50] purging heresy, maximizing profits, the majority's prosperity, etc.).

Currently, this is most blatantly recognizable in the so-called corporate raiders (in Germany often called *Heuschrecken*, i.e. 'locusts') that – mostly, but not always (!) – do everything in their might to increase revenue, oblivious to their possibly immediate responsibility for employees, which should not be sacrificed on the altar of profit maximization.

Additionally, utilitarianism's claim to be able to decide what is best for a spatially and temporally far remote world[51] seems presumptuous to me. Did not nuclear energy once seem to be the magical formula for satiating the world's hunger

---

48   On the victim-conception implicit in modernity's dispositional ethics *cf.* R. Girard, G. Vattimo, *Christentum und Relativismus*, Herder, Freiburg 2008.

49   Just think of the fate of South America's indigenous peoples whose forced displacement helped with the ongoing exploitation of mineral resources. Undoubtedly, this benefited the greatest amount of people the most. Still, it remains an injustice, because the protection of indigenous living species has ethical priority.

50   This is something that should be taken very seriously. Michael Wildt has illustrated stringently how the 'ethics' that drove the Holocaust's elites, those making up the top level of the *Reichssicherheitshauptamt*, the 'ethics' that drove the *Einsatzgruppen* commanders in the East, the heads of the concentration camps and the generals of the *Waffen-SS*, how those 'ethics' were subordinate to a consequentialist ethics: 'Only success mattered. It justified their deeds as well as their ideas. The deed legitimised itself. This generation's worldview was distinguished not so much by specific political beliefs but rather by a specific structure of political thinking. Politics always aimed at the absolute, the totality, and was not allowed to be subjected to regulating norms or any kind of moral laws whatsoever'. M. Wildt, *Generation des Unbedingten. Das Führungskorps des Reichssicherheitshauptamtes*, HIS Verlag, Hamburg 2008, p. 854.

51   On a systematic criticism of utilitarianism as a strategy for optimisation see R. Spaemann, *Über die Unmöglichkeit einer universalteleologischen Ethik* [in:] *id., Grenzen. Zur ethischen Dimension des Handelns*, Klett-Cota, Stuttgart 2001, pp. 193–212.

for energy? Asbestos the ultimate means of insulation? The car-friendly city the solution to our demands for mobility?

If the end justifies the means, you only have to find ends general enough, and anything goes. Early thinkers such as John Rawls had to reintroduce the principle of fairness in their theories of justice in order to overcome utilitarianism's principle of maximization, which was ignorant of justice.[52] For example, in the debate on economic ethics, it is a known fact that increasing the GDP does not necessarily ensure a just distribution of the generated surplus value in accordance with the accepted norms of allotment. It is even less true that an increase in wealth, at least when defined solely as GDP growth, brings forth an equal increase in the feeling of well-being. Thus, the poor kingdom of Bhutan's current example teaches the affluent West to give more thought to a 'gross domestic sense of happiness', which anything but correlates with GDP-growth indicators.[53]

If not contingent upon other ethical principles, utilitarianism eventually remains as an instrumental strategy of optimization, which, while definitely capable of creating (mostly technical) positive effects, is not capable of offering ethical orientation, but instead passes the ethical questions down to the technicians.

Of course, I do not want to claim that economic decisions obviously securing survival and human prosperity should not be made according to a shrewd weighing of choices. I am simply trying to shed light on what way of thinking clearly does *not* contribute to an ethically sustainable foundation of economics, and, of course, in what way and to whom ethically relevant behaviour is answerable. Whether the chairman cited above was a technician is not recorded, but with his words he gives himself in to an answerability that no longer has to answer to anyone, as its 'anyone' is only a cold 'more' whose boundaries are infinite.

Elemental ethics today: Limited while unconditional responsibility

Drawing on the Stoa, this section will try to illuminate the approach to ethics introduced here as an ethics of boundaries that is not taken in by a functional reductionism. In the third chapter of his work *De officiis*[54], Marcus Tullius Cicero distinguished three levels of obligation (responsibilities one is obliged to):
– MORES are normative factualities: that which is customary. They have to be respected *a priori*, but this – as we would say today – factual normativity is

52 J. Rawls, *Eine Theorie der Gerechtigkeit*, Suhrkamp, Frankfurt am Main 1975.
53 S. Klein, *Die Glücksformel. Oder wie die guten Gefühle entstehen*, S. Fischer, Gütersloh 2008.
54 M.T. Cicero, *De Officiis – Vom Pflichtgemäßen Handeln*, lateinisch und deutsch, übersetzt, kommentiert und herausgegeben von H. Gunermann, Reclam, Stuttgart 1984.

not endowed with an intrinsic ethical authority. The second level Cicero speaks of are

- LEGES, the republican rights agreed upon in free public speeches and debates. These, the laws, are already invested with a high degree of authority. Cicero opposes this legal positivism with
- HONESTUM (the honourable), which is, in fact, the sphere of our voluntary self-restraint. In doing so, Cicero explicitly distinguishes HONESTUM from an UTILE (the useful); that which is *honestum* is done for its own sake, while a true *utile* can only be legitimate in connection with this authoritative character of the *honestum*.[55]

In turn, the *honestum* is defined in regard to the 'nature of a thing'. This idea of a 'thing naturally right', i.e. the tradition of natural law, while marginalized in post-modernity, has never disappeared.[56] Of course, we cannot draw on the tradition of a similar meta-constitution supposed to be above all other positively set laws; trying to remember what might be imperatively binding 'by itself' does not, however, seem to have disappeared completely behind all the neo-constructivist interpretations of obligation.

To give an example: by definition, it is an imperative part of a judge's role or obligation to be impartial, despite the fact that biased sentences might be quicker, cheaper, or more profitable. Similarly, promises are universally understood to be binding statements because that is their nature – hence the dictate to give them but rarely. It is improper to say that in spite of my pledge I have found something better, more profitable, healthier, or more comfortable. The free, that is to say, un-enforceable promise is a preference for something or someone that is at the core of freedom. Therefore, a medical doctor has to heal; his self-conception cannot derive from a possible obligation towards cutting costs or furthering research or any other notion 'irrelevant to the thing itself'; if it did, he would no longer be a medical doctor.[57] Lastly, those carrying economic responsibility are supposed to provide meaningful products and services that serve humankind, but that do not, while definitely allowed to benefit the producer, neglect the requirements for a positive outcome, as Joseph Schumpeter has suggested. In my opinion, it is this *aporia* which the 'Occupy' movement has reacted to.

---

55 Ch. Schröder, *Verantwortung – Profil eines komplexen Begriffes*, [in:] U. Meier, B. Sill (eds.), *Zwischen Gewissen und Gewinn. Werteorientierte Personalführung und Organisationsentwicklung*, Friedrich Pustet, Regensburg 2005, p. 337.

56 Recently, again R. Spaemann, *Die Aktualität de Naturrechtes*, [in:] *id., Philosophische...*, *op. cit.*, pp. 60–78.

57 The doctor – patient relationship is, after all, a moral relationship necessarily based on the doctor's intention to secure the patient's well-being and/or the alleviation of the patient's suffering. If the doctor abandons this obligation, he is no longer a doctor.

To put it in a philosophical nutshell: the factual demands of a moral relationship's essence define the 'unconditionally good'. None of the particular factual demands can call on a totalitarian hierarchy, as the following – regretfully little known – totalitarianism-critical narrative by Thomas Aquinas shows well: Everybody has to meet their own ethical demands. Once, this used to be called conscience, pertaining to the fact that there is no all-encompassing ethical theory that everything else is derivable from.

At present, we can observe a growing openness towards the communicative self-evidence of a factual morality and the increasing willingness to use concepts of human dignity (and their formulations as human rights) as discursive limits.

Consequently, ethical as well as, interestingly, economic discourse cites Adam Smith's famous 'invisible hand' less frequently than it cites Kant's dictum of 'dignity and value', whose authority and decisive power are never questioned.[58] As Kant wrote in *Groundwork of the Metaphysics of Morals*,

> That which has a price can be replaced by something different, something equivalent; that which is above all prices and does not allow for an equivalent, that has dignity.[59]

The transcendent legitimation of the idea of human dignity, which Kant gives in the following, is unfortunately rather rarely quoted – perhaps out of 'unintentional interest', as one may be tempted to say: Kant, the demolisher of proofs of God, surely could not have promoted a philosophical legitimation based on a concept of transcendence?! Kant's somewhat idiosyncratic argument which he makes for a dignity which cannot be derived from economic factors goes as follows: thinking about dignity as derived from the category of 'price' cannot even 'be attempted [...] without violating the SANCTITY [my emphasis – U.M.] of dignity itself.'[60] Emile Durkheim will draw on this thought later on by introducing the 'sacrality of the person'.[61]

---

58 N.E. Bowie, *Business Ethics. A Kantian Perspective*, Blackwell Publishers, Malden 1999.

59 German quote taken from GMS BA 77. More precisely: I. Kant, *Grundlegung zur Metaphysik der Sitten* (1785), [in:] *id., Werke*, vol. 7, Frankfurt am Main 1982, p. 68.

60 *Ibid.*, p. 69.

61 Also, the context in which Kant formulates his conception of dignity is significant. It is found in the chapter on the theory of virtue in the *Metaphysics of Morals*, more precisely in the subchapter on 'sycophancy'. To Kant, dignity is not primarily a defensive right, such as in Article 1 of the German Basic Law, but a mandate for shaping one's own self which grows from this dignity: 'Do not become people's slaves. – Do not let your rights be trampled on without repercussions. – Do not take up debts without being able to guarantee for their restitution. Do not accept benefactions which you have no need of, and do not become parasites or sycophants or even beggars (only to be distinguished from the former by means of degree). Be thrifty, in order not to become poor. – Lamenting and whimpering, even screaming due to bodily pain is not worthy of you [...]. – Kneeling down or prostrating, even in the worship of divine entities, thus objectifying yourself, runs counter to your human dignity, just as the

Still, we are left with the realization that most decisions in life have to be made by means of weighing up the choices, and that 'the functional good' therefore determines our everyday life as well as the fields of our professional decision-making (Colgate or Elmex, public transit or car, e-car or fuel-saving car, Monica or Michelle?) and even when deliberating issues of consumer responsibility in regard to economic, business, and everyday ethics.

It starts to become clear that most fields of decision-making are still located within the sphere of rational assessments indebted to the principle of the weighing of alternatives. Nevertheless, there are several discernible segments of life in which this categorical limit of an unconditional 'ought', as acknowledged by Kant, has been clearly situated normatively.

The limits of an ethics of trade-off, understood as benefit maximization *Traditions of moral 'no-go areas' in Western thought*

With the origins of the modern constitutional state, Western societies have already successively subjugated themselves to limitations of a possible weighing of choices: a government's or a majority's potential political and legislative aims are no longer generally justifiable.

The constitutional state and the limitation of majority decisions

From the Magna Charta of 1215 to the Habeas Corpus Act of 1679, to the Virginia Bill of Rights of 1776 and the step-by-step extended civil rights of the U.S. American Bill of Rights of 1789, which eventually led to the Universal Declaration of Human Rights in 1948, Euro-American constitutional development has not only wrested rights from the absolutist monarch's despotism, but also from the democratic parliament's majority power and thus from a purely rationally oriented discourse.[62] This development betrays an underlying conviction that hails from natural law: namely, that some essential things in life, in this case civil rights due to the unalterable nature of a human as a human, may no longer be

---

invocation of the divine in images; for you thus humble yourselves not in front of an ideal which your own reason submits you to, but in front of an idol which you have unreasonably made up.' Quote after K.P. Liessmann, *Lob der Grenze. Kritik der politischen Urteilskraft*, Zsolnay Verlag, Wien 2012, p. 65.

62 N. Brieskorn, *Menschenrechte. Eine historisch-philosophische Grundlegung*, Kohlhammer, Stuttgart 1997.

subjected to modification – not even through democratic majorities – and cannot be allowed to be at the mercy of majority-voting and its trade-off discourses.

With this, Western constitutional democracies did not only pass on norms – incidentally originating in Judeo-Christian thought – protecting personality rights,[63] such as those of the Decalogue, but also retained a scepticism towards an easily corruptible discourse, which is not immune to being instrumentalized by utilitarianism.[64]

Thus, it is safe to say that the idea of 'unalienable basic or human rights' preserves and sanctions the admonition not to keep the discourse on fundamental basic norms open for too long: some things can be traded off against others – others can never be!

No grandstand view in sight: Thomas Aquinas' criticism of the possibility of an ultimate trade-off

In a regretfully little-known section of his work,[65] the church father Thomas Aquinas narrates a – as one would say today – moral dilemma: Royal bailiffs are hunting down a criminal hiding at his wife's place. For our modern tastes, aspiring towards ultimate solutions, Thomas distinguishes his definitions of responsibilities in a surprisingly irritating way: what is the wife supposed to do? In Thomas' opinion, she is responsible for her husband's private well-being and should hide him. What are the attorneys supposed to do? They are supposed to help implement the law (and promote the common good). And finally, the crucial question: Which obligation has the higher priority? What criteria, according to Thomas Aquinas, are at our disposal when we want to decide on the best course of action? Aquinas' answer is somewhat disturbing: only God knows.

This passage challenges totalitarian ethical claims that perceive themselves as authorities on the common good. Thomas remains modest. Since ethical

---

63 On the origin of human rights *cf.* K. Hilpert, *Menschenrechte und Theologie. Forschungsbeiträge zur ethischen Dimension der Menschenrechte*, Universitätsverlag, Freiburg 2001, pp. 59–87.

64 This is apparent, *inter alia*, in the fact that for a long time, the fathers of the American constitution could conceive of neither Native Americans nor Afro-American slaves and their descendants as legal persons entitled to invoke the Bill of Rights. All too often, their view was distorted by (plantation) business considerations as well as racist ideologies, which played a decisive role in – now quite literally – trading off the rights of the indigenous and African 'human commodities'.

65 Th. Aquinas, *Summa theologica*, I–II, quaestio 19, articulus 10, as quoted in R. Spaemann, *Die schlechte Lehre vom guten Zweck*, [in:] *id., Grenzen..., op. cit.*, p. 399.

obligations arise from specific moral circumstances, we are not to strive for the knowledge of that which benefits everybody. Only God possesses this knowledge.

This conviction seems to me to be an important corrective against all totalitarian temptations of modernity, a modernity which tends to glorify absolute instrumentality. Thomas Aquinas teaches us that we do not possess the final answer on the ultimate question of the sense behind things. Democracy needs religion. Also in its defence against totalitarian tendencies!

Modernity, having lost its trust in the concept of 'the good', may not be able to do this anymore. This does not mean, however, that it silently bears this inability to find ultimate solutions; on the contrary, it grimly tries to solve the paradox, to dismantle it, and eventually to eliminate it.[66]

Thomas Aquinas may be able to teach us something: SOME THINGS CAN BE TRADED OFF AGAINST OTHERS, OTHERS CAN NEVER BE. Maybe the secret to a humane 'solution' lies in living with this tension of not being able to find a quick solution that reveals all things' ultimate purpose, while contradictions will 'cancel' themselves out eventually in the long term. To use the words of a contemporary critic of totalitarianism: 'Nothing is true without its opposite.'[67]

Bringing to mind what is always destructive: The theory of the Intrinsece Mala, or Where the ends can never justify the means

So far, we have taken a closer look at Thomas Aquinas' critical reminder of the necessity to limit profit maximization, as the weighing of alternatives. Now, we can consider an ethical tradition that assumes not so much that we can find the answer in our quest for ethical consistency by positively asking what is TO BE DONE, but rather, more modestly, contemplates what is most certainly NOT TO BE DONE to preserve universal well-being.

This expresses an ethical experience less concerned with what helps establish the individual's happiness (which is, indeed, a central purpose of ethics as the theory of good life[68]), but rather with what is to be refrained from in order to realize life's purpose.

---

66   It might be useful to conduct a cultural-critical inquiry into our inability to sustain supposed and actually existing paradoxes in many areas of our everyday lives, into our preoccupation with finding smooth solutions, with eliminating problems and solving contradictions, and – ultimately – our preoccupation with the 'whole'.

67   Martin Walser in an interview: 'Wealth makes independent. But also ugly.' In: 'Frankfurter Allgemeine Sonntagszeitung' 9.09.2007, 36, 38. This quote is one of Walser's life maxims; he often mentions it and also uses it in his novels.

68   O. Höffe, *Lebenskunst und Moral – oder macht Tugend glücklich?*, C.H. Beck, München 2007.

In ethics as well as in the philosophy of law, the prohibiting commandment ('Thou shalt not kill!') usually carries more weight,[69] as it is more difficult to tell how an individual may find their own happiness, their content with themselves (*eudaimonia*), and eventually, their life's goal. Prescriptive commandments, on the other hand, suffer from the defect that we cannot know what benefits the other person in the end, although it is definitely possible to contextualize 'failure to render assistance'.

Thus, throughout the history of thought and of convictions, a canon of unconditional prohibitions has emerged,[70] which offers orientation even today when the truth about the individual's unobjectifiable nature is presupposed.

Interestingly, this longstanding tradition of 'intrinsically wrongful actions' (*intrinsece mala* or *malum ex genere*) readopts the relationships of responsibility that make us humans as individuals and in which we become persons:
- the right to life and limb,
- authentic communication,
- personal sexuality,
- the integrity of an individual's personality,
- our relationship with the ultimate meaning of life.

In the following section, I will give a brief overview of this tradition's historical development:
- In works as early as Aristotle's *Nicomachean Ethics*, we can find an argumentation that assigns to certain behaviour the quality of being 'intrinsically bad', and irremediably so, even when serving a good cause. Among these are adultery, larceny, and homicide:

> All these things are condemned because they are intrinsically wrong; not only in excess or in their lack. Committing them, one can never come close to the right thing to do, but only be guilty of misconduct.[71]

- In line with the idea of the *intrinsece mala* already established by Aristotle, Thomas Aquinas stresses the fact that actions such as intentional lying, homicide (i.e. killing innocents), adultery (i.e. breaking loyalty vows taken in 'valid'

---

69 Prohibitive, rather than prescriptive commandments, dominate jurisdiction even today. E. Schockenhoff, *Grundlegung der Ethik. Ein theologischer Entwurf*, Herder, Freiburg in Breisgau 2007, here Zweiter Teil, I, 3.2d: *Handeln und Unterlassen oder Handeln durch Tun und Handeln durch Nicht tun*, pp. 490–498.

70 For a historical overview: E. Schockenhoff, *Naturrecht und Menschenwürde. Universale Ethik in einer geschichtlichen Welt*, Grünewald, Mainz 1996, here chapter IV, 4.1 (*Die negativen Verbote des Naturrechtes*) and 4.2 (*Die in sich schlechten Handlungen*), pp. 200–232.

71 Aristoteles, *Die Nikomachische Ethik*, 1107, 10–14, C.H. Beck, München 1998, p. 141.

marriages), as well as larceny,[72] apostasy[73] and also blasphemy,[74] are always intrinsically wrong, regardless of any possible supposedly good consequences; they cannot be justified by being the means to ends worth striving for. With this, Thomas Aquinas draws on ideas of St. Augustine, who had already criticized instrumental ethics in the early church: the end does not justify the means![75]

— In the context of unbound modernity's breaches in human rights, the Second Vatican Council, expanding the teachings on the *intrinsice mala*, named the interdicted deeds which can never be reconciled with a person's dignity. Under the premise that a believer should discern the presence of Christ in those who are suffering, it introduced a canon of actions intrinsically wrong which the 20th century nevertheless deemed *de facto* justified by the invocation of various notions of 'greater good':

> Furthermore, whatever is opposed to life itself, such as any type of murder, genocide, abortion, euthanasia or wilful self-destruction, whatever violates the integrity of the human person, such as mutilation, torments inflicted on body or mind, attempts to coerce the will itself; whatever insults human dignity, such as [...] disgraceful working conditions, where men are treated as mere tools for profit, rather than as free and responsible persons; all these things and others of their like are infamies indeed. They poison human society, but they do more harm to those who practice them than those who suffer from the injury. Moreover, they are supreme dishonor to the Creator (*Gaudium and Spes* 27).[76]

The long enumeration of many depersonalizing actions can be summarized as the unconditional demand for respect towards the dignity of human life,

---

72 With good reason, commentators point out Thomas Aquinas' several inconsistencies, since he justifies petty larceny of food in another section. E. Schockenhoff, *Naturrecht und Menschenwürde...*, *op. cit.*, p. 204. The fact that Thomas erred in other areas, such as in his evaluation of women according to natural law, is another issue concerning the Dominican from Aquin.

73 References to Thomas cited in E. Schockenhoff, *Grundlegung der Ethik...*, *op. cit.*, p. 398.

74 According to Thomas Aquinas, habitual blasphemy is 'the language of hell' and a sign of damnation: S. th. II–II quaestio 13 art. 4, *cf*.: B. Häring, *Das Gesetz Christi*, vol. 2, E. Wewel, Freiburg 1963.

75 In *Contra Mendacium* (VII, 18), Augustine writes: 'Who would, in the face of actions intrinsically wrongful, such as larceny, fornication and blasphemy, dare to claim that those were no longer sins when done for the right reasons; or, even less convincingly, conclude that they were justifiable sins?' PL 40, 528; see also E. Schockenhoff's perceptive considerations in *Grundlegung der Ethik...*, *op. cit.*, p. 453ff.

76 *Pastoralkonstitution über die Kirche in der Welt von heute* (*Gaudium et spes*), No. 27. English version available at the Vatican's homepage: *Pastoral Constitution on the Church in the Modern World 'Gaudium et Spes' Promulgated by His Holiness, Pope Paul VI on December 7, 1965,* http://www.vatican.va/archive/hist_councils/ii_vatican_council/documents/vat-ii_const_19651207_gaudium-et-spes_en.html (accessed: 1.09.2012).

whose bodily, mental and economic dimensions the Council deemed necessary to respect and possible to define.

– In his 1993 encyclical *Veritatis Splendor*, Pope John Paul II confirms the above-mentioned teachings on inacceptable actions. He, too, believes those actions to be intrinsically anti-personal to such a degree that no good can come of them.[77] He continues his argument by critically consolidating earlier theories – above all, in regard to their moral-philosophical foundation, which is consequentialism:

> Consequently, circumstances or intentions can never transform an act intrinsically evil by virtue of its object into an act 'subjectively' good or defensible as a choice.[78]

Experience teaches us that we shudder to think of a person said to be capable of everything; some deep intuition senses the ultimate amorality of his actions, which no longer acknowledge any boundaries; he is willing to sacrifice everything – and, even more likely, everybody – for his 'greater good'.

'Stop Signs' for today: Unconditional boundaries for humanity's sake

As a last point I would like to summarize these moral-philosophical debates on contemporary *intrinsece mala* and their historical roots, which set up moral boundaries without recourse to utilitarianism. One can indeed identify 'unconditional boundaries for the sake of human dignity' which are not merely contingent on historical traditions.[79] Thus, one can identify the following 'stop signs' derived from ethics, which adhere to the principle that a person is not objectifiable and which conceives of responsibility as an immediate responsibility, ensuing from 'the nature of an entity'. These 'stop signs' can do so because they are sceptical towards recourses to ends and purposes perceived to be ultimately good:

---

77 John Paul II, *Enzyklika Veritatis splendor, Der Glanz der Wahrheit*, Christiana Verlag, Stein am Rhein 1993, ch. IV: *Die sittliche Handlung*. Here, the pope recalls a dictum from Paul's Epistle to the Romans (Rom 3,8), essentially saying: 'Though shalt not do evil to bring about good.'

78 *Veritatis splendor*, Nor. 81. English version available at the Vatican's homepage: Ioannes Paulus PP. II, *Veritatis Splendor*, http://www.vatican.va/holy_father/john_paul_ii/encyclicals/documents/hf_jp-ii_enc_06081993_veritatis-splendor_en.html (accessed: 1.09.2012).

79 Accordingly, E. Schockenhoff, *Grundlegung der Ethik...*, *op. cit.*, pp. 397–422; also E. Schockenhoff, *Naturrecht und Menschenwürde...*, *op. cit.*, pp. 209–232; R. Spaemann, *Moralische Grundbegriffe, op. cit*; *cf.* also H. Küng, *Anständig wirtschaften – Warum Ökonomie Moral braucht*, Piper, München – Zürich 2010, pp. 239–287.

– On the Goodness of Life:

It is unconditionally and intrinsically wrong to kill an innocent human being intentionally. No hardship – not even when weighed against another person's life – justifies annihilating the life of a human being. His or her right to live is unalienable.

– On the goodness of the morally autonomous person's integrity:

It is reprehensible to torture a human being. Torture breaks a person's core, objectifies him or her to such an extent that he or she is no longer a subject. This is valid independently of (legal or ethical) guilt.

– On the goodness of communicative identity:

It is intrinsically wrong to violate another's rights to truthfulness in relationships of trust and to break promises when having given them consciously and considered them carefully. A promise's intrinsic nature is to be kept. Without a mutual pledge of truthfulness, the exchange of arguments and indeed any communicative community are *per se* impossible.

– On the goodness of the unity of body and soul in sexuality:

It is contradictory to functionalize and instrumentalize the voluntary provision of a person's body as this would mean violating the personal nature of the other, who can expect unconditional acceptance in love.

– On the goodness of an axiomatic affirmation of reality:

It is a danger to meaning itself if meaningful existence and the existence of meaning are generally disputed. Whether in affirmation or contradiction, even non-theistic explanations of life presuppose the desirability of life to some extent. This general desirability of *Dasein* and *Sein* must not be negated.

To sum this up normatively:

♦ ON THE GOODNESS OF LIFE:
Never question the right to live!

♦ ON THE GOODNESS OF PERSONAL INTEGRITY:
Never violate anybody's freedom!

♦ ON THE GOODNESS OF COMMUNICATIVE IDENTITY:
Never break a promise!

♦ ON THE GOODNESS OF THE BODY-SOUL UNITY IN SEXUALITY:
No abuse; never!

♦ ON THE GOODNESS OF MEANINGFUL EXISTENCE:
Never declare everything meaningless!

Merely reminding ourselves of the unconditional boundaries to our ethical actions does not yet specify how the integrity of a person is violated, what exactly a 'consciously given promise' is, whether any form of AIDS prevention is already a form of 'instrumentalized sexuality', or whether minimum wage could be the logical consequence of the ban on objectification inherent in Kant's Categorical Imperative. Nevertheless, I hope that the desirable boundaries to an ethics of weighing up the choices have become clear, as well as the occasions on which we have to say: Some things can be traded off against others – others can never be!

It thus becomes clear that the tradition of unconditional 'oughts' is very close to the great religions' moral semantics, such as the Decalogue in Judaism and Christianity, the Surah 17 in Islam, and also the wisdom teachings and guidelines in Hinduism (the virtues of the path of Yoga)[80] and Buddhism (the eightfold path and the five precepts of Buddhism).

It may also be questioned – making use of the aforementioned scepticism of Jürgen Habermas – whether these unconditional 'oughts' can be generated by the judgment of reason alone, although the latter doubtlessly may corroborate them; perhaps a spiritually and also ritually grounded 'sacral motivation' is a prerequisite for being able to obey these 'unconditional commandments', which make us human, but make us inhuman if we subordinate them to other considerations.

And it is not hard to perceive that these 'unconditional commandments' also constitute the core of our human rights, which form the foundation for all Western constitutions.

If these human rights are deemed 'sacred', then we should consider very carefully whether it is really advisable to cancel out the 'sacred' as a legitimation and a guarantee for the inviolability of these rights in our constitutional democracies.

It is true that this reminder of the guardrails of a 'minimum-level ethics' has not yet outlined ethical behaviour in its entirety, providing meaning and rendering reality comprehensible; using a more modest approach, I have, however, tried to show which circumstances render the endowment with meaning and the comprehension of reality most certainly impossible.

Coming to a close on this ethics of boundaries, let us now synoptically formulate an ethics of principles that may offer some ethical orientation beyond avoiding the obstruction of personhood as outlined above. While the former section was about absolute 'stop signs' referring to the intrinsically inhumane, these principles shall be formulated positively: modifying Michael A. Pagano's grid for business ethics, the following 'moral check list' is to be understood as a General Guide suggesting traditional as well as contemporary orientation standards to help (like an ethical filter) distinguish what is beneficial towards a 'good life'. This basic ethical guide necessitates rational appraisal and opens up possibilities for humane behaviour, but also requires the above-mentioned absolute norms, which may not be subject to the weighing of alternatives.

---

80 1. Non-violence: A-Himsa 2. Truthfulness: Satya 3. Non-stealing: A-Steya 4. Chastity: Brahmacharya 5. Non-greediness: A-Parigraha, form the core morals of Hinduism.

Democracy has the task to find humane solutions in particular cases of the clash of interests.

The following principles may help form the bridge between the unconditional demands, which protect the core of what makes us human, and conditional norms, which open up possibilities to lead a good life.

The core of positive responsibility: Moral guideposts as ethical principles in decisions of responsibility

In the following, I shall up sum up my line of argumentation by introducing ethical viewpoints of the Western tradition which can give an ethical orientation a distinctive basis, 'ethical guideposts for everyday use', so to speak: As outlined above, one can attribute different degrees of responsibility (CAN, SHOULD, and MUST norms) to ethical principles for behaviour.

Whereas the aforementioned norms were MUST norms for leading a humane life, the Meier-Pagano Filter shall be understood as a SHOULD checklist. This is due to the fact that it is rather difficult to predict a positive outcome when imagining a successful life; one can determine with more certainty the circumstances under which a good life is made impossible.

If we want to sketch a canon of responsibility ethics, we should pre-eminently concern ourselves with the aspect of an operationizable ethical orientation. Those wishing to limit their actions to the ethical ones should espouse the following principles. A rational ethics can hardly get around them when striving to be the measure for a successful and good life:

The Meier-Pagano Filter for Humane Ethics
Guideposts leading towards the Good

LEGALITY PRINCIPLE Are my actions lawful? (in a working democracy!)	CATEGORICAL IMPERATIVE Are my actions generalizable? Do they (ab-)use another person? (I. Kant + German Basic Law Art. 1)	IMPARTIALITY FILTER What would my best friend say (who is not involved)? (J. Rawls)
PUBLICITY TEST Could I publicly justify my actions on TV? (J. Habermas)	RESPONSIBILITY AS AN ESSENTIAL ACCORDANCE	ECOLOGICAL IMPERATIVE Will my behaviour reduce my children's/grand-children's degrees of freedom? (H. Jonas)

GOLDEN RULE	UTILITARIAN WEIGHING	ESCHATOLOGICAL PRINCIPLE
Would I want the consequences of my actions to apply to myself? (Jesus/Buddha/Mohammed and all religions)	OF CHOICES Weighing up all my actions' consequences, would they benefit or harm more people? (J.S. Mill, J. Bentham)	OF MEANING Imagining my final hour, would my actions stand up to judgment? (Ignatius of Loyola)

A democratic education for youth should thus endorse both its religious roots as well as the sacred nature of its unconditional ethical demands, but nevertheless have the courage to critically question the historical constrictions of religious morals due to their political instrumentalization and setting them against the historically evolved principles of the democratic culture of weighing interests against another, both in non-violent discourse. For the culture of weighing interests against one another without recourse to violence is a vital moral tradition belonging to our spiritual heritage as well.

One could also close this essay by quoting Charles Taylor:

> [My] notion is that modern culture, in breaking with the structures and beliefs of Christendom [during the period of enlightenment and the ensuing democratization of authoritarian societies], also carried certain facets of Christian life further than they ever were taken or could have been taken within Christendom. In relation to the earlier forms of Christian culture, we have to face the humbling realization that the breakout was a necessary condition of the development.[81]

When heeding these ethical – and, at their origin, also religious – guideposts and judging an individual situation accordingly, our actions can hardly transgress the boundaries set for humanity as such.

Bibliography

Aristoteles, *Die Nikomachische Ethik*, C.H. Beck, München 1998.

Assländer M., *Grundlagen der Wirtschafts- und Unternehmensethik*, Metropolis Verlag, Marburg 2011.

Beck U., *Der eigene Gott. Friedensfähigkeit und Gewaltpotential der Religionen*, Verlag der Weltreligionen, Franfurt am Main 2008.

Berger P.L., *The Heretical Imperative*, Doubleday, Garden City, NY 1979.

Bertelsmann Stiftung (ed.), *Woran glaubt die Welt*, Verlag Bertelsmann Stiftung, Gütersloh 2009.

---

81 Ch. Taylor, *A Catholic Modernity* – lecture given in 1996 at the University of Dayton (Ohio), quote after H. Jonas, *Braucht der Mensch Religion? Über Erfahrungen der Selbsttranszendenz*, Suhrkamp, Freiburg am Main 2006, p. 98.

Bowie N.E., *Business Ethics. A Kantian Perspective*, Blackwell Publishers, Malden 1999.

Brantl J., *Verbindende Moral. Theologische Ethik und kulturvergleichende Humanethologie*, Freiburg in Breisgau 2001.

Brieskorn N., *Menschenrechte. Eine historisch-philosophische Grundlegung*, Kohlhammer, Stuttgart 1997.

Bucksteeg M., Hattendorf K., *Führungskräftebefragung 2010*, available at: http://www.wertekommission.de/content/pdf/kampagne/Fuehrungskraeftebefragung_2010.pdf (accessed: 17.09.2014).

Buss E., *Die deutschen Spitzenmanager. Wie sie wurden, was sie sind. Herkunft, Wertvorstellungen, Erfolgsregeln*, Oldenbourg Wissenschaftlicher Verlag, Oldenburg 2007.

Cicero M.T., *De Officiis – Vom Pflichtgemäßen Handeln*, lateinisch und deutsch, übersetzt, kommentiert und herausgegeben von H. Gunermann, Reclam, Stuttgart 1984.

'Frankfurter Allgemeine Sonntagszeitung' 9.09.2007, 36, 38.

Fried E., *Lebensschatten. Gedichte*, Wagenbach, Berlin 1981.

Girard R., Vattimo G., *Christentum und Relativismus*, Herder, Freiburg 2008.

Habermas J., *Moralbewusstsein und kommunikatives Handeln*, Suhrkamp, Frankfurt am Main 1983.

Habermas J., *Politik und Religion*, [in:] F.W. Graf, H. Meier (eds.), *Politik und Religion. Zur Diagnose der Gegenwart*, C.H. Beck, München 2013.

Häring B., *Das Gesetz Christi*, vol. 2, E. Wewel, Freiburg 1963.

Heidegger M., *Was heißt denken?*, Kohlhammer, Stuttgart 1992.

Hilpert K., *Menschenrechte und Theologie. Forschungsbeiträge zur ethischen Dimension der Menschenrechte*, Universitätsverlag, Freiburg 2001.

Höffe O., *Einführung in die utilitaristische Ethik*, A. Francke Verlag, Tübingen 2003.

Höffe O., *Lebenskunst und Moral – oder macht Tugend glücklich?*, C.H. Beck, München 2007.

Huber S., *Der Religionsmonitor 2008: Strukturelle Prinzipien, operationale Konstrukte, Auswertungsstrategien*, [in:] Bertelsmann Stiftung (ed.), *Woran glaubt die Welt*, Verlag Bertelsmann Stiftung, Gütersloh 2009.

Ioannes Paulus PP. II, *Veritatis Splendor*, available at: http://www.vatican.va/holy_father/john_paul_ii/encyclicals/documents/hf_jp-ii_enc_06081993_veritatis-splendor_en.html (accessed: 1.09.2012).

John Paul II, *Enzyklika Veritatis splendor, Der Glanz der Wahrheit*, Christina Verlag, Stein am Rhein 1993.

Jonas H., *Das Prinzip Verantwortung*, Suhrkamp, Frankfurt am Main 1984.

Jonas H., *Braucht der Mensch Religion? Über Erfahrungen der Selbsttranszendenz*, Freiburg 2006.

Kant I., *Grundlegung zur Metaphysik der Sitten* (1785), [in:] *id.*, *Werke*, vol. 7, Frankfurt am Main 1982.

Klein S., *Die Glücksformel. Oder wie die guten Gefühle entstehen*, S. Fischer, Gütersloh 2008.

Küng H., *Anständig wirtschaften – Warum Ökonomie Moral braucht*, Piper, München – Zürich 2010.

Lammert N., *Glaube Politik und Demokratie*, [in:] U. Kropac, U. Meier, K. König (eds.), *Jugend, Religion und Religiosität. Resultate, Probleme und Perspektiven der aktuellen Religiositätsforschung*, Pustet, Regensburg 2012.

Lewis C.S., *Die Abschaffung des Menschen*, trans. from English M. Gisi, Johannes Verlag Einsiedeln, Freiburg 2003.

Liessmann K.P., *Lob der Grenze. Kritik der politischen Urteilskraft*, Zsolnay Verlag, Wien 2012.

Meier H., *Politik, Religion und Philosophie*, [in:] W. Graf, H. Meier (eds.), *Politik und Religion. Zur Diagnose der Gegenwart*, C.H. Beck, München 2013.

Meulemann H., *Säkularisierung oder religiöse Erneuerung? Weltanschauung in 22 Gesellschaften: Befunde und Hinweise einer Querschnittsbefragung*, [in:] Bertelsmann Stiftung (ed.), *Woran glaubt die Welt*, Verlag Bertelsmann Stiftung, Gütersloh 2009.

Pastoral Constitution on the Church in the Modern World 'Gaudium et Spes' Promulgated by His Holiness, Pope Paul VI on December 7, 1965, available at: http://www.vatican.va/archive/hist_councils/ii_vatican_council/documents/vat-ii_const_19651207_gaudium-et-spes_en.html (accessed: 1.09.2012).

Rawls J., *Eine Theorie der Gerechtigkeit*, Suhrkamp, Frankfurt am Main 1975.

Ruland B., *Wernher von Braun. Mein Leben für die Raumfahrt*, Burda, Offenburg 1969.

Schockenhoff E., *Grundlegung der Ethik. Ein theologischer Entwurf*, Herder, Freiburg in Breisgau 2007.

Schockenhoff E., *Naturrecht und Menschenwürde. Universale Ethik in einer geschichtlichen Welt*, Grünewald, Mainz 1996.

Schröder Ch., *Verantwortung – Profil eines komplexen Begriffes*, [in:] U. Meier, B. Sill (eds.), *Zwischen Gewissen und Gewinn. Werteorientierte Personalführung und Organisationsentwicklung*, Friedrich Pustet, Regensburg 2005.

Shell Deutschland Holding (ed.), *Jugend 2010. Eine pragmatische Generation behauptet sich*, Fischer-Taschenbuch Verlag, Frankfurt am Main 2011.

Sinn H.-W., *Kasino-Kapitalismus. Wie es zur Finanzkrise kam, und was jetzt zu tun ist*, Econ, Berlin 2010.

Spaemann R., *Die Aktualität de Naturrechtes*, [in:] *id., Philosophische Essays*, Klett-Cotta, Stuttgart 1994.

Spaemann R., *Die schlechte Lehre vom guten Zweck*, [in:] *id., Grenzen. Zur ethischen Dimension des Handelns*, Klett-Cotta, Stuttgart 2001.

Spaemann R., *Moralische Grundbegriffe*, C.H. Beck, München 2008.

Spaemann R., *Philosophische Essays*, Reclam, Stuttgart 1994.

Spaemann R., *Über die Unmöglichkeit einer universalteleologischen Ethik*, [in:] id., *Grenzen. Zur ethischen Dimension des Handelns*, Klett-Cotta, Stuttgart 2001.

Strauss L., *Naturrecht und Geschichte*, Koehler, Stuttgart 1956.

Wieland J., *Gesellschaftliche Verantwortung der Unternehmen*, [in:] J. Wieland et al. (eds.), *Unternehmensethik im Spannungsfeld der Kulturen und Religionen*, Kohlhammer, Stuttgart 2006.

Wildt M., *Generation des Unbedingten. Das Führungskorps des Reichssicherheitshauptamtes*, HIS Verlag, Hamburg 2008.

Dariusz Góra-Szopiński
Nicolaus Copernicus University
Toruń (Poland)

Partnership in Innovation for the Good of Civil Society: A New Conceptual Framework

The Catholic Church has a proper and everlasting aim of evangelisation that remains both inimitable and impossible to abandon.[1] At the same time, though, the modes of its activity may vary from one period of time to another. Ours is a time of rediscovering the value of civil society, its moral sovereignty and legal priority over any state-run institutions. The collapse of Communism in 1989 might have signified the end of the world for the political regimes behind the Iron Curtain, but it also represented the end of the holiest secular faith for a good number of prominent minds in the Western world.[2] From then on, political institutions constructed along the lines of a socialist-like, authoritarian submission to the omnipotent secular State have been constantly called to reorganisation and devolution according to different, more society-centred formulas. Nowadays, it is common to talk in abundance about globalisation and market-oriented issues, but the core of the question remains social. As the German economist Ludwig Erhard put it in the 1940s, free economy means the same as social economy.[3] The two expressions are synonymous and signify an off-the-state approach, a grassroots or – if you wish – spontaneous order that emerges throughout the activity of civil society. The time has also come for the Church to revise its classical Church-and-State lines of reasoning and consider heading towards some more society-centred approach. The time has come for reasoning in terms of Church-and-Society conceptual framework.

---

1   Matthew 28:19.
2   P.L. Berger, *Social Ethics in a Post-Socialist World*, 'First Things' 1993, 4, 2, pp. 9–14.
3   Erhard's original phrase about 'freie oder soziale Marktwirtschaft' was adopted as the genuine name of the doctrine of social market economy.

A classical approach

The classical approach, in the case of the Roman Catholic Church, was developing until the mid-20th century. Its leading idea may be articulated by the formula: WE ARE SOCIETY. The Church considered itself as the right society, rightly governed and perfect in the legal sense of the term, which meant the ability to achieve the goals the society states for itself.[4] The outside world was regarded as semi-justified, to put it mildly, not very interesting from the cognitive point of view, and even dangerous from the moral one. The sense of inner righteousness dominated the analyses of the relation between the inner and outer spheres of this perfect entity. 'Civil society' as we understand it today remained neither desirable nor worthy of interest.

Such out-of-context, immutable and self-righteous perfectibility was put into question particularly at the Second Vatican Council (1962–1965). An eyewitness reporter explained at that time:

> The theology which has been entrenched for the last four hundred years, then, might fairly be described as 'non-historical' or even 'anti-historical'. It favours speculation which is not called to the bar of historical fact, past or present; moreover, it often seems to fear principles which would make it face such a bar. It sometimes discourages speculation altogether, and confines itself to making commentaries on a theoretical structure once built up, in the late Middle Ages, in the past. It would be fair to name this theology 'anti-historical orthodoxy', because it defends a system of propositions as orthodox, while refusing to commit itself to the work of investigating that system's historical justification, or making it relevant to the historical realities of the present. It would be fair to call it 'anti-historical orthodoxy', but a more neutral designation is simply 'non-historical'. For it defends an orthodoxy suspended, as it were, outside of history, in mid-air.[5]

Catholic theologian Michael Novak, the author of these words, developed his statements under the influence of Lord Acton, a century-older Catholic commentator of Vatican I (1870). Yet in the 19th century, Acton had been able to describe the ruling school of NON-HISTORICAL ORTHODOXY 'as afraid; as, in the end, intellectually lazy; as isolated from contact with unbelievers; as jealous of its authority; as unscrupulous in its treatment of other schools; as fearful of sources of evidence outside its own system'.[6]

Whilst the reforms undertaken at Vatican II have radically changed the state of affairs within the Catholic Church, the attitude described here as NON-HISTORICAL ORTHODOXY remains essential for the reasoning within the Orthodox Church as well as some sectarian denominations of Protestantism.

---

4   A. Ottaviani, *Institutiones iuris publici ecclesiastici*, vol. 1, Typis Polyglottis Vaticani, Roma 1947, pp. 44–45.
5   M. Novak, *The Open Church: Vatican II, Act II*, Darton, Longman & Todd, London 1964, p. 56.
6   *Ibid.*, p. 57.

The reforming efforts

The Catholic endeavour during Vatican II was motivated by a commonly shared effort of introducing oneself in an updated way (that is what the Italian word *aggiornamento* means) to the global society. The premise of the new Vatican theology was articulated best by the Polish cardinal Karol Wojtyła, who one day would become the Supreme Pontiff of the transforming Catholic community. Wojtyła pointed to the fact that it is not only the outside world that shall learn from the Church, but, conversely, it is also the Church that has something to learn from the world outside. The idea was expressed from the very first words of the document stating the positioning of the Church within the world of its times, the Constitution *Gaudium et spes*:

> The joys and the hopes, the griefs and the anxieties of the men of this age, [...] these are the joys and hopes, the griefs and anxieties of the followers of Christ.[7]

The Council Fathers experimented with a number of concepts and expressions that had not been adequately explained. One of these expressions referred to the 'signs of the times' revealed, as it seems, throughout the movements of the outside world. The concept was best explained in the works of Marie-Dominique Chenu, one of the advisors to the bishops, but not a decision-maker at the assembly. According to Fr. Chenu, the Church had ceased to dictate to the outside world what it should think or do. The Church is now called to grasp and understand what appears in the events of the secular world, which progresses in a fully autonomous way.[8]

While the general impact of the conciliar reform was positive and responded well to the expectations of many, a number of difficulties appeared which revealed the crisis of the post-conciliar Church. In declaring its convinced orientation towards the world outside, the Church found itself inexperienced in models and methods:

> From the outset its aim was to involve as many people as possible in the Church's decision-making process. The Dutch theologians who worked on the project frankly admitted that, finding no ecclesiastical models that were of any use, they had learned from the experience of large firms like Philips and General Motors which faced the same problem: how could people be made to feel involved in an excessively large institution?[9]

---

7 *Pastoral Constitution on the Church in the Modern World 'Gaudium et spes'*, Vatican II, 1965, no. 1.

8 M.-D. Chenu, *Les signes des temps. Réflexion théologique*, [in:] Y. Congar, M. Peuchmaurd (eds.), *L'Eglise dans le monde de ce temps. Constitution pastorale 'Gaudium et spes'*, Cerf, Paris 1967, vol. 2, pp. 214–215.

9 P. Hebblethwaite, *The Runaway Church: Post-Conciliar Growth or Decline*, Seabury Press, New York 1975, p. 47.

But even before came the problem of the language. The Church enthusiastically engaged in a 'dialogue' with the world. Optimistic and even ultra optimistic about the good intentions of their secular partners, the Church intellectuals made use of and borrowed on a large scale from secular languages of such domains as sociology, theory of management, psychoanalysis, and even political ideologies. The result was best described in a book by Alain Besançon, *La Confusion des lonques* (*The Confusion of Languages*). The author concluded his argument this way: 'Among all the functions of this [new] Catholic jargon one is to be noted in particular. It is a sign of UNIFORMITY that hides the non-existence of UNITY or rather substitutes the lost one'. (highlighted by author.)[10] The ultra optimism about the good intentions of every possible partner in dialogue led to the conclusion about the unity of goals proclaimed by all humankind. Wasn't it true that every single man and woman, as well as their communities no matter where in the world, were dreaming about love and peace and justice? Wasn't it true that even the secular social sciences of that time came to the conclusion about the 'end of ideology' and the 'convergence' in world progress? Wasn't THAT the very aim of the United Nations, the global parliament full of good intentions?

The dominant trace of the post-conciliar reformist way of reasoning was the deficiency of institutional thinking. The authors seemed to ignore the subtle level of interest, which plays a key factor in realist analyses of social reality. In particular, the state remained a 'big absent' of the debates.[11] This did not prevent, however, the personnel of the Church, now liberated from its traditional distinctive traces (cassock, tonsure, etc.), altogether with newly bolstered lay persons, from beginning to imitate, even in their fashion style, the professional culture of corporate business and state bureaucracy.[12]

It was good to develop the dialogue with the outside world; it was fine to focus on similarities and common causes. But the word 'crisis' that marks the period of the 1960s through 1980s had particularly much to do with a generalised loss of identity, ideological disorientation, permeability of institutional frontiers, and simple ignorance covered by loads of fashionable parlance.[13]

---

10 A. Besançon, *La confusion des langues. La crise idéologique de l'Eglise*, Calmann-Lévy, Paris 1978, p. 127.

11 E. Poulat, *Le grand absent de Dignitatis humanae: l'Etat*, 'Le Supplément. Revue d'éthique et de théologie morale' 1990, 21, 175, pp. 5–27.

12 E.D. McCarraher, *The Saint in the Grey Flannel Suit: The Professional-Managerial Class, 'The Layman' and American-Catholic-Religious Culture, 1945–1965*, 'U.S. Catholic Historian' 1997, 15, 3, pp. 111–118.

13 D. Góra-Szopiński, *Złoty środek. Kościół wobec współczesnych wizji państwa*, Adam Marszałek, Toruń 2007, pp. 173–181.

New framework proposal

The contemporary Church experience briefly described above provides a preliminary synthesis concerning the proper relation between the Church and civil society. We did not have time to discuss in detail the other term of the relation: the world that exists outside the Church in a continuous way. We leave aside the question whether the world outside can do without the Church and which of the two parts shall be more motivated in maintaining appropriate mutual relations. The post-conciliar Church approved, definitely as it seems, that the world outside – civil society – has its own autonomous ways of development and its own business to carry on. It seems rather logical that the Church cannot count on the outside world to help it to develop its own, supernatural aim of saving souls. But it is the Church's task to convince the world that the aim of saving souls might be advantageous and beneficial for the good of the whole community of men and women that constitute the body of civil society. The proposal developed here is the following: before advancing its own noble aim to the outside world, the Church may also look around and elicit the secular goals that are fostered and developed in a distinctive way so as to make them associated with its own activity, in due respect to one's own specificity and identity. Let's illustrate this proposal with two examples: one general and one detailed.

One of the key challenges of contemporary public policy happens to be expressed by the word 'innovation'. The legacy of technological revolution, as well as years of economic crises and regime changes, has shown our contemporaries the complexity of the social realm. Even if it sounds bold, changing the political realm might be as easy as introducing some legislative revisions. It is much more difficult to amend the economic system. Yet the most complex task consists of changing the realm of culture. A good portion of scientists and intellectuals of the 20th century neglected this third dimension of social reality and produced more or less technocratic programs of improvement limited to the two former spheres. Such was also the position expressed by the Institute for Market Economy Research, a leading Polish think tank with sound achievements in modernising this post-communist country. Yet with the passage of time, a different kind of reflection arose:

> After several years of experience in transforming and modernizing, a growing sense appeared that the regime alone, the rules of the game, plus the current socio-economic policy is not enough to effectively stimulate the process of transformation and development. Something very important lacked in this puzzle [...]. An entire new area of interest emerged, which was the fundamentals of cultural development. [...] The Washington consensus which still quite recently used to be the global model of economic policy was insufficient in recognizing the cultural determinants. In the long run though, it is the culture which is crucial to the development of nations.

Institutions and current regulations are important as well, but they shall basically remain in keeping with the cultural background. The same is with the current socio-economic policy.[14]

If we agree that the core of the social realm is the culture and that the amendments within the realm of culture might be called innovation, the time has come to ask about its content. How is innovation understood by its promoters? Where do they intend to aim innovation? How much will they influence the life of ordinary members of civil society? And – to supplement the research – at what extent do these (secular) innovations go together with the (religious) task of transforming human culture that is proper for the Church?

If we want to go deeper into detailed projects, we may look for the case study of the National Program Foresight Poland 2020. It is a project developed under the guidance of the Polish Ministry of Science, with around 3000 participants representing the research, educational, business, industrial, and social milieus. As a result, analyses have led to eliciting the four factors determining the development of the country in the years to come. They will be: globalisation, inland capacity of reforming, knowledge economy, and social acceptance for change.[15] A question may arise if there is a place for the Church to coordinate its mission with any of the four factors? Or rather, let's put it this way: Is it possible that the Church would not feel involved in any of them at all? The suggestion that all the four determinants merit careful scrutiny and co-development by the Church might be in order.

Conclusion

After the times of dead silence and separation from the outside world and also after the years of openness so excessive that it became dangerous for its own identity, the Catholic Church may nowadays develop its mission in cooperating with external innovation initiatives. According to the conciliar constitution *Gaudium et spes*, all that is good for humanity is also good and worth considering for the Church itself. As a result, anything good that happens within civil society

---

14   J. Szomburg, *W poszukiwaniu idei dla Polski – czyli krótka historia Instytutu Badań nad Gospodarką Rynkową*, available at: www.ibngr.pl/O-Instytucie/Historia (accessed: 31.10.2013). Each year the Institute organises a nationwide Citizen Congress, a vibrant and inspiring assembly of individuals, managers, public officials, and third sector activists engaged in the task of making their country a better place. Statistically speaking, as it goes for Poland, an overwhelming majority of the Congress participants shall be members of the Church. Unfortunately though, the activity of the Citizen Congress has not been rewarded with the attention of any official Church representation so far.

15   E. Bendyk, *Foresight: sztuka i techniki zarządzania przyszłością*, IBnGR, Gdańsk 2013, p. 33.

might be fruitfully backed up and fostered through the Church community. After the 50 years that have passed since the Vatican Council, it sounds even banal for the Catholics to engage in good initiatives throughout civil society as private persons. But the question raised in this paper does not concern Church members as private persons. It concerns the official engagement of the Church body and the common good of civil society. To make this engagement reliable, individuals that consider themselves members of the Church should first reflect upon what it means to be a Christian and whether engagement in the outside world actually deserves the name of 'apostolate'.

Bibliography

Bendyk E., *Foresight: sztuka i techniki zarządzania przyszłością*, IBnGR, Gdańsk 2013.

Berger P.L., *Social Ethics in a Post-Socialist World*, 'First Things' 1993, 4, 2.

Besançon A., *La confusion des langues. La crise idéologique de l'Eglise*, Calmann-Lévy, Paris 1978.

Chenu M.-D., *Les signes des temps. Réflexion théologique*, [in:] Y. Congar, M. Peuch-maurd (eds.), *L'Eglise dans le monde de ce temps. Constitution pastorale 'Gaudium et spes'*, Cerf, Paris 1967.

Góra-Szopiński D., *Złoty środek. Kościół wobec współczesnych wizji państwa*, Adam Marszałek, Toruń 2007.

Hebblethwaite P., *The Runaway Church; Post-Conciliar Growth or Decline*, Seabury Press, New York 1975.

McCarraher E.D., *The Saint in the Grey Flannel Suit: The Professional-Managerial Class, 'The Layman' and American-Catholic-Religious Culture, 1945–1965*, 'U.S. Catholic Historian' 1997, 15, 3.

Novak M., *The Open Church: Vatican II, Act II*, Darton, Longman & Todd, London 1964.

Ottaviani A., *Institutiones iuris publici ecclesiastici*, vol. 1, Typis Polyglottis Vaticani, Roma 1947.

Pastoral Constitution on the Church in the Modern World 'Gaudium et spes', Vatican II, 1965.

Poulat E., *Le grand absent de Dignitatis humanae: l'Etat*, 'Le Supplément. Revue d'éthique et de théologie morale' 1990, 21, 175.

Szomburg J., *W poszukiwaniu idei dla Polski – czyli krótka historia Instytutu Badań nad Gospodarką Rynkową*, available at: http://www.ibngr.pl/O-Instytucie/Historia (accessed: 31.10.2013).

Mariusz Sztaba
John Paul II Catholic University of Lublin
Lublin (Poland)

Postmodernism and Neoliberalism as Modern Ideologies Threatening Today's Civic Society: An Educator's Afterthought in Terms of Catholic Church Social Doctrine

The mission of the Catholic Church is based on supernatural character and salvation. This religious and supernatural role of the Church, however, and its mission are not separated from history and mundane aspects, being the Church's great field of activity. We may talk about the social aspect of the Church's mission, which is its 'secondary' calling, for it can't be implemented without the original one. The Church grew into this kind of mission awareness for ages, covering with its pastoral care all dimensions of human existence, including the Total Picture of social life with its particular dimensions: cultural, political, economic and international. This care is expressed in the social teachings of the Church[1] as well as in scientific, interdisciplinary philosophical approach formed by Catholic social doctrine.[2]

Among the many social life aspects involving the Church's wisdom, there is a problem of civic society, understood as democracy in practice. The Church is interested in this form of reality not from organizational, or legal point of view, but looks more at its ontological and ethical-moral foundations, as well as its true aim of existence.[3] That is why these phenomena and situations, which question

1 Pontifical Council for Justice and Peace, *Compendium of the Social Doctrine of the Church*, USCCB, Washington, DC 2005. Hereinafter referred as CSDCH.
2 M. Sztaba, *Wychowanie społeczne w świetle nauczania Karola Wojtyły – Jana Pawła II*, Catholic University of Lublin Scientific Society, Lublin 2012, pp. 152–162.
3 M. Sztaba, *Troska błogosławionego Jana Pawła II o etyczno-moralne podstawy życia społecznego*, Tyniec, Cracow 2011, pp. 97–101.

meaning and foundations of civic society, are deeply analysed. Postmodernism is certainly one of them, as this thoughtstream negates the principality of all rules, spreading a philosophy of cognitive, axiological and theological relativism. Another dangerous phenomenon is neoliberalism striving for marketisation of social life, by measuring it with demand-supply logic, defining the citizen as a consumer only. These are today's main dominating ideologies.[4]

In this paper, I wish to analyse the problems mentioned above in terms of the Church's social doctrine. Before I go to the main aspect, I would like to highlight the challenge of providing a uniform definition for the problematic character of civic society. Then I would like to present main civic society ideas in terms of the Church's social doctrine. My afterthought will constitute a background for proper postmodernism and neoliberalism analysis. The analysis is completed and closed with educational conclusions and postulates.

Problematic and unambiguous definition of civic society

The term 'civic society' may be defined as an ideal norm describing a value of social order as well as a form of social, political, cultural and economic reality. That's why the idea of civic society may not be ideologically and politically precised.[5]

The historical experience in Central and Eastern Europe contains four models of society: a) classical model based on civic society general features; b) imperfect model related to communist times degenerations; c) ethical model, idealistic form created as an anti-communist opposition; and d) transformational model created after restoring independence subsequent to 1989.[6]

Despite many forms and models of civic society, few significant features may be selected. According to the literature, civic society is created by:

---

4 Without detailed analysis of definition of ideology, as this term is one of less perceptible terms in social sciences (D. McLellan), one may say, that ideology is a system of opinions, dominating vision of the world, political doctrine, regime of truth, for it creates a 'language' of social and political discourse, set of assumptions and rules of society functioning and functioning of an individual human within it. The ideology is a paradigm, according to T. Kuhn, as – thanks to the set of rules, doctrines and theories – it puts intellectual cognitive process in order. Ideology in such meaning is always connected to power. It is not a surprise, then, that ideology dominating in a certain time and place generates social illusions, strengthened more by the authorities which use them. This fact is confirmed by the history of last ages: fascism, communism, nationalism, etc. (A. Heywood, *Ideologie polityczne*, trans. from English M. Habura, N. Orłowska, D. Stasiak, Polish Scientific Publishers PWN, Warsaw 2007, pp. 19–30).

5 J. Mariański, *Społeczeństwo i moralność: studia z katolickiej nauki społecznej i socjologii moralności*, Biblos, Tarnów 2008, p. 143.

6 *Ibid.*, p. 146.

non-governmental organisations and civic associations of public sector, citizen-ship approach and collective awareness, cooperation and collaboration of citizens in public area, citizens' rights: civil, political and social, basic and citizen virtues (e.g., fraternity, solidarity, equality, trust, common good, cooperation, observance of common rules, cooperation), free market and private property.[7]

Civic society creates a specific space between private and state spaces, con-stituting a part of democracy, being a practical democracy in practice, both as an engine of democratic changes and as a guarantee of the *status quo*. Civic so-ciety creates a social space, wherein citizens may feel safe and which is protected against excessive state and market interference.[8]

The idea of civic society in the Church's social doctrine

In social doctrine of the Catholic Church, the idea of civic society is rooted in the ideology of human dignity, being a centre of social life, i.e. its basic and ultimate criterion.[9] It is impossible to support

> [...] personal dignity without providing care to the family, groups, societies, local organizations, briefly speaking – without supporting associations and institutions of economic, social, cultural, sportive, leisure, professional and political character, created by people spontaneously in order to stimulate their real social increase.[10]

The Church decisively sees the difference between civic society and free mar-ket, indicating the bonds between these two sectors.[11]

The political community remains in service for civic society, which is its justification for existence. The state should create a legal framework for social entities to act and support them, providing assistance[12] when they can't manage by themselves their tasks related to common good.[13] The Church, lead by the basic truth about the human person as a free being, who is able to create connections and who is also open to transcendental aspects, strictly opposes the tendencies

---

7 *Ibid.*, pp. 143–149.
8 As an initiative of John Paul II and Institute for Human Sciences, several dozen scientists from all over the world participated in a meeting concerning the problem of civic society in Europe, at Castel Gandolfo, 10–12 August 1989. The result of their scientific discourse was the paper of K. Michalski (ed.), *Europa i społeczeństwo obywatelskie. Rozmowy w Castel Gandolfo*, Znak, Cracow 1994.
9 CSDCH, pp. 105–151; M. Sztaba, *Troska..., op. cit.*, pp. 67–229.
10 CSDCH, p. 185.
11 *Ibid.*, p. 419.
12 *Ibid.*, pp. 419–420.
13 *Ibid.*, pp. 168, 417–420.

which strive to 'swallow' civic society into the state, as it is done in totalitarian ideologies or individualistic political ideologies.[14]

The above rule concerns also the relations between civic society and free market. The Church clearly teaches here that

> [...] the social-economic system must be marked by the twofold presence of public and private activity, including private non-profit activity. In this way sundry decision-making and activity-planning centres come to take shape. The use of certain categories of goods, collective goods and goods meant for common utilization, cannot be dependent on mechanisms of the market, nor does their use fall under the exclusive competence of the State.[15]

The Church's social doctrine states:

> [...] civile society is the sum of relationships and resources, cultural and associative, that are relatively independent from the political sphere and the economic sector [...]. The purpose of civil society is universal, since it concerns the common good, to which each and every citizen has a right in due proportion. This is marked by a planning capacity that aims at form associtions, working to develop and express therir preferences, in order to meet their fundamental needs and defend their legitimate interests.[16]

The main tasks of civic society, according to the Church, are the following: a) developing a person's social aspect; b) developing social initiatives, exceeding state areas, and creating fields for active presence and direct activities of citizens; c) initiating new and positive methods of using human rights, increasing quality of democratic life; d) overcoming ideological differences and looping for connecting aspects, instead of dividing ones, by generating bonds in terms of cooperation and solidarity; e) creating public ethics, based on solidarity and true cooperation as well as fraternal dialog; f) implementation and reinforcement of 'subjectivity of the society' principle[17]; g) stimulating the development of 'proper economic democracy'[18] and h) interesting social opinion to many aspects of international life, with emphasis put on human rights observance.[19]

Civic society essence and strength is expressed in the fact that:

> The complete number of relations between social units and intermediate societies, created and appeared on a basic level, thanks to the citizen's creative subjectivity [...] innervates and strengthens social tissue which creates a foundation for true commonwealth of the people, making higher forms of socialization possible.[20]

---

14 CSDCH, p. 417.
15 *Ibid.*, p. 356.
16 *Ibid.*, p. 417.
17 *Ibid.*, pp. 419–420.
18 *Ibid.*, p. 356.
19 *Ibid.*, p. 443.
20 *Ibid.*, p. 185.

The Church has great expectations related to civic society, while it is also aware of many threats which concern it both from outside and inside. Civic society from inside 'is varied and divided, with many ambiguities and contradictions: it is also a place where many different interests interact, with presence of constant threats of domination of the stronger upon more helpless ones'.[21] External threats come from various ideologies, which simplify the vision of world and society creating reductive visions of man.[22]

That's why the Church, as an expert in aspects of humanity as well as a moral authority, in a particular manner emphasises the spiritual and ethical-moral dimensions of civic society. It takes care of common and timeless moral values,[23] indicating the need of general ethical consensus. It indicates basic values, such as: life from conception to natural death; equity, justice, peace, fraternity, human rights, patriotism, etc.,[24] as well as fundamental social life principles, which include: primacy of person and subjectivity (personalism); common good and common wealth use; helpfulness; participation; solidarity; as well as social love and justice.[25]

Basic values and social life principles related to the integral idea of human dignity act for development of each one as well as for the common good. They provide the chance for real understanding in matters which concern things worth being experienced by humans and what makes a life truly human. They become a guarantee of social order. The Church, by noticing philosophical and theological aspect of reality, provides metaphysical legitimacy to these values, protecting them against the dictatorship of relativism and changeable fashion trends.[26]

---

21 *Ibid.*, p. 418.
22 'Creation', 'creating' is a favorite term of all ideologies. The ideologies, instead of making efforts to discover the nature of things and truth about the world, prefer to create, i.e. to make them up, in order to manipulate them in the future.
23 They include: personal dignity, truth, good, national freedom, responsibility, love and personalistic norm. See M. Sztaba, *Troska...*, *op. cit.*, pp. 259–302.
24 I describe basic social values necessary in public and political, economical and international as well as cultural life, indicating the importance of Christian religious values in the paper: *Wychowanie społeczne...*, *op. cit.*, pp. 299–340; W. Szymczak, *Wartości w społeczeństwie obywatelskim*, [in:] E. Balawajder (ed.), *Społeczeństwo obywatelskie: modele teoretyczne i praktyka społeczna*, Catholic University of Lublin Press, Lublin 2007, pp. 27–45.
25 CSDCH, pp. 160–208.
26 J. Mariański, *Kościół a społeczeństwo obywatelskie*, [in:] S. Fel, J. Kupny (eds.), *Katolicka nauka społeczna: podstawowe zagadnienia z życia społecznego i politycznego*, Księgarnia św. Jacka, Katowice 2007, pp. 186–195.

Postmodernist civic society deconstruction

Each era has its own ideology. In his analysis of postmodernism, Andrew Heywood noticed that it caused and still causes emerging new ideological movements and transforming the already existing ones: pacifism, the gay movement, radical feminism and ecologic ideologies, as well as plenty of different 'post-isms', e.g., postliberalism (neoliberalism), postmarxism, postfeminism, etc. Moreover, he noticed the influence of postmodernism on globalisation processes.[27]

The ideology of postmodernism (it's genesis, development stages, main ideas and representatives,[28] has been precisely described and analysed in literature with detailed listings of antinomies and threats, both for societies and the whole culture understood in its classical terms (science, art, morality and religion).[29] Here, I would like to mention only these contents (theses) of postmodernism which affect civic society idea itself and negate the meaning of its functioning.[30] The society is created by people – citizens living in a precise reality. That's why first I wish to present the ontological concept of reality. Then I wish to present the postmodernist vision of man in order to show the postmodernist ideas of society.

POSTMODERNIST ONTOLOGY. The postmodernist deconstruction deprived reality of any meaning. The logocentrism was replaced with 'grammatology', indicating that language and scripture based on changeable rules are the most important factors. Postmodernists reject idea of an internal essence of each thing, applying antiessentialism. Their most important categories describing reality are: difference, ambiguity, and ambivalence. They reject such ideas as: subject, person, substance, existence, soul and truth. The postmodernist ontology, negating the non-variance and ontic rationality principles, is generally anti-systemic, which directly conditions its anthropology and vision of society.[31]

POSTMODERNIST ANTHROPOLOGY. Postmodernists question rationality and the spiritual dimension of man, speaking much about his carnality, vitality and sexuality. They negate human nature, defining man as a 'network of ideas and desires' (Richard Rorty). Man is no longer an autonomic subject, a self-aware and independent decision-making centre; instead, he has become a constantly lin-

---

27   Cf. A. Heywood, *Ideologie polityczne, op. cit.*, pp. 35–36.

28   Finding leading thinkers of postmodernism is a problematic task. These may be the following: Jacques Derrida, Michel Foucault, Jean-François Lyotard, Richard Rorty and Zygmunt Bauman.

29   A. Bronk, *Zrozumieć świat współczesny*, Catholic University of Lublin Scientific Society, Lublin 1998, pp. 23–74; S. Kowalczyk, *Idee filozoficzne postmodernizmu*, Polwen, Radom 2004; A.E. Szołtysek, *Filozofia wychowania moralnego*, Impuls, Cracow 2009, pp. 325–339.

30   Postmodernism itself is full of ambivalences and paradoxes, or even absurd (A. Bronk, *Zrozumieć..., op. cit.*, pp. 29–34, 69–74).

31   S. Kowalczyk, *Idee filozoficzne..., op. cit.*, pp. 53–64.

guistically and discursively created identity. Postmodernist anthropology is anti-humanist and anti-personalist. The depersonalisation of man is related to its na-turalistic self-creationism (self-fulfilment).[32]

POSTMODERNIST VISION OF SOCIETY. There is no systematic postmodernist concept of society. There are, however, partial and ambivalent projects of societies presented by individual representatives of described ideology. As postmodernism has negated the logocentrism and internal essence of everything, (including the social nature of man with its need for organisation and cooperation),[33] and reality is perceived through linguistic games, that's why the natural and ontological com-monwealth has been replaced by postmodernism with a cultural ethnocentrism having the idea of solidarity based on temporal and spatial vicinity. The social community is just a 'creation of time and coincidence' (R. Rorty). The postmod-ernists prove to have a negative approach to the idea of nation, national State and civic society, concentrating more on cosmopolitan global society. Even though their papers include terms such as solidarity, justice, equity, pluralism and ethics, they have more specific content and scope.[34]

The reluctance for civic society is caused by postmodernist ontological, an-thropological and axiological assumptions. It is clearly visible in Rorty's proposal of society. Being a decisive follower of democratic systems based on parliamen-tary power, he proposed a complete separation between the political and public life from the private and personal life. Rorty's utopia is related to domination of care for expanding human freedom through its own autonomy and creating its in-dividuality. Rorty also thought that the best manner to resolve political problems is an ironic attitude, striving for exteriorisation of politics.[35]

The postmodernist way of thinking and activity has no place for civic soci-ety. The problem of social life in the analysed ideology is logically inconsistent. First, without personal 'material', there may be neither society nor community. Second, the maximisation of pluralism and variety, with a rejection of the specific uniformity and social nature of man, loses the social and community foundation. Third, the proposed values are in fact verbal mottos, with no national explanation. Fourth, postmodernist society is permissive, sceptic, relative, culturally narcis-sistic and egotist, with no room for common good.[36] Some researchers of social phenomena – Niklas Luhmann and Jean Baudrillard use direct name of 'death of society'.[37]

32 *Ibid.*, pp. 65–75.
33 M. Sztaba, *Wychowanie...*, *op. cit.*, pp. 191–260.
34 S. Kowalczyk, *Idee filozoficzne...*, *op. cit.*, pp. 76–100.
35 M. Żardecka-Nowak, *Wspólnota i ironia: Richard Rorty i jego wizja społeczeństwa liberal-nego*, Catholic University of Lublin Press, Lublin 2003.
36 A. Bronk, *Zrozumieć...*, *op. cit.*, pp. 36–39.
37 'The fight' against postmodernism in order to create happy new socialist society is prepared – even initiated – by the 'late left wing'. Its main representatives are: Perry Anderson, David

Anti-civic philosophy of neoliberalism

The ideology of neoliberalism is strictly related to postmodernism. They are both reflected in globalization processes, which are defined as the international face of neoliberalism (A. Saad-Filho, D. Johnson).[38]

Neoliberalism and globalization are multi-faceted phenomena. The analysis includes an interesting element: the influence of these ideologies on understanding society and its functioning. To be more precise, we look for an answer to the question of whether in times of neoliberalism and neoliberal globalism[39] there is any room for civic society?

In order to obtain an adequate answer for the above question, we first need to make a key differentiation between classical liberalism and neoliberalism. Then we need to point the neoliberal ontology and anthropology in order to present a vision of society implemented in globalization processes.

According to the research and everyday experience, neoliberalism is a treason of classical liberalism. In terms of the problem discussed herein, we may indicate few primary theses of classical neoliberalism that support civic society. They are the following: a) moral education, forming moral character and social feelings as the foundation of freedom; b) preparation for a role of active member of civic society, forming a sense of common good and social virtues; c) education and self-education as property of principle implementation; d) primacy of family in education with the auxiliary function of the state, being a guarantee of equity before law and tolerance; e) implementation of basic principles of liberalism, such as: freedom, equity, property, tolerance, and civic society.[40]

Neoliberalism[41] diverged from classical liberalism by making radical changes that caused a lack of space for civic society in it. In order to explain this thesis, we will present the reality created with neoliberalism. Then we will indicate neoliberal anthropology in connection with axiology, eventually showing the understanding of society in terms of the analysed ideology.

NEOLIBERAL REALITY. Neoliberal reality is fully created by the market discourse. Market logic is the most important factor, i.e. logic of unlimited profit and

---

Harvey, Frederic Jameson and Terry Eagleton (B. Kuźniarz, *Goodbye Mr. Postmodernism: teorie społeczne myślicieli późnej lewicy*, Nicolaus Copernicus University Press, Toruń 2011).

38   E. Potulicka, J. Rutkowiak, *Neoliberalne uwikłania edukacji*, Impuls, Cracow 2012, pp. 326––327; M. Lewartowska-Zychowicz, Homo liberalis *jako projekt edukacyjny. Od emancypacji do funkcjonalności*, Impuls, Cracow 2010, pp. 235–236.

39   A. Heywood, *Ideologie polityczne, op. cit.*, pp. 328–329.

40   K. Wrońska, *Pedagogika klasycznego liberalizmu: w dwugłosie John Locke i John Stuart Mill*, Jagiellonian University Press, Cracow 2012, pp. 219–239.

41   Theoretical foundations of neoliberalism and its practice is analysed in the paper of E. Potulicka and J. Rutkowiak, *Neoliberalne..., op. cit.*, pp. 39–67.

growth. The hegemony of market growth leads almost to complete state disarming (depoliticization) and depriving it of power by depreciation of public life political character; dismantling forms of power competitive to the capital, i.e. state democratic procedures; building a uniform cultural space (consumerism); creating own power structures (corporations), etc. Such a situation puts market ideas as reality: persons and human relations defining matrices. All this results in monism and destruction of the *homo politicus* ideal, so important for classical liberalism and civic society. Neoliberalism reduced the political area of life and society to the economic sphere and free choice, including the political one – to shopping (J.A. Schumpeter). *Homo liberalis* was conceptualized from politics and 'captured' in the economy. Liberal and ethical democracy was replaced with market democracy. The accumulation of capital power owned by great corporations lead to transferring the political phenomena from official stages to the corporatism shadow zone (U. Beck).

The hegemony of market discourse causes dislodging huge areas of social life from public control, which gradually and increasingly decreases the role of citizen (M.J. Sandel, R.D. Putman).[42] The aforementioned neoliberal intentions are supported by globalization processes.[43]

NEOLIBERAL ANTHROPOLOGY AND AXIOLOGY. The 'death' of *homo politicus* and the reduction of *homo liberalis* to shopping freedom makes neoliberalism create and implement new market personality models.[44] In the centre of market discourse focus, there is human identity and manners of its submission to manufacturers and service providers. The process of identity creation concerns, i.e. autonomy, understood as freedom of choice from an available pool, proposed by markets, economic situations and fashion. Market identity using a strategy of seduction and control, creates consumable identity (B.R. Barber), being a flattened and de-intellectualised identity. The unification of a consumer's identity, being a purely functional identity, favours creations similar to the marketing of illusions of high ideas and originality of life style of modern human beings (N. Klein). The ideal man proposed by neoliberalism – *homo oeconomicus* – is really a falsification of *homo oeconomicus*, who was free thanks to its freedom of husbandry, which has now been replaced by a freedom of unlimited market pool.[45]

---

42 M. Lewartowska-Zychowicz, Homo liberalis..., *op. cit.*, pp. 219–238.
43 E. Potulicka, J. Rutkowiak, *Neoliberalne...*, *op. cit.*, pp. 331–335. Globalism seen in economical, political and civilisation/cultural aspects is a modern utopia (Ł. Stefaniak, *Utopizm: źródło myślowe i konsekwencje cywilizacyjne*, Catholic University of Lublin, Lublin 2011, pp. 189–203).
44 In neoliberalism, we meet many categories (groups) of people necessary for this ideology to function. They are: corporatism oligarchy, so-called new producers, simple works producers, consumers, 'human waste', criminals. I will concentrate on consumers only, as basic category of neoliberal reality (E. Potulicka, J. Rutkowiak, *Neoliberalne...*, *op. cit.*, pp. 311–321).
45 M. Lewartowska-Zychowicz, Homo liberalis..., *op. cit.*, pp. 239–252.

The process of consumer identity is co-created by media and education. The latter has already been dominated by market discourse. Today's education, using market logic, becomes a product, implementing the corporate economy educational program, which destroys the idea of citizenship and foundations of civic society.[46]

NEOLIBERAL SOCIETY. Neoliberalism sees society as 'suspect'. That's why a new type of society has been created, which is woven from contractual relationships. Society is a group of individuals, with no aim of existence as such (D. Boaz). Neoliberalism creates an atomistic vision of society, taking a sense of common good away from the people. It separates society from democracy, stopping it and weakening the spirit of citizenship, which, as a consequence, favours the desubjectivization of society. That's why civic society is less and less mentioned; instead, more and more we hear about 'society of ownership' (R. Legutko), 'shareholders' society' (A. Aldridge), 'consumers' society' (J. Baudrillard), 'spectacle society' (G. Debord),[47] and 'commercial communities'.[48]

In neoliberalism, *homo politicus* has been reduced to *homo oeconomicus* or even to *homo consumens*. Neoliberalism made an equals sign between a citizen and consumer. Neoliberal man is an indefatigable, permanently efficient producer and insatiable consumer. Consumption is the basic principle of individual and social existence. It remains a unique social act, making it possible for an individual to participate in social life, constituting its basic participation mechanism at the same time (M. Douglas). Human defines himself through the freedom to consume. The lack of 'commercial community' access results in alienation and isolation from the world.[49]

The virtues of such and the individual are, e.g. egoism, competition, fight for success and efficiency. Neoliberal propagated 'social philosophy' leads to breaking apart social solidarity, which results in attacks on organisations of social self-management. For both the market and corporations claim to be the sole and only real independent authority and educator.[50]

Social reality is dominated by market discourse and logic, which makes it similar to Friedman's vision of flat worlds.[51] Individuals and societies are focused on meeting needs related purely to existence and consumption, often artificially created by market, less and less interested in higher needs, including those related to common good, citizenship, democracy and democratic society (S. Sinha). All

---

46 M. Lewartowska-Zychowicz, Homo liberalis..., *op. cit.*, pp. 252–263; E. Potulicka, J. Rutkowiak, *Neoliberalne...*, *op. cit.*, pp. 13–37.

47 E. Potulicka, J. Rutkowiak, *Neoliberalne...*, *op. cit.*, pp. 49–51, 328–331.

48 M. Lewartowska-Zychowicz, Homo liberalis..., *op. cit.*, pp. 244–246.

49 *Ibid.*

50 *Ibid.*, pp. 332–335, 342–343.

51 *Ibid.*, pp. 339–341.

the situations mentioned above make social life researchers write about 'non-civic society' or even 'anti-civic society' functioning (J. Czapiński).[52]

Postmodernism, neoliberalism and globalisation are not an academic abstraction or illusionary problem. These ideologies involve every aspect of social life, generating real threats for individuals and societies. This paper is focused on threats caused by the analysed ideologies for the essence and functioning of civic society. At the end of our divagations, we turn back to the social doctrine of the Catholic Church to use its light to draw the conclusions and postulates on overcoming difficulties met by the civic society from the above-mentioned ideologies.

Catholic Church against ideological threats of civic society – educational implications

The Church sees every ideology as a great threat to life of an individual human being and the whole society. It is expressed in a totalitarian vision of society and State[53] as well as in the reductionist, falsified concepts of man.[54] Postmodernism, neoliberalism and globalisation, the result of the two former ones,[55] altogether as co-existing leading ideologies are not able to give any adequate answer to crucial questions and challenges[56] of people and societies. That's why the Church, exposing false and evil nature of every ideology, proposes instead its own, profound thought on 'complex reality of human existence in the society in the international context, analysed in terms of Church's faith and tradition'.[57] The Church encourages all people of good will to learn its social teachings and use it in their lives.[58]

In terms of the Church's social doctrine, each social question is based on integral anthropology, i.e. the science about man, including the whole truth about the person.[59] This makes the Church, wishing to 'catch' the ontological,

---

52 *Ibid.,* pp. 342–345.

53 CSDCH, pp. 48, 417.

54 *Ibid.,* pp. 124–125; A. Maryniarczyk, K. Stępień, (eds.), *Błąd antropologiczny*, PTTA, Lublin 2003.

55 Globalisation is an ambivalent process. It brings certain benefits but also many threats, particularly in the finance-economic aspect. John Paul II said during the VII Session of Papal Academy of Science in Vatican on April 2001: 'globalisation is neither *a priori* good nor evil. It will be such as it will be created by people [...]. Globalisation, such as any other system, must serve the man, solidarity and common good'. The globalisation processes 'demand' purification from ideological tendencies (M. Sztaba, *Troska..., op. cit.*, pp. 182–196).

56 CSDCH, p. 100.

57 *Ibid.,* p. 72.

58 Historical description and essence of social teaching of the Church is found in CSDCH, pp. 60–104.

59 *Ibid.,* pp. 124–152.

anthropological and axiological foundation of civic society[60] focus on the transcendence and originality of the person of man's social nature and human rights.[61] The adequate anthropology allows the creation of new social life adjusted to each human existence and humanity in total. It also helps to build healthy civic society, which is not seen as a threat to the State or market, completing them, with preservation of its own autonomy instead.

The proper forming of relations between members of civic society as well as between the State and market is supported by the principles of social life created by the Church's social doctrine.[62] Each of these principles favours generation of true and creative relations between the three abovementioned sectors of public life. Their learning and implementation results in correctness and efficiency of the above relations. Naturally, care for the form of civic society requires the care for the quality of State and democracy[63] as well as economic life, in terms of the globalisation processes (problems of labour, workers' rights, property, entrepreneurship, finance, etc.).[64]

Benedict XVI, in his encyclical *Caritas in veritate*, emphasised that the basic rule of Church's social science is 'love in truth' (*caritas in veritate*). This principle has a special meaning for the development in the globalised society, considering the problem of justice and common good. It is practically expressed in moral criteria.[65] Church constantly points at the fact that there can be no genuine society without spiritual and moral values.

There is a great challenge in front of neoliberally entangled education, in terms of the creation of the civic society. Even though many economists (e.g. J. Stiglitz, J. Sachs, A. Greenspan, R. Wade) clearly speak about errors of neoliberal doctrine, proposing to rethink the rules of world functioning, persons and institutions responsible for education still do not see the need of delivering it from neoliberal influence.[66]

The Catholic Church, facing so many threats in the modern world, postulates the 'healing' of education, calling for 'great educational and cultural activity'.[67] The Church itself undertakes activities related to social education, seeing them as lifetime objectives and encouraging the remaining educators to undertake such

---

60 M. Sztaba, *Wychowanie...*, op. cit., pp. 191–352.

61 CSDCH, pp. 108–159.

62 *Ibid.*, pp. 160–208. These principles are also analysed in paper: M. Sztaba, *Wychowanie...*, op. cit., p. 478–509.

63 CSDCH, pp. 377–427.

64 *Ibid.*, pp. 255–376.

65 Benedict XVI, Encyclical, *Caritas in Veritate. On Integral Human Development in Love and Truth*, available at: http://www.vatican.va/holy_father/benedict_xvi/encyclicals/documents/ hf_ben-xvi_enc_20090629_caritas-in-veritate_en.html (accessed: 29.06.2009).

66 E. Potulicka, J. Rutkowiak, *Neoliberalne...*, op. cit., pp. 11–12, 29–34, 339–355.

67 CSDCH, p. 376.

initiatives.[68] The Church in its education activity, i.e. in teaching and upbringing, remains aware of the basic truth that

> [...] person and society are in constant coexistence and relationship. Whatever one does for the person, is also a good made for the society, and whatever is done for the society, results in good of the individual.[69]

The Church encourages lay followers to use its social doctrine, and is involved in sensible activity for civic society through service to humans, culture, politics and economy.[70] It sees its main participation in civic society as protecting every person and its rights related to moral aspect of revitalisation.

Bibliography

Benedict XVI, Encyclical, *Caritas in Veritate. On Integral Human Development in Love and Truth*, available at: http://www.vatican.va/holy_father/benedict_xvi/encyclicals/documents/hf_ben-xvi_enc_20090629_caritas-in-veritate_en.html (accessed: 29.06.2009).

Bronk A., *Zrozumieć świat współczesny*, Catholic University of Lublin Scientific Society, Lublin 1998.

Heywood A., *Ideologie polityczne*, trans. from English M. Habura, N. Orłowska, D. Stasiak, Polish Scientific Publishers PWN, Warsaw 2007.

John Paul II, *Christifideles Laici: On the Vocation and the Mission of the Lay Faithful in the Church and in the World*, available at: http://www.vatican.va/holy_father/john_paul_ii/apost_exhortations/documents/hf_jp-ii_exh_30121988_christifideles-laici_en.html (accessed: 29.06.2009).

Kowalczyk S., *Idee psychologiczne postmodernizmu*, Polwen, Radom 2004.

Kuźniarz B., *Goodbye Mr. Postmodernism: teorie społeczne myślicieli późnej lewicy*, Nicolaus Copernicus University Press, Toruń 2011.

Lewartowska-Zychowicz M., Homo liberalis *jako projekt edukacyjny. Od emancypacji do funkcjonalności*, Impuls, Cracow 2010.

Mariański J., *Społeczeństwo i moralność: studia z katolickiej nauki społecznej i socjologii moralności*, Biblos, Tarnów 2008.

Mariański J., *Kościół a społeczeństwo obywatelskie*, [in:] S. Fel, J. Kupny (eds.), *Katolicka nauka społeczna: podstawowe zagadnienia z życia społecznego i politycznego*, Księgarnia św. Jacka, Katowice 2007.

Maryniarczyk A., Stępień K. (eds.), *Błąd antropoligiczny*, PTTA, Lublin 2003.

---

68 M. Sztaba, *Wychowanie...*, *op. cit.*, pp. 353–554.

69 *Christifideles Laici: On the Vocation and the Mission of the Lay Faithful in the Church and in the World*, available at: http://www.vatican.va/holy_father/john_paul_ii/apost_exhortations/documents/hf_jp-ii_exh_30121988_christifideles-laici_en.html (accessed: 29.06.2009).

70 CSDCH, pp. 541–574.

Michalski K. (ed.), *Europa i społeczeństwo obywatelskie. Rozmowy w Castel Gandolfo*, Znak, Cracow 1994.

Pontifical Council for Justice and Peace, *Compendium of the Social Doctrine of the Church*, USCCB, Washington, DC 2005.

Potulicka E., Rutkowiak J., *Neoliberalne uwikłania edukacji*, Impuls, Cracow 2012.

Stefaniak Ł., *Utopizm: źródło myślowe i konsekwencje cywilizacyjne*, Catholic University of Lublin Press, Lublin 2011.

Szołtysek A.E., *Filozofia wychowania moralnego*, Impuls, Cracow 2009.

Sztaba M., *Troska błogosławionego Jana Pawła II o etyczno-moralne podstawy życia społecznego*, Tyniec, Cracow 2011.

Sztaba M., *Wychowanie społeczne w świetle nauczania Karola Wojtyły – Jana Pawła II*, Catholic University of Lublin Scientific Society, Lublin 2012.

Szymczak W., *Wartości w społeczeństwie obywatelskim*, [in:] E. Balawajder (ed.), *Społeczeństwo obywatelskie: modele teoretyczne i praktyka społeczna*, Catholic University of Lublin Press, Lublin 2007.

Wrońska K., *Pedagogika klasycznego liberalizmu: w dwugłosie John Locke i John Stuart Mill*, Jagiellonian University Press, Cracow 2012.

Żardecka-Nowak M., *Wspólnota i ironia: Richard Rorty i jego wizja spoleczeństwa liberalnego*, Catholic University of Lublin Press, Lublin 2003.

Part II
Practical Approach

TOSHIKO ITO
Mie University
Mie (Japan)

Nuclear Disaster and the Quest for Meaning in the Civil Society: Religion in Japanese Educational Institutions Today

Introduction: The disaster of 2011 and post-institutional religion

Disasters are apt to supplant a scientific outlook with a religious outlook in many people's minds. The Great East Japan Earthquake is a case in point. On 11 March 2011, Japan's Atlantic coast was struck by a strong earthquake that caused a series of tsunamis and resulted in widespread flooding. As an immediate consequence, Japan's worst-ever nuclear accident occurred at the Fukushima Dai-ichi power plant, instantly turning the name of Fukushima into a household word across the world. With the north-eastern coastal area of Japan's main Honshu Island largely devastated, with some 16,000 dead and nearly 3,000 missing, as well as a harrowing uncertainty over the eventual outcome of the nuclear accident, many Japanese people turned to spirituality for solace. A charity song entitled *Flowers will bloom (Hana wa saku)*, which purports to deliver a message from the deceased earthquake victims to those left behind, touched the hearts of many across the country and rose through the pop music charts.[1] The average Japanese,

---

1 The song was produced by NHK (*Nippon Hōsō Kyōkai*), Japan's national public broadcasting organization, with a view to raising money for the disaster recovery effort. With its lyrics written by Iwai Shunji and its music composed by Kanno Yoko, the song was created by two previously obscure artists from the stricken Miyagi prefecture. As the lyrics voice the perspective of the dead, the song echoes another recently successful song using the same perspective, *Do not stand at my grave and weep (sen no kaze ni natte)*, which is based on a poem originally written by Mary Elizabeth in 1932 and translated into Japanese by Man Arai in 2003. It entered the pop charts in January 2006 following its performance on the tenth anniversary of the Great Hanshin ('Kobe') Earthquake.

who mostly self-identify as non-religious, have since taken an increasing interest in religion, as witnessed by the fact that a number of religious books have become best sellers[2] and numerous magazines have run special issues on religion. According to the 'Research Survey on Religious Consciousness among Students' (*Gakusei shūkyō ishiki chōsa*), which has been conducted every three years since 1995 by the Institute for Japanese Culture and Classics of Kokugakuin University (*kokugakuin daigaku nihon bunka kenkyūsho*) and the Japanese Association for the Study of Religion and Society (*shūkyō to shakai gakkai*), the percentage of students who self-identify as religious has more than doubled from 7.5% in 2010 to 16.1% in 2013.[3]

The disaster not only changed the attitudes of average people toward religion, it also affected the roles played by temples and shrines, the religious institutions that, respectively, embody Buddhism and Shintō. These are Japan's main two religions, which have co-existed in a symbiotic relationship for centuries. Traditionally, neither Buddhist temples nor Shintō shrines discharge any clear-cut pastoral duties towards a well-defined parish, and their publicly visible activities are limited to the celebration of few ceremonies. The ministrations of a Buddhist temple, for instance, are limited almost exclusively to burial and memorial services. A book entitled *No Need for a Funeral* (*sōshiki wa iranai*), a best seller in 2010, questioned even this limited role. However, the disaster of 2011 proved to be a major turning point for the traditional religious institutions, as memorial services for disaster victims provided the institutions with a new public role. Understanding that their services provided much-needed support to the victims,[4] they began to search opportunities to serve the country's secular civil society beyond their customary institutional boundaries.

Moreover, in a change promoted by both policy makers and academics, educational institutions have placed increasing emphasis on religious matters. This development was initiated by policy makers, who in 2006 revised the 'Fundamental Act of Education' (*kyōiku kihon hō*) for the first time since its enactment

---

2   K. Isa, *Quest for Religion now* (*ima shūkyō o shiritai*), 'Asahi Shimbun' 15.11.2011. In 2011, special issues related to religion were favourably received: a special section devoted to Buddhism and Shintō in *Diamond* magazine (July), and special issues on Buddhism and, respectively, Zen Buddhism in *President* magazine (August and October). In addition, books on religion became best sellers, such as Daisaburō Hashizume's *Profound Christianity* (*fushigina kirisutokyō*), published in May, and Akira Ikegami's *Watch the World with Knowledge of Religions* (*shūkyō ga wakareba sekai ga mieru*), published in July.

3   K. Isa, *The Great Earthquake as an Opportunity to Seek the Meaning of Life* (*daishinsai kikkake ikiru imi jimon*), 'Asahi Shimbun' 27.03.2013.

4   The support effort after the disaster left many priests and monks with mixed feelings: their support was happily received by victims, but most of the support activities were identical to the activities of common people and did not necessarily require any training in religious traditions.

in 1947. This amendment calls for more attention to 'religious teaching', and has caused a noticeable shift in educational institutions under the national standard curriculum, the 'Government Guidelines for Teaching' (*gakushū shidō yōryō*). The current 'Guidelines' mandate direct and indirect religious instruction in primary and secondary education, reflecting the revised 'Fundamental Act on Education', whose new provisions recently came into force: in primary schools in 2011, in lower secondary schools in 2012, and in higher secondary schools in 2013. According to the official instruction manual, the 'Ministry of Education, Culture, Sports, Science and Technology' (*Monbukagakushō*) (MEXT), this change aims to improve pupils' morals. The guidelines require that the mandatory 'moral education class' (*dōtoku no jikan*: literally, path of virtue) in primary schools and in lower secondary schools be strengthened through the promotion of religious sentiment, while the elective subject of 'ethics' (*rinri*) in higher secondary schools be enriched by the knowledge of religion and reflection on its teachings.

Japan's religious revival is also being promoted through new academic courses recently introduced on the initiative of scholars in fields related to religion. In 2011, two academic associations – the Japanese Association for Religious Studies (*Nihon shūkyō gakkai*) and the Japanese Association for the Study of Religion and Society (*shūkyō to shakai gakkai*) – jointly launched a certificate in Religious Culture (*shūkyō-bunka-shi*) for undergraduate students. In 2012, scholars and practitioners at Tōhoku University unveiled a course to train interfaith chaplains (*rinshō-shūkyō-shi*) at its graduate school. These developments reflect the clear intention to strengthen the bond between religion and civil society.

Niklas Luhmann (1927–1998) argued in his systems theory that secularisation is not a crisis of religion to be lamented but an opportunity for religion to seize, as religion gains room for more flexibility for its performance as a result of secularisation. In a secularised society, the performance of religion can be expanded all the more because of (in spite of) the decreasing number of believers[5] – not within the framework of the institutionalised function of the church (*Organisation*) – but in the framework of welfare and social work (*Diakonie, Liebesaktivismus, Sozialarbeit*).[6] The loss in system functions opens a new perspective for giving additional performance in the public space.[7] The present situation in Japan seems to correspond to the conception of Luhmann in a certain sense.

---

5 N. Luhmann, *Die Funktion der Religion*, Suhrkamp, Frankfurt am Main 1977, p. 264. 'Wir müssen mit der Möglichkeit rechnen, daß unter der Bedingung eines Rückzugs aus vielen anderen Funktionsbereichen, eines Verzichts auf ‹social control› und Legitimierung politischer Macht, die Chancen für Religion steigen.' (N. Luhmann, *Die Religion der Gesellschaft*, Suhrkamp, Frankfurt am Main 2000, p 145).

6 N. Luhmann, *Die Religion...*, *op. cit.*, p. 243.

7 *Ibid.*, p. 305.

Religious background in Japan

Ambiguity of religious consciousness

According to the 'World Value Survey' of 2005, only 6.5% of Japanese respondents say that religion is 'very important'.[8] While 11.7% of Japanese respondents say that they are members of religious organisations, only one-third of them claim to be active members.[9] This, however, does not mean that Japanese people are indifferent to religious practices. The average Japanese celebrate Christmas, meditatively listen to the tolling of the bell at their local Buddhist temple on New Year's Eve, intended to stamp out worldly desires and visit a Shintō shrine on New Year's Day to pray for a happy new year. In addition, they marry in a Christian church, have their children baptised at a Shintō shrine and are buried in the graveyard of a Buddhist temple.

The Japanese have traditionally observed three teachings: Shintō, Buddhism and Confucianism. Shintō is an indigenous teaching which combines animism, ancestor worship and emperor worship while lacking both a founding figure and any formalised doctrine.[10] Buddhism was introduced to Japan from India via China and Korea during the sixth century.[11] Because this teaching was regarded as a matter of scholarship rather than belief, only the elite studied it at first: it was not until the 13th century that Buddhism began to spread among the common people. Buddhism and Shintō coexisted harmoniously through an allocation of separate roles: while Shintō rules the affairs of this world, Buddhism rules the affairs of the next. Added to this mix was Confucianism, a doctrine based on the teachings of the Chinese philosopher Confucius (551–479 BC). Introduced to Japan at the same time as Buddhism,[12] Confucianism served primarily as an ethical code during the feudal period of the shogunate (1603–1867), as its emphasis on fealty underpinned and legitimised highly hierarchical social relations.[13] The

---

8   World Value Survey Association, *WVS 2005 CODEBOOK*, p. 108, available at: http://www.wvsevsdb.com/wvs/WVSAnalize.jsp?Idioma=I (accessed: 31.12.2013). In total, 13.1% found religion 'rather important', 35.7% 'not very important' and 44.8% 'not at all important'.

9   *Ibid.*, p. 140.

10   The use of the extant term 'Shintō' dates back to the year 720 and appears in the *Chronicles of Japan* (*nihon shoki*). Shintō's signature views the Emperor as a descendant of the gods, which is often regarded as an article of faith invented no earlier than the second half of the 19th century, reflecting the Meiji period's surge of national awareness.

11   According to the *Chronicles of Japan*, Buddhism was officially introduced to Japan in 552, when Seong of Baekje (?–554), a king of a Korean Kingdom, sent Emperor Kinmei (510–571) a bronze statue of Buddha and several sutras.

12   Confucianism war introduced to Japan in 513 by Chinese scholars.

13   Confucianism divides ethics into five categories of interpersonal relations: lord and vassal, father and son, elder brother and younger brother, wife and husband, and friends. This teaching contributed to stabilise the feudal system in Japan for centuries.

three teachings, which are classified into religions today, were seamlessly interwoven in the pre-modern period.

It was not until the end the country's seclusion policy (1639–1853) and the beginning of modernisation in the Meiji period (1868–1912) that the Japanese first encountered Western teachings that were incompatible with their own traditions. The Japanese term *shūkyō*, the equivalent of the English term 'religion', came to denote such teachings.[14] The Japanese tend to associate *shūkyō* with exclusive teachings in stark contrast to the inclusive teachings familiar to them.[15] In particular, the term *shūkyō* refers to teachings that are closed to other teachings, are formally organised, have founders and leaders, and that are characterised by formal doctrines and internal formations, such as orders. Teachings described as *shūkyō* are matters of identity. However, Japanese people seldom identify themselves with formal teachings, which is why they describe themselves as non-religious, even as they observe religious practices.

Ambiguity of religious education: The reforming efforts

Religious education before 1945

The term *shūkyō* hints at an ambiguous relation between religion and education in modern Japan. In the country's formative period as a nation state, educational policy tended to promote the conventional teachings, which were not recognised as *shūkyō*, while it tended to repress the non-conventional teachings, which were called *shūkyō*. This made the relation between religion and education much more complex.

Christian teachings are *shūkyō* especially in the sense of their incompatibility with Japan's traditional teachings. The country's initial encounter with Christianity dates to the visit of a Portuguese Catholic missionary, Francis Xavier (1506–1552), in 1549. At first, Christianity was propagated with permission of the rulers, but it began to be repressed at the end of the 16th century as it came to be perceived as a threat to peace. After a peasant revolt in the town of Shimabara, staged mostly by Christians between 1637 and 1638, the rulers decided to ban

---

14 The use of the term *shūkyō* in the Western sense of *religion* emerged around 1874 (*cf.* T. Ama, *Why Are the Japanese Non-religious? (nihonjin wa naze mushūkyō nanoka)*, Chikumasshobō, Tokyo 1996, p. 74).

15 The Japanese have been called religious only in the sense of natural religion, not in the sense of revealed religion. *Cf.* T. Ama, *Why are the Japanese...*, *op. cit.*, p. 11. See also S. Fujiwawa, *Problems of Teaching about Religion in Japan. Another Textbook Controversy against Peace?*, 'British Journal of Religious Education' 2007, 29, 1, p. 46; *id.*, *Japan*, [in:] G.D. Alles (ed.), *Religious Studies. A global View*, Routledge, London 2008, p. 192.

Christianity. Claiming that Western Christians had engaged in sedition, Japan broke off relations with Portugal and imposed a strict policy of national seclusion.[16] It was not until 1873 that the country lifted the ban on Christianity as a concession to the West. In 1899, freedom of belief was guaranteed in Article 28 of the 'Constitution of the Empire of Japan' (dai-nippon teikoku kenpō). Despite this change, religion remained stigmatised as a result of the long-term ban.

The treatment of religion in schools was beset by ambiguity as a result of the complex principles established when framing the modern State. The 'Imperial Rescript on Education' (kyōiku chokugo) required educational institutions to propagate imperialistic policies and Confucian ethics, a decision which committed education to the country's expansionary militarism from the Rescript's promulgation (1890) to the end of World War II (1945). The 'Imperial Rescript on Education' rests on 'State Shintō', a politicised form of Shintō engineered to meet the propaganda requirements of the imperialist nation State. State Shintō romanticised the Japanese nation as a large family in which the emperor, who ruled Japan as a legitimate descendant of the gods, acted both as a benign pater familias and as a living god. Reflecting the spirit of the 'Imperial Rescript on Education', the curriculum was dominated by a subject called moral training (shūshin).

In 1899, the Ministry of Education (monbushō) issued Resolution No. 12, which demanded that, in conformity with the principle of the separation of State and religion, all religions and religious practices be excluded from schools. In 1935, the Ministry issued Notification No. 8 concerning Resolution No. 12, which stipulated that the Resolution required religion to be excluded from schools, but permitted the inclusion of religious sentiment. Moreover, the Resolution encouraged religious sentiment in schools, as such sentiment was seen to be helpful towards moral education. The Ministry of Education expected that religious sentiment, in conjunction with State Shintō, would serve as a bastion against undesirable Western ideologies such as liberalism and Marxism, which were seen as threats to the country's imperial aspirations. Moreover, the Ministry of Education expected that religious sentiment would unite the nation in supporting the expansionist policies adopted under the imperial system. The Ministry assumed that moral education based on religious sentiment would be compatible with the principle of the separation of state and religion, because religious sentiment was not attached to a particular religion or denomination.

---

16   During this period, everyone was forced to become a member of a Buddhist temple as proof that they did not adhere to Christianity.

Religious education after 1945

After World War II, the occupying Allied Powers identified State Shintō as a major contributory factor to the outbreak of the war, since State Shintō dignified naked military aggression with the appearance of legitimacy flowing from the Emperor's putative divine descent. Accordingly, State Shintō was branded an ultra-nationalist ideology with religious overtones. In 1945, the occupying authorities issued the Shintō Directive (*shintō shirei*), which demanded the abolition of government sponsorship, support, perpetuation, control and dissemination of State Shintō. As a result, moral training – a central curricular subject until 1945 – was abandoned without any replacement.

The constitution of Japan (*nihonkoku kenpō*) was adopted in 1946 and reflects the priorities laid out by the occupying authorities. It guarantees freedom of religion in Article 20[17] and prescribes the exclusion of religion from public schools: 'The state and its organs shall refrain from religious education or any other religious activity'.[18] The 'Basic Act on Education', which was passed in 1947, excludes religion from public schools in Article 9: 'The schools established by the national and local governments shall refrain from religious education or other activities for a specific religion'.[19] The same Article, however, also called for religion to be part of the curriculum: 'The attitude of religious tolerance and the position of religion in social life shall be valued in education'.[20] These two somewhat contradictory stipulations have caused much controversy about religious education in public schools. In Japan, religious education is thought to consist of three categories: sectarian education (denominational education), the inculcation of religious sentiment (cultivation of religious sentiment) and education concerning religious knowledge (teaching about religion). There is universal agreement that education concerning religious knowledge is legally recognised in public schools and that sectarian education is prohibited. There is disagreement, however, regarding the inculcation of religious sentiment. Some insist that it is legally recognised even in public schools; others oppose this view, as they say it infringes upon freedom of religion. The former regard religious sentiment as a feeling of awe which is common to all religions; the latter regard religious sentiment as a feeling of awe which must depend on a particular religion.

---

17 'Freedom of religion is guaranteed to all. No religious organisation shall receive any privileges from the State, nor exercise any political authority. No person shall be compelled to take part in any religious act, celebration, rite or practice' (Prime Minister of Japan and his Cabinet, *Constitution*, available at: http://www.kantei.go.jp/foreign/constitution_and_government_of_japan/constitution_e.html (accessed: 31.12.2013).

18 *Ibid.*

19 MEXT, *Fundamental Act of Education* (*kyōiku kihonhō*), available at: http://www.mext.go.jp/b_menu/kihon/data/07080117.htm (accessed: 31.12.2013).

20 *Ibid.*

The *Government Guidelines for Teaching*, through which the Ministry of Education guides the implementation of the national standardised curriculum, prescribes the detailed contents of school education in accordance with the 'Fundamental Act on Education'. The first edition of the non-binding guidelines was issued in 1952. The revised second edition was issued in 1958 and its contents were then made legally binding. Since then, the guidelines have been revised approximately every ten years and they continue to apply to all schools throughout the country. The second edition (1958) introduced a special subject for moral education outside of regular subjects and allocated one teaching unit per week (45 minutes in elementary school; 50 minutes in lower secondary school) to the new moral education class. Since their introduction, such classes have been taught in every elementary school (grades 1–6) and lower secondary school (grades 7–9).[21] In one sense, the class on moral education is similar to the central subject of morals training prior to 1945: they both offer moral education detached from regular subjects, accompanied by religious overtones, such as references to superhuman beings.

The first revision of the *Basic Act on Education*, which was passed in 2006,[22] increased the emphasis on religious education. The article concerning religious education gained an additional phrase: education must not only further 'the attitude of religious tolerance and the position of religion in social life' but also facilitate 'general learning regarding religion'.[23] Introduced at the initiative of policy makers, this revision strengthened religious education in the current *Government Guidelines for Teaching*.

---

21 Denominational private schools are allowed to teach religious education in place of moral education.

22 The revised law specifies two requirements: 'respect of tradition and development of patriotism' and 'cultivation of religious sentiments and reinforcement of moral education'. The first requirement was accepted, but the second requirement was rejected.

23 According to Article 15 of the *Fundamental Act of Education* (2006), 'The attitude of religious tolerance, general knowledge regarding religion, and the position of religion in social life shall be valued in education. (2) The schools established by the national and local governments shall refrain from religious education or other activities for a specific religion' (MEXT 2006).

Religious education as moral education:
Change of the *Government Guidelines for Teaching* initiated by policy makers

Religious sentiment and moral education in elementary and lower secondary schools: moral education class

According to the *Government Guidelines for Teaching*, the aim of moral education lies in 'cultivating morality as a foundation for developing Japanese citizens with a proactive attitude'.[24] Therefore, moral education is considered the basis on which school education rests. Moral education consists of four elements: 'regarding self',[25] 'relation to others',[26] 'relation to nature and the sublime',[27] and 'relation to groups and society'.[28] The third element – 'relation to nature and the sublime' – speaks to aesthetic sensitivity and seeks to impart reverence for the transcendental, placing especial emphasis on religious sentiment.

In 1997, the Ministry of Education unveiled a new scheme of moral education entitled *Education of the Heart* (*kokoro no kyōiku*). Under this scheme, which has been developed and practiced in Japan since 1998,[29] the heart (*kokoro*) is considered the wellspring of moral sensitivity; its education is expected to bring out all that is good and holy in human nature. The cultivation of moral awareness

---

24 MEXT, *Government Guidelines for Teaching. Elementary School. General Provisions* (*shōgakkō gakushū-shidō-yōryō. sōsoku*), available at: http://www.mext.go.jp/component/a_menu/education/micro_detail/__icsFiles/afieldfile/2011/04/11/1261037_1.pdf (accessed: 31.12.2013). MEXT, *Government Guidelines for Teaching. Lower Secondary School. General Provisions* (*chūgakkō gakushū-shidō-yōryō. sōsoku*), available at: http://www.mext.go.jp/component/a_menu/education/micro_detail/__icsFiles/afieldfile/2011/07/22/1298356_1.pdf (accessed: 31.12.2013). Japanese citizens are expected to 'apply a spirit of respect for human dignity and reverence for life in specific activities at home, school and other social situations, have a generous spirit, respect traditions and culture, love [their] country and hometown which have fostered such traditions and culture, create culture with a distinctive character, honour the public spirit, make an effort to develop the democratic society and state, respect other countries, contribute to world peace and the development of the international community and the preservation of the environment, and have interest in exploring possibilities for the future' (*ibid.*).

25 It includes moderation, diligence, courage, sincerity, freedom and order, self-improvement and love of truth.

26 It includes courtesy, consideration and kindness, friendship, thanks and respect, and modesty.

27 It includes respect for nature, respect for life, aesthetic sensitivity and nobility.

28 It includes public duty, justice, group participation and responsibility, industry, respect for family members, respect for teachers and people at school, contribution to society, respect for tradition and love of nation, and respect for other culture. The forth field – relation to group and society – tacitly introduces Shintō as part of Japanese tradition.

29 T. Ito, *Erziehung des Herzens als Rezept gegen Jugendkriminalität*, 'Neue Züricher Zeitung' 20.06.1998.

thereby relies on sentimentality at the expense of rational thought. To further these priorities, MEXT began to distribute in 2002 a supplemental learning booklet titled *Notebook for the Heart* (*kokoro no nōto*).[30] It posits a close connection between moral values and spiritual experience. The *Notebook* for fifth and sixth grade, for example, has a chapter entitled '*Fill yourself with awe*'. The chapter first proclaims the existence of an invisible, mystic world: 'Nature, which supports all life, is filled with mysterious providence. There is an invisible, mystic world. There is a world which lies beyond human understanding'.[31] This explanation is followed by a question: 'What encounter have you had with something that lies beyond human understanding and that moved you deeply?'[32] Awe, presented as a guiding principle in moral education class, is construed as a moving experience of the transcendental world, an experience which students are expected to have already made.[33] Religious sentiment derived from transcendental experience is thus expected to enrich moral sentiment. In the market for moral orientation, the demand for religious sentiment is rising steadily.

In 2013, policy makers announced that 'moral education class' would be upgraded from special subject to regular one so that moral education can be more heavily weighted in evaluation reports. This change will be implemented pending the partial revision of the *Government Guidelines for Teaching*, which is expected to be ratified in 2015. The *Notebook for the Heart*, whose print distribution was replaced by a downloadable version as a result of a budget cut in 2011, is now being revised for a new print edition. The revised booklet – newly entitled *Our Morals* (*watashitachi no dōtoku*) – is due to be distributed again from April 2014. It is expected to include biographical profiles of great personalities, such as Inazo Nitobe (1862–1933), the author of *Bushido: Soul of Japan* (1900), and episodes involving personalities of worldwide fame, such as Naoko Takahashi (1972–), a marathon runner and Olympic gold medallist at the 2000 Games. Moreover, the booklet aims to promote appreciation of Japan's traditional culture and to curb undesired behaviour such as bullying, which is widely seen as a rising phenomenon. As policy makers expect the booklet to contribute to the prevention of undesired behaviour by means of cultivating moral sentiment, the expectations that underpin the *Notebook of the Heart* are emblematic of the whole thinking in this area.

---

30 The booklet, which was created under the direction of the Jungian clinical psychologist Hayao Kawai (1928–2007), has been criticised for its over-emphasis on psychological factors (cf. T. Ito, *Das Herz als Hoffnung. Moralerziehung im heutigen Japan*, 'Die Deutsche Schule' 2005, 97, 2).

31 MEXT, *Notebook for the Heart* (*kokoro no nōto*), vol. 3, Tokyo 2002, p. 68.

32 *Ibid.*, p. 69.

33 According to MEXT's commentary in *Government Guidelines for Teaching*, students of this age group are capable of recognising the world beyond human understanding and the providence of nature (MEXT 2008, p. 57).

Briefly stated: policy makers now recommend moral education based on religious sentiment in tune with the country's traditions.

Education concerning religious knowledge and moral education in upper secondary schools: 'ethics'

While primary and lower secondary schools assign the cultivation of 'morality as a foundation for developing Japanese citizens with a proactive attitude'[34] to a special subject, 'moral education class', upper secondary schools assign it to an optional subject of ethics in the field of 'civics' (*kōmin*). This consists of three subjects: 'contemporary sociology' (*gendai shakai*), 'politics and economy' (*seiji keizai*) and 'ethics'. 'Ethics' aims to make the students contemplate four issues:

> [...] self-building during the period of adolescence as well as their way of life, raising their practical will of character-building, establishing self-direction while living together with others, and developing ability and attitude as citizens with good judgement, based on respect for human being and reverence for life.[35]

'Ethics', therefore, is regarded as an advanced course in 'moral education class'.[36] It is not expected that 'moral education class' deals with actual religion, but the class obviously depends on religious sentiment to enrich moral sentiment, especially after the introduction of the supplemental booklet. However, in stark contrast to 'moral education class', 'ethics' deals with major religions directly in order to impart the necessary civic virtue of good judgement.

The current *Government Guidelines for Teaching*, which reflect the revision of the *Fundamental Act of Education*, increase religious topics in 'ethics'. 'Ethics' consists of three parts: 'our problems of living today', 'our way of being and living as a human being', and 'the present age and its ethics'.[37] The second part – 'our way of being and living as human being' – which consists of 'self-awareness as a human being' and 'self-awareness as a Japanese citizen living in an international society' is relevant to religious education. Through 'self-awareness as human beings', students are expected to deepen their understanding of human nature and culture by studying great personalities in philosophy, religion and art. It places,

---

34 MEXT 2008.
35 MEXT, *Government Guidelines for Teaching. Upper Secondary School* (*kōtogakkō gakushū-shidō-yōryō*), available at: http://www.mext.go.jp/a_menu/shotou/new-cs/youryou/kou/kou.pdf (accessed: 31.12.2013).
36 The current *Government Guidelines for Teaching* makes the role of 'ethics' as a subject for moral education in upper secondary school clearer that in the light of *Education for the Heart* (MEXT 2009, p. 23).
37 MEXT 2009, p. 33.

therefore, special emphasis on knowledge about religion, from which students are expected to derive values.

'Ethics' textbooks are offered by a number of widely different publishers under their own editorial principles, but their contents concerning 'self-awareness as a human being' quite uniformly follow the governmental *Guidelines*. The textbooks recommend readings for the students' contemplation, which are selected from philosophy of diverse periods and from diverse religions. These readings supposedly deepen and widen the students' contemplation, but they leave virtually no room to think about moral issues critically nor to develop the students' ability to make independent moral judgements. This is because the values the students need to acquire from each reading are strictly pre-determined in the *Guidelines*, according to which every reading in philosophy and religion needs to deliver a certain unambiguous message concerning values. The students are expected to learn, for example, the value of neighbourly love from Christianity, the value of life from Buddhism and the value of compassion from Confucianism. Under the assumption that every reading imparts a predetermined virtue, students are given no room to discuss a reading or derive anything from it except the prescribed message. Furthermore, the selection of readings implies that the religions that are not mentioned in the textbooks are unworthy of study because they have no virtues to offer.[38] As the textbooks present arbitrarily chosen readings as a means of dictating arbitrarily determined virtues, beyond which no critical thinking or independent judgement is encouraged, philosophy and religion are exploited as a means of indoctrinating students with certain virtues allegedly necessary for citizens of good judgement, as if there existed a single objectively right way to describe a religion. The textbooks foster a shallow and blinkered manner of reading that defies every principle of critical thinking and scholarly practice.

As for 'self-awareness as a Japanese citizen living in an international society' – the second point of the section 'our way of being and living as human being' – students are expected to deepen and widen their self-awareness as self-directed people by acquiring the supposedly proper Japanese view of human beings, of nature and of religion. The students are asked to study Shintō, the country's indigenous teaching, in this context in which it serves as the vehicle that conveys the supposedly proper outlook required of a Japanese citizen.

According to the *Guidelines*, the study of religion should deepen and widen the contemplation undertaken by students, but the effective narrowing of this study demanded by the *Guidelines* serves little else except for religious indoctrination with a political bias.

---

38 The *Guidelines* of 2009 refered to the intrinsic value of Islam for the first time: students should learn the value of mutual aid from Islam. Islam had never been mentioned previously (MEXT 2009).

Studying religion for civil education: New initiatives by scholars

Expertise in religion as a contribution to civil society: 'Specialist in Religious Culture'

In 2011, the Japanese Association for Religious Studies[39] and the Japanese Association for the Study of Religion and Society[40] launched a new programme for undergraduate students to be certified as Specialists in Religious Culture, which is run by the Center for Education in Religious Culture (*shūkyō bunka kyōiku suishin sentā*) (CERC), a research facility affiliated with Kokugakuin University (Tokyo).[41] This programme aims to improve the understanding of religion by training specialists who can contribute to civil society through their expertise in religion.

To qualify for the examination, undergraduate students need to acquire 16 credits for courses offered by the programme[42] in four compulsory fields (introduction to world religions, introduction to religious studies, religions in the contemporary world, Japanese religions) and in one optional field concerning the history of specific religions. The examination, which consists of multiple-choice questions and open-ended questions, assesses the ability to understand religious culture, basic knowledge of major religious traditions and general knowledge of the contemporary world.[43] The programme has administered two examinations

---

39 The Japanese Association for Religious Studies, which was founded in 1930, represents religious studies in Japan. Members include scholars of religion and theologians.

40 The Japanese Association for the Study of Religion and Society was founded in 1993. Its members are social scientists who study religion.

41 Nobutaka Inoue, the founding director of this centre, has held for many years that religion needs to be taught 'in combination with culture', because most Japanese people are prejudiced against religious instruction, while they acknowledge the necessity of teaching culture. The so-called 'religious culture education', which promotes understanding of both Japanese and foreign religious culture, is readily accepted even at public schools. This conception is quite parallel to that of Québec's subject Ethics and Religious Culture (ERC) (*cf.* S. Fujiwara, *Has Deconfessionalization Been Completed? Some Reflections upon Québec's Ethics and Religious Culture (ERC) Program*, 'Religion & Education' 2011, 38, 3), that of Brandenburg's subject 'Lebenskunde, Ethik und Religionskunde (LER)', and Zurich's subject 'Kultur und Religion (KUR)' (*cf.* T. Ito, *The Discourse of the Religious in Value-education: Origin, Development and Prospects* (*kachi-kyōiku no bunmyaku niokeru shūkyō-sei o meguru gensetsu. Sono raireki, henyō, tenbō*), 'Bulletin of the Faculty of Education, Mie University' 2007, 58).

42 There are eight universities which offer this program: Kwansei Gakuin University (a private non-denominational Christian university), Kōgakkan University (a private university offering qualifications for Shintō priesthood), Kokugakuin University (a private university offering qualifications for Shintō priesthood), Taishō University (a private university based on the Tendai school of Buddhism), Tsukuba University (a state university), Tōhoku University (a state university), Tenri University (a private university as an independent part of the secular mission Tenrikyō) and Hokkaidō University (a state university).

43 Center for Education in Religious Culture (CERC), available at: www.cerc.jp/index_eng.html (accessed: 31.12.2013). The first examination was held in November 2011 at six universities.

every year since its launch in 2011, but it still struggles with basic problems such as the definition of criteria for assessing expertise in religion, as the current examination 'risks promoting stereotypical understanding of each religion'.[44]

Religious practice in civil society: Interfaith chaplains

Following the disaster of 2011, religious practitioners turned out in force to offer counselling in the public space while refraining from proselytising. Even scholars in the study of religion, accustomed to keeping their academic distance, began to take part in the effort.

Practitioners from across the religious spectrum held a number of ecumenical services and set up a jointly-run initiative to support the bereaved families in the stricken area. The Counselling Room for the Heart (*kokoro no sōdanshitsu*), headquartered at Tōhoku University, was composed of members of monastic orders, scholars of religion, medical professionals and specialists in bereavement counselling. They set up Café de Monk and held monthly memorial services. Concluding from their experience that these activities met a need of the public, they developed and launched a programme to train interfaith chaplains. The endowed Department for Practical Religious Studies (*jissen shūkyōgaku kifu-kōza*), newly created for the purpose at the Graduate School of Art and Letters at Tōhoku University in 2012, offers programmes focused on four areas: the ability to 'engage in attentive listening and spiritual counselling', the cultivation of 'inter-faith dialogue and religious co-operation', the willingness to 'co-operate appropriately with non-religious organisations' and the provision of 'broadly conceived religious counselling'.[45] The initiative aims to contribute to civil society by training religious leaders as interfaith chaplains,[46] also known as 'Japanese-style chaplains'.[47]

The examination was taken by 92 candidates, 58 of whom passed. The examination is held twice a year.

44 S. Fujiwara, *On Qualifying Religious Literacy. Recent Debates on Higher Education and Religious Studies in Japan*, 'Teaching Theology and Religion' 2010, 13, 3, p. 230.

45 H. Takahashi, *The Aim of the Department for Practical Religious Studies and the Concept of Rinshō Shūkyō-shi*, 'Department of Practical Religious Studies' 2012, 1, p. 7.

46 *Ibid.*, p. 6.

47 Department of Practical Religious Studies, 'Practical Religious Studies Newsletter' 2012, p. 1.

Conclusion: Religion and the civil society in the age of nuclear catastrophe

In general, the Japanese are wary of religion and tend to eschew most of its formal manifestations. This tendency is rooted in the country's political history: religion was restricted for a long period by the ban on Christianity, resulting in a cultural bias against it. In addition, Shintō is viewed with suspicion by many who remember its complicity in legitimising the ultra-nationalistic and militaristic ideology of the country's imperial past.[48] Despite such reservations, the Japanese agree on the need for religious education. Policy makers argue for religious education, stressing its benefit of moral orientation. They expect that religious sentiment and knowledge, which religious education should deliver, will foster the essential civic virtues of moral orientation and judgement. Scholars argue for religious education stressing its benefit of social orientation. They expect that religious understanding and caring, which is acquired from their instruction, can contribute to civil society through deeper understanding and effective caring.

Luhmann claims that in a secularised society, acts of religion can be engaged in far beyond the institutional framework of welfare and social work. The current change in the relation of public education and religious education, brought about by the initiative of policy makers and scholars in religious studies, support the relevance of Luhmann's observation.

In the aftermath of the disaster of 2011, the song that took the perspective of the deceased earthquake victims entered Japan's pop music charts. In this song, the voices of the deceased empathise not only with those suffering in the present, but also with those who are yet to be born. Such empathy towards future generations is needed especially in an age of nuclear disaster, when the span of concern needs to exceed the span of our lives. A disaster of the kind and magnitude that befell Japan in 2011 has serious consequences far beyond the present generation, as the radioactive half-life period of plutonium lasts a hundred thousand years. Our imagination needs to reach far beyond the present generation. Religious education needs to facilitate and foster such imagination, if acts of religion in Luhmann's sense are to take hold. In a secular society, religion can unfold its benefits

---

48 The sarin gas attack perpetrated by the Aum Shirikyo cult in Tokyo in 1995 deepened such reservations. Yet the Japanese, especially the young, do show a considerable interest in religion. The wildly popular animation films directed by Hayao Miyazaki weave a rich tapestry of religious symbolism in which spirits, ancient gods and magical creatures play central roles. A best-selling *manga* graphic novel featuring two religious founders as protagonists, Hikaru Nakamura's *Saintly Young Men*, has been serialised in monthly instalments since 2006. The fictional narrative chronicles the events that transpire between Jesus Christ and Gautama Buddha as they share a Tokyo apartment while taking a vacation on Earth. The work received a Tezuka Osamu Cultural Prize in 2009.

free from all institutional bonds. Yet if institutional religion seeks to forestall such liberation, and if religious education curtails the understanding or practice of religion, which is obviously the situation brought about by policy makers and scholars in Japan today, the secular age will be a bane to religion rather than an opportunity. Solidarity with those living a hundred thousand years ahead, which is required in an age of nuclear disaster, depends on the decisive rejection of every kind of curtailment.

Bibliography

Ama T., *Why Are the Japanese Non-religious?* (*nihonjin wa naze mushūkyō nanoka*), Chikumashobō, Tokyo 1996.

Center for Education in Religious Culture (CERC), available at: www.cerc.jp/index_eng. html (accessed: 31.12.2013).

Department of Practical Religious Studies, 'Practical Religious Studies Newsletter' 2012, 1.

Fujiwara S., *Has Deconfessionalization Been Completed? Some Reflections upon Québec's Ethics and Religious Culture (ERC) Program*, 'Religion & Education' 2011, 38, 3.

Fujiwara S., *Japan*, [in:] G.D. Alles (ed.), *Religious Studies. A Global View*, Routledge, London 2008.

Fujiwara S., *On Qualifying Religious Literacy. Recent Debates on Higher Education and Religious Studies in Japan*, 'Teaching Theology and Religion' 2010, 13, 3.

Fujiwawa S., *Problems of Teaching about Religion in Japan. Another Textbook Controversy against Peace?*, 'British Journal of Religious Education' 2007, 29, 1.

Isa K., *Quest for Religion Now* (*ima shūkyō o shiritai*), 'Asahi Shimbun' 15.11.2011.

Isa K., *The Great Earthquake as an Opportunity to Seek the Meaning of Life* (*daishinsai kikkake ikiru imi jimon*), 'Asahi Shimbun' 27.03.2013.

Ito T., *Das Herz als Hoffnung. Moralerziehung im heutigen Japan*, 'Die Deutsche Schule' 2005, 97, 2.

Ito T., *Erziehung des Herzens als Rezept gegen Jugendkriminalität*, 'Neue Züricher Zeitung' 20.06.1998.

Ito T., *The Discourse of the Religious in Value-education: Origin, Development, and Prospects* (*kachi-kyōiku no bunmyaku niokeru shūkyō-sei o meguru gensetsu. Sono raireki, henyō, tenbō*), 'Bulletin of the Faculty of Education, Mie University' 2007, 58.

Luhmann N., *Die Religion der Gesellschaft*, Suhrkamp, Frankfurt am Main 2000.

Luhmann N., *Die Funktion der Religion*, Suhrkamp, Frankfurt am Main 1977.

MEXT, *Fundamental Act of Education* (*kyōiku kihonhō*), available at: http://www.mext. go.jp/b_menu/kihon/data/07080117.htm (accessed: 31.12.2013).

MEXT, *Government Guidelines for Teaching. Elementary School. General Provisions* (*shōgakkō gakushū-shidō-yōryō. sōsoku*), available at: http://www.mext.go.jp/component/a_menu/education/micro_detail/__icsFiles/afieldfile/2011/04/11/1261 037_1. pdf (accessed: 31.12.2013).

MEXT, *Government Guidelines for Teaching. Lower Secondary School. General Provisions* (*chūgakkō gakushū-shidō-yōryō. sōsoku*), available at: http://www.mext.go.

jp/component/a_menu/education/micro_detail/__icsFiles/afieldfile/2011/07/22/
1298356_1.pdf (accessed: 31.12.2013).

MEXT, *Government Guidelines for Teaching. Upper Secondary School* (*kōtogakkō gakushū-shidō-yōryō*), available at: http://www.mext.go.jp/a_menu/shotou/new-cs/youryou/kou/kou.pdf (accessed: 31.12.2013).

MEXT, *Notebook for the Heart* (*kokoro no nōto*), vol. 3, Tokyo 2002.

Prime Minister of Japan and his Cabinet, *Constitution*, available at: http://www.kantei.go.jp/foreign/constitution_and_government_of_japan/constitution_e.html (accessed: 31.12.2013).

Takahashi H., *The Aim of the Department for Practical Religious Studies and the Concept of Rinshō Shūkyō-shi*, 'Department of Practical Religious Studies' 2012, 1.

World Value Survey Association, *WVS 2005 CODEBOOK*, available at: http://www.wvsevsdb.com/wvs/WVSAnalize.jsp?Idioma=I (accessed: 31.12.2013).

Eugeniusz Sakowicz
Cardinal Stefan Wyszyński University
Warsaw (Poland)

The Resolution of Conflicts and Building Unity: M. Fethullah Gülen's Pedagogical Proposition

An overview of M.F. Gülen's pedagogical themes

The contemporary world has a multicultural and multireligious character. It is not just the national capitals and metropolises that are inhabited by people representing various cultures and religions, but cities, big towns and small towns as well. More and more often, schools, Catholic parishes and other Christian churches and communities have a multi-ethnic and multicultural character. The media significantly influence the attitudes of people of various cultures. Education cannot ignore the pluralism of cultures.

Children and youngsters are not brought up and educated in an ideological vacuum. Our era has been described as the 'end of history' (Francis Fukuyama), and has seen the 'clash of civilisations' (Samuel Huntington) and propagation of an irrational fear of media-generated phenomena, e.g. Eurabia (Oriana Fallaci). It is also a time of 'crossing the threshold of hope' (John Paul II). The 20th century saw the accumulation of unforgiveness, intolerance, anti-dialogue, countless conflicts (both local and global), the undermining of the foundations of the unity of all humanity and the loss of healthy concepts of upbringing. The bitter fruit of such anti-human visions of life is the destroyed dictionary of basic terms and concepts. Exceptionally intolerant individuals willingly speak about tolerance, regardless of the geographic and cultural latitude, religions and worldview. Politicians appeal for dialogue even though they do not want to have anything to do with it. On the other hand, some people perceive dialogue as a sign of weakness, helplessness and thus a betrayal of one's identity. Many people who willingly talk about unity do not do anything to enable its existence. People who start conflicts are keen to solve them.

Every epoch, including the one we live in, has its visionaries. They are not confined to the sociological boundaries of specific religions, cultures or worldviews. They follow the principles of humanism, the common good, in the name of love, which is an unconditional affirmation of 'otherness'.

It is not an exaggeration to say that M. Fethullah Gülen is the representative of Islam who also serves all of humankind. Gülen's honourable title, *Hodjaefendi* ('master teacher'), identifies him as a religious scholar and teacher whose religious knowledge and, above all, wisdom have been widely recognised. Various circumstances and situations have prepared Gülen for his mission, and his life and work are the best proof of that. The atmosphere of his home was surely the source of his ideas and deeds. He has also followed the principles of his spiritual patrons, the great thinkers who served God and people in everyday life. The Turkish thinker also has an impressive body of writing. Many of his publications are devoted to education. The ideas initiated by Gülen have been adopted by the Gülen Movement. Gülen's interfaith and intercultural activity is worthy of particular attention.

Hodjaefendi is the educator who implements the precepts of Islam in his life's mission with a conviction about the exceptional character of his religion. On the one hand, he is not afraid to describe it as the best among the existing and possible systems of belief. On the other hand, he shows respect for the followers of other religions, similar to John Paul II, who was open and well disposed to all people without exception. The most important precept of Islam is the belief in one and only God. Love and morality play a central role in everyday life. Gülen stresses the special significance of the latter in the process of education. His vision of life has been inspired and shaped by Sufism, the mystical tradition that proclaims love. He emphasised the need to shape life in the spirit of forgiveness, tolerance and openness. John Paul II and Benedict XVI have been guided by similar principles.

According to Gülen's teaching, Muhammad is the first educator in Islam. Both the circumstances of the Prophet's life and the example set by Him carry an educational message. In the 'school of the Prophet', students gain a better understanding of God's will and wish to fulfil it in their lives. Muhammad clearly defined the conditions and criteria of good education meant to serve individuals and the entire community, and to lead to eternal happiness in paradise. The pedagogy of the Qur'an and Muslim tradition is the most important for all Muslims, including those whose education is strictly secular. The Holy Book is said to contain the answers to all questions raised by man. The basics of upbringing are part of the Qur'an-based Muslim tradition that highlights the importance of acquiring knowledge. In speeches delivered to Muslims during his apostolic trips all over the world, John Paul II often quoted the holy surahs of the Qur'an. On the threshold of the 21st century, John Paul II kissed the Qur'an in a gesture of deepest respect.

Humans do not bring themselves up on their own. The family, school, Islamic community as well as the mass media are authorities with an important educational function. One may say that, to some extent, the environment holds control over an individual who lives in it and interacts with other people. Various groups with influence over the upbringing of children and youth should work together. An environment guided by destructive educational principles can have an exceptionally negative impact on a young person. Under such circumstances, young people lose their spiritual power or use it to do evil deeds. As Gülen argues, the harmonious cooperation of all groups and authorities involved in education and upbringing is crucial. John Paul II and Benedict XVI expressed the same ideas throughout their pontificates.

The origins and main points of reference of education according to Gülen are clear. He respects the legacy of the past in order to reach out to the future with an even greater enthusiasm. Intangible values are of paramount importance in the approach to the education that Gülen has initiated. According to the Turkish intellectual, education faces the challenge of globalisation, but he is not afraid of it. On the contrary, he tackles the difficult dilemmas of globalisation with great determination. Education has to take into account everything linked with globalisation. John Paul II and Benedict XVI noticed both the threats and opportunities it brings. John Paul II even taught about the global solidarity among people as an effective antidote against the destructive influence of dehumanising tendencies in the world today.

While opposing individualism in education, Gülen rejects projects ignoring the individual, as he believes them to be deleterious to all that is noble in a human being. There should be interaction and harmony between the individual and community, in the context of education. Gülen stresses that, in every kind of education, the focus should be on the mind, heart and spirit of the individual. From this follows the importance of anthropology as a starting point for the complex and difficult process of education and upbringing. According to the Turkish thinker, it is the individual person that is important in Islam, not the notion of a human being. Gülen asserts that Islam embodies the most valuable achievements in human science. No sphere is alien to an educator. Therefore, a true teacher should accept the intellect as a criterion of humanity and analyse desire or anger in the light of rationality. At the same time, Gülen points out the existential dimension of education.

The Turkish scholar has conducted numerous undertakings aimed at serving humanity and thus neutralising the sources of violence. He overcomes evil with good, social chaos and unrest with peace. The state of crisis, tension or unsettled interhuman relations may eventually bring positive effects if they are appropriately diagnosed, solved or counteracted. According to Gülen, harmony between science and religion as well as interreligious dialogue are conducive to the resolution of conflicts and building of unity. Every citizen, as Hodjaefendi emphasises, should be up to date with the life of society and the problems it experiences. The structures of understanding and unity should be built based on the political realities of life.

Values should be internalised in the process of upbringing so that they help people change the world. The affirmation of cultural values and traditional values is a key goal of education. Gülen sees the need for the patriotic dimension of education. Only someone who loves and respects their nation, its tradition, religion and past, who recognises that 'history is the teacher of life', can genuinely respect other nations with their cultural richness, despite historical tragedies and disasters. John Paul II shared this conviction. On numerous occasions, he declared his love for the fatherland – Poland – that had experienced various forms of 'oppression and misery'.

Gülen's wish has been to shape the 'golden generation', i.e. girls and boys, and then women and men who will be aware of the mission they should carry out in the modern world. The 'golden generation' is a community of noble, pure, ardent, faithful and decent people who change the world through the life they live. According to Gülen's idea, the teachers of the 'golden generation' should embody all that is the most noble in Islam. The Golden Generation Worship and Retreat Center is located in Saylorsburg, Pennsylvania, where the Turkish educator has been living for more than ten years.

Teachers and educators enjoying authority and respect among students are credible witnesses of what and whom they serve. In Gülen's approach, the work of a teacher is not just an ordinary job but a worthy mission. The ideas of the Turkish theorist of education have been adopted and implemented by various institutions, organisations and foundations, both in Turkey and around the world, including Poland. His educational vision has been implemented in the strictly educational dimension by schools as well as through the media serving as forums for discussion. The special character of schools associated with the Gülen Movement is not only reflected in how they have originated and developed but in their names as well. Scattered around the world, they are referred to as 'Turkish schools' and 'schools of tolerance'. The focus on the individual, as well as the community where he or she lives, constitutes the essence of each school. The curriculum and educational priorities foster the development of the potential of individuals. Education in Gülen's schools combines humanities with science. School staff are fully dedicated to their educational service. Schools linked with the Gülen Movement can be found on all continents, and they stand out not only because of their number but, above all, because of their standards and atmosphere. These schools are willing to collaborate with the local authorities, thus assuming co-responsibility for the communities in which they function. Their contacts with key figures in the world of politics and business as well as journalists are particularly significant.

In a sense, Gülen is a visionary who perceives the world from God's perspective. Inspired by a profound experience of faith in God, his theory of education has a prophetic dimension. The Turkish 'teacher of teachers' and 'educator of educators' is fully convinced that every individual should be continually educated for dialogue, affirmation of other people, mutual acceptance, tolerance and respect in society, including the respect for the views of other people. Gülen's vision of Muslim education is wholly original, an elaboration of valuable intuitions of Islam. The system of educational theory that can be built based on his words and works is not a utopia. It is founded on a profound belief in God, fidelity to the Islamic creed, openness to the world and its challenges, and deeds conforming to God's will. This theory is oriented towards the intellectual and spiritual renewal of Muslims and non-Muslims, all people of good will.

Interfaith and intercultural activity

Interfaith and intercultural dialogue is a major aspect of Gülen's work. Representatives of various, often very different, cultures, nations, religions and ideologies should choose dialogue if they want to live in peace and harmony. Solving conflicts and building unity is the task of every individual, regardless of whether or not they believe in God. Gülen's interfaith and intercultural work,[1] discussed only briefly in this paper, was inspired by his desire to promote kindliness, understanding and harmony among all people.

The Necessity of Interfaith Dialogue, which was authored by the Turkish scholar, was presented at the Parliament of the World's Religions which convened in December 1999 in Cape Town, South Africa. In this document, Gülen argues that there is no alternative to dialogue – it is a necessity. People of various nationalities, living in various political systems share many common values, more than they could expect. No boundaries, including political borders, may restrict the idea and pragmatism of dialogue. The context, time and circumstances in which Gülen presented this document were special. Cape Town is located near the Cape of Good Hope where the people of South Africa have experienced the drama of racial segregation for decades. The period of apartheid has led to a deep division of society into 'white' and 'coloured' people – the 'masters' and the 'slaves'. Another consequence was that the persecuted people questioned some religious truths, including the belief in Divine Providence in their life and Divine Justice. It should be noted that the first free, democratic elections, held in South Africa in 1994, were preceded by a time of intensified interreligious dialogue.

---

1 *Działalność międzywyznaniowa i międzykulturowa*, available at: http://pl.fgulen.com/content/ view/3/2/ (accessed: 10.08.2012).

The uncertainty about the future of the State and fear about how power will be transferred from the dominating racist group to the newly-elected government were common among the participants of the joint prayers, regardless of their race or religious tradition.[2]

Hodjaefendi is deeply convinced that through dialogue, mutual understanding can be achieved regardless of historical, political and religious considerations, including the tragic legacy of the past. Dialogue is not a static process; hence, it should be continually developed and intensified in order to promote mutual understanding among people of different worldviews, cultures and religions (it is one of the key objectives of dialogue in general, as indicated by John Paul II and Benedict XVI). Gülen supported the establishment of the Istanbul-based Journalists and Writers Foundation in 1994, which has achieved much in the field of intercultural and interreligious dialogue. Gülen's involvement in various forms and manifestations of dialogue has won broad acclaim.

The Turkish thinker and scholar leads a very active life. He meets various cultural, religious and political personages from nearly all over the world; these are not merely courtesy visits. During his meeting with Pope John Paul II on 9 February 1998 in the Vatican, he proposed joint actions towards breaking the spiral of hatred among people in the Middle East. The international community may not remain indifferent to conflict, including military actions and hatred prevailing in this part of the world where the three great religions – Islam, Judaism and Christianity – were born. People in the Middle East should undertake cooperation and dialogue.[3] The cooperation called for by Gülen constitutes a dialogue of works, i.e. dialogue of social involvement, whose value and significance was often stressed by John Paul II.

According to Kardaş, Hodjaefendi's meeting with John Paul II, spiritual leader of the Catholic Church, was one of the most conspicuous moments in his project for the dialogue of civilisations. The hallmarks of this project were: understanding instead of prejudice, respect instead of anger, peace instead of fighting and wars. In other words, working for understanding in any possible form and with the aid of any acceptable methods. In the following decade, the Gülen Movement managed to establish numerous institutions and academies promoting dialogue all over the world.[4]

---

2 A. Musiałek, *Dialog religijny w Republice Południowej Afryki*, 'Collectanea Theologica' 2009, 79, 3, p. 169.
3 *Letter presented to Pope John Paul II by Fethullah Gülen during his historic visit to the Vatican on February 8, 1998*, [in:] A. Kardaş, *Praktyczny wymiar dialogu w nauczaniu Fethullaha Gülena*, [in:] M. Lewicka, Cz. Łapicz (eds.), *Dialog chrześcijańsko-muzułmański. Historia i współczesność, zagrożenia i wyzwania*, Nicolaus Copernicus University Press, Toruń 2011, pp. 81–83.
4 A. Kardaş, *Praktyczny wymiar...*, *op. cit.*, p. 89.

In his document on the proposed actions for peace, Gülen emphasised that knowledge and religion do not exclude each other but actually constitute two different aspects of the same truth, from which they are derived. The path towards the resolution of conflicts and building of unity is paved by education fostering the reconciliation of science and religion as well as interreligious dialogue (discussed below). During his meeting with the pontiff, Gülen observed:

> From time to time, humankind has been negating religion in the name of science, or vice versa, arguing that the two represent contradictory world views. All knowledge belongs to God, and religion comes from God. So how can the two contradict each other? Our joint efforts focused on interreligious dialogue can improve, to a significant extent, mutual understanding and tolerance among people[5].

The spirit of that Vatican meeting was also present at the international symposium 'In the Footsteps of Our Common Ancestor Abraham', organised in Harran in Turkey. It was attended by representatives of three monotheistic religions: Islam, Judaism and Christianity.[6] It is worth noting the highly symbolic meaning of the venue – Harran. It was from here that Abraham, recognised by monotheistic religions as a paragon of faith, fulfilled God's will and set off on his journey to the Land of Canaan.[7] Gülen proposed the establishment of the Abrahamic University of Harran, an idea that has not been implemented yet.

Hodjaefendi also talked to the retired archbishop of New York, Cardinal John O'Connor, who passed away in 2000, about a year and a half before the terrorist attack on the World Trade Center. It should be remembered that Cardinal O'Connor was a vocal opponent of abortion (for several years now, New York has had the highest proportion of abortions in relation to its population). He also opposed the demands of the gay movement, spoke against capital punishment, and condemned anti-Semitism. Beyond doubt, the problem of abortion and the aggressive promotion of homosexuality should be the subjects of interreligious and intercultural dialogue. After 9/11, New York has become, in a sense, the center of all global events. The escalation of hatred in various parts of the world, combating terrorism, the civil wars in countries of Islamic culture in North Africa and the Middle East should be viewed from the perspective of 11 September.

After the terrorist attacks on the WTC, Gülen published a press statement condemning the attacks as a gross violation of world peace. What is more, these acts of violence not only cost the lives of thousands but also undermined the integrity of Muslims. In his statement, Gülen asserted that terror must never be

---

5 *Ibid.*
6 See: *The Journalists and Writers Foundation. Towards Universal Peace*, Istanbul 2011, p. 7.
7 For a discussion on Abraham and the prophets, also in the context of interreligious dialogue, see E. Sakowicz, *Dialog Kościoła z islamem według dokumentów soborowych i posoborowych (1963–1999)*, UKSW Press, Warsaw 2000, pp. 322–324, 334–353.

used in the name of Islam or to achieve any Islamic objectives. A terrorist cannot be a true Muslim, nor can a Muslim be a terrorist. A Muslim can only be a representative and symbol of peace, well-being and happiness.[8]

Between 11–13 April 2003, the University of Texas at Austin hosted a symposium dedicated to the heroes of peace. The outcome of the conference was a list of peacemakers over 5,000 years of human history. The peaceful heroes included Jesus Christ, Buddha, Mahatma Gandhi, Martin Luther King, Mother Theresa of Calcutta. M. Fethullah Gülen was mentioned as a contemporary peacemaker. That neither meant that the individual persons were of equal stature nor was a manifestation of religious relativism. The outstanding 'holy men' of a particular religion (a Judeo-Christian term for persons who have played an exceptional role in the history of Judaism and Christianity) should be perceived from the perspective of those they were emulating. Gülen should thus be viewed from the angle of Muhammad. What is more, the 'heroes of peace' prove that peace is a universal human value indeed. It starts and ends with human conscience, the deep self, heart and thought. Every religion uses its peculiar language consistent with its doctrinal identity to talk about the spiritual dimension of peace. The building, promoting and strengthening of peace requires tremendous effort, patience and commitment. War is an act of existential cowardice, while building peace and unity is an act of heroism.

The existential dimension of education and upbringing

Various complex conflicts always have an existential dimension. Ultimately, disagreements, fighting and wars among people are an anthropological, existential disaster. Therefore, the existential dimension of education and upbringing has to be recognised first in order to neutralise the sources of conflict, and undertake positive efforts to restore unity where it has been lost.

Hodjaefendi observes:

> At birth, the outset of the earthly phase of our journey from the world of spirits to eternity, we are totally impotent and extremely needy. By contrast, most animals come into the world as if mature or as if they have been perfected beforehand.[9]

---

8   N. Akmman, *W prawdziwym islamie terroryzm nie istnieje. Wywiad z Fethullahem Gülenem*, [in:] E. Çapan (ed.), *Terroryzm i zamachy samobójcze. Muzułmański punkt widzenia*, trans. from English J. Sander, Dialog, Warsaw 2007, pp. 17–24. See also I. Albayrak, *Islam and Terror: From the Perspective of Fethullah Gülen*, available at: http://www.Gülen.org (accessed: 10.06.2006).

9   M.F. Gülen, *Education from Cradle to Grave*, [in:] M.F. Gülen, *Essays-Perspectives-Opinions*, The Light, Somerset, New York 2007, p. 71.

Education seeks to respond and gradually release humans from their defence-lessness and helplessness even though these human frailties will never disappear.

It should be stressed that Gülen presents human life as an earthly journey whose destination is eternity, and that education accompanies people on this journey, giving them protection and preparing them for mature life. The Turkish teacher emphasises: 'We are born helpless as well as ignorant of the laws of life and must cry out to get the help we need.'[10]

Education makes us aware of the existence and significance of the laws that govern our life. It is a response to our cry for help, a cry that comes not only from infants but also accompanies us, to a greater or lesser extent, at all stages of our life and development – from conception until natural death. By assisting us, education and upbringing serve life – they are life. They help us achieve true humanity, develop all our potential abilities and predispositions. Thus they prepare us for the 'blissful, eternal life in another, exalted world'.[11]

The 'purification of our emotions' is part of the process of education. Nursing a grudge, resentment and sense of harm or injustice is ultimately destructive to the individual harboring such negative feelings. The upbringing of a young person is aimed at liberating them from emotional evil. Only the mind can control emotions. Therefore, reason and common sense are required in educational activities. On many occasions, John Paul II stressed the necessity of 'clearing one's memory' and reinterpreting history as a process leading to mutual forgiveness and true reconciliation.

The consistent guidance of young persons while their humanity matures – this is what upbringing is about – will prevent them from being overwhelmed by selfishness and egoistic love of themselves. These two are at the root of all discord and divisions. Education and upbringing is about the training of the mind and feelings. Intellectual exercise, Gülen argues, is what makes an individual spiritually inspired. Only such people are able to effectively tackle conflicts and creatively serve reconciliation, without which unity does not exist. The theory of education seeks to develop the innate good abilities of an individual as well as amend their views while respecting an individual's freedom.

Hodjaefendi emphasises the particular significance of education for the existence of the individual and the community. B. Jill Carroll actually asserts 'neither the individual nor the society can achieve their true potential without education'. Education is thus a means thanks to which 'people can become true beings as God has created them. Hence, education becomes the chief goal of life'.[12] 'True beings',

---

10 *Ibid.*, p. 71.
11 *Ibid.*, p. 72.
12 B.J. Carroll, *Dialog cywilizacji. Muzułmańskie ideały Gülena a dyskurs humanistyczny*, trans. from English J. Surdel, Dunaj Instytut Dialogu, [Warsaw], [s.a], p. 70.

aware of their own value and value of another person's life, will never disseminate hatred. Instead, they will always be the defenders of life, advocates of understanding and reconciliation.

Education for the reconciliation of science and religion

The resolution of conflicts and building of unity should take place at the level of the science–religion relationship, as I have already indicated above. The conflict between science and religion reached its zenith towards the end of the 20th and turn of the 21st centuries. Scholars, scientists, some religious leaders as well as 'ordinary' people have been drawn into this absurd conflict, and the consequences of this antagonism can be felt in education. The religious commitment has been regarded as a senseless waste of time and the biggest obstacle to the progress of our civilisation. Hodjaefendi believes that the issue of antagonism between religion and science will be solved by education, which should be conducted in a new way. The combination of religious and scientific knowledge will create a generation of noble enlightened people. Their hearts, Gülen argues, will glow with religious knowledge and spirituality. Only such people will be fully aware of the reality and processes taking place.[13]

According to Gülen, the conflict between religion and science emerged when

[...] scientific studies developed in opposition to the Church and medieval Christian scholasticism [...]. This conflict resulted from two factors: the Church did not accept new discoveries and scientific ideas, while the rising middle class wanted to break free from the limitations of religion.[14]

A consequence of this conflict was the separation of religion from science. It was not a purely theoretical separation of these two realities. Theory never exists on its own and for its own sake. It is always propagated by specific people. Hence, there appeared a hiatus between science and religion, while simultaneously, many people renounced the latter. This is the root of all human disagreements, disorientation and disharmony in social and political life.

The Turkish scholar views this phenomenon from the perspective of the history of ideas. He carries out a synthesis of the dispute between science and religion that has also given rise to other disputes. 'This development [or rather: breakdown of the religion–science relationship – E.S.] has ultimately led to materialism and communism.' As Gülen continues, he reveals his historiosophic interpretation of

---

13   Th. Michel, *Fethullah Gülen as Educator*, available at: http://www.thomasmichel.us/gulen-educator.html (accessed: 2.07.2012).

14   M.F. Gülen, *Education from Cradle...*, op. cit., p. 81.

reality: 'In the field of social geography, humanity has had to face striking and dramatic elements of Western culture such as global exploitation, endless conflicts of interests, two world wars and division of the world into blocks'.[15]

While the conflict between science and religion has existed in Western culture for centuries, it has been virtually unknown in the world of Islam. It is worth mentioning that the background of the debate over faith and knowledge was Europe's economic and military power through which this continent controlled the world. The hegemony of the West over the rest of the world, including the East, has lasted for centuries. Gülen points out that the science–religion dispute has been part of the discourse conducted in numerous intellectual circles. This misunderstanding has been generating ever-increasing discord among people.

While trying to elucidate the problem, Gülen offers the following historical summary:

> The Enlightenment movements in the 18th century viewed man solely in terms of the intellect. Subsequently, the positivist and materialist movements saw man as a merely material or corporal being. In consequence, spiritual crises appeared, one after another. It will not be an exaggeration to state that these crises and the lack of spiritual satisfaction were the main factors behind the conflict of interests that has been rampant over the last two centuries, culminating in the two world wars.[16]

The above interpretation is not universally accepted. Empirical historians flatly reject it while materialist historians are not interested in it. One should admire Gülen's courage in expressing such views and opinions that call for serious scientific studies to be undertaken and then followed up by discussion.

The Turkish thinker resolves the conflict between science and religion by evoking the Qur'an. This Holy Book provides incontrovertible evidence of the harmony and cooperation between religion and science. The Qur'an offers a solution to the most difficult disputes and dilemmas, both religious and scientific. According to the Holy Book of Islam, the above conflict is fictitious. The Qur'an, Gülen argues, 'is the universe codified and recorded in writing. In its authentic meaning, religion neither contradicts science and scientific work nor does it impose any limitations on them'.[17]

Islam encompasses the entire reality and recognises the creative interaction of religion and science. Hodjaefendi testifies not only before his co-believers but also before people of other religions and non-believers that:

> Religion provides guidance to sciences: it identifies their true objective and points at universal human values as a signpost for sciences. Things would have been

---

15 *Ibid.*
16 *Ibid.*
17 *Ibid.*, p. 84.

different if this truth had been understood in the West and this relationship between religion and knowledge had been discovered. The world of science would not have brought more destruction than benefits and would not have paved the way for the production of bombs and other kinds of lethal weapons.[18]

The Turkish intellectual argues that 'scientific' materialism has nothing to do with science. The combination of the terms 'scientific' and 'materialism' signifies a cognitive error propagated around the world by Marxist philosophy for decades. Materialism that has wrought havoc in man's spiritual life, as well as 'the pollution of the environment', Gülen emphasises,

> [...] has its roots in 'scientific' materialism. The pollution results from the idea, con-ceived by the 'scientific' lack of faith, that nature is an accumulation of things whose only valuable function is the satisfaction of man's material needs. In reality, nature is something more than matter. There is a peculiar saintliness about it because it is an arena where God's Beautiful Names are revealed.[19]

Applying the term 'scientific' to phenomena that contradict science (e.g. lack of faith) also constitutes serious abuse that should be flatly rejected. Promoting the concept of 'scientific lack of faith' is a contamination of the human mind, much more dangerous than the pollution of water, soil or air. This concept causes the 'disintegration' and disorientation of man.

In his discourse, Hodjaefendi often evokes the fundamental truth about God the Creator, just as John Paul II used to do. In light of this truth, the peculiar para-digm of reality, Gülen solves the most difficult problems using very simple, vivid language. The beauty of nature reminds people about the Creator of the world. Human coexistence with the world of animate and inanimate nature, governed by 'scientific' laws, gives Gülen (as well as the readers of his works and those who listen to his speeches) a lot to think about. Like the poet who sees more than an ordinary observer of everyday life, the Turkish scholar enthusiastically remarks, 'Nature is a display of beauty and meanings [...]!' Then he adds:

> [...] the human heart and mind become like a honeycomb that lures the mind, which hovers about like a bee, and encourages contemplation. From it flows the honey of faith, virtue, love of humanity and all living creatures because of the Creator; help to others, self-sacrifice so that others can live, and ministry to all creatures.[20]

This help and sacrificing one's life for the good of others is nothing else but upbringing, education and pedagogy.

The dispute over religion and science has not only been going on in the Western world but also where West meets East, e.g. in Turkey. Throughout the

---

18   M.F. Gülen, *Education from Cradle...*, *op. cit.*, p. 84.
19   *Ibid.*
20   *Ibid.*, p. 85.

20th century, the modernisation of the state was criticised with greater or lesser intensity. According to its opponents, modernisation was aimed at adapting what was the best and the worst in European civilisation. Secularisation began to be viewed as the outcome of an anti-religious trend. The critics of the modern history of Turkey observed that a profound dislike of religion lay at the basis of the modernisation process. As a result of these ideological disputes, the debate on religion secularisation became one of key importance. As a result, it was demanded in public discourse that every thinker or activist declare on whose side they were on: in favor of religion or secularisation. According to Michel, since Gülen has chosen to maintain a distance from the dilemma above, he has come in for criticism from various groups in Turkey's political life, both believers and non-believers. Gülen has not taken the side of either of the polarised parties. Instead, he has proposed a debate on the future, which has turned out to be a successful idea in the social dimension.

Gülen approved the direction of the reforms, including the modernisation of Turkey, but with one significant qualification. The process will be successful only if it takes into account the development of the entire human being. In relation to education, this requirement means that its mainstream should adopt a new style that will creatively and comprehensively respond to the shifting challenges of today's world. Gülen schools and his educational theory do not envision the restoration of the past, the Ottoman past in particular, or the science and education specific to that historical era. Gülen insists that schools associated with his name are oriented towards the future. In order to emphasise his standpoint, he quotes an old Turkish proverb: 'If you do not adapt to the new conditions, the outcome will be exclusion'.[21]

Gülen's tackling of the doubts concerning the dispute over science and religion turned out to be a crushing critique of materialism. Human beings have an inalienable value. They are not the objects that can be irresponsibly used, abused and manipulated. This conclusion stems from the proper understanding of relationships between the realities described by Christianity and the Latin terms *fides* and *ratio*. This problem was emphasised in the teaching of John Paul II and Benedict XVI. These great men of God spoke with one voice; their teaching relied on the same Divine authority.

Hodjaefendi does not limit himself to presenting his thoughts on the reconciliation of science and religion. In a letter presented to Pope John Paul II by Fethullah Gülen during his historic visit to the Vatican on 8 February 1998, already referenced above, Gülen offered an 'invitation to work for the reconciliation between religion and science'.[22] While working for this reconciliation, one should

---

21 Th. Michel, *Fethullah Gülen..., op. cit.*
22 A. Kardaş, *Praktyczny wymiar..., op. cit.*, pp. 81–83.

pay attention to the sovereignty of the individual. In the name of science and religion, one should courageously oppose the violation of the fundamental human rights: to be born, to live and to die a dignified natural death. 'Matters of the heart' can only be handled by someone who has sorted out their inner self, who knows that science does not contradict religion and vice versa. The reconciliation of science and religion, religious freedom, the right to live and die a dignified death, and protection of human life in general were keynotes of the teachings of John Paul II and Benedict XVI.

The significance of interreligious dialogue

Dialogue, in its various forms and manifestations, is the surest means of solving conflicts and building unity. The fate of the world depends on dialogue. Without it, the world condemns itself to annihilation. Dialogue is not just a declaration. It requires responsibility from the parties that participate in it.

Gülen proposes the dialogue that is based on solid foundations: deep faith in God, abiding by the Islamic creed, openness to the world and its challenges, and deeds that follow God's will. Education preparing for dialogue is aimed at the intellectual and spiritual renewal of Muslims as well as people of other religions and worldviews. Without this renewal, any changes in the life of society will be a mere illusion.

Bediüzzaman Said Nursi (d. 1960), a modern Muslim scholar who is an authority for Gülen, indicated the perspective of the future in interhuman relations. An important role is played by dialogue. Whether conducted by individuals, groups or communities, dialogue is always oriented towards the present and the future. As Gülen points out:

> [...] when Bediüzzaman said that 'controversial topics should not be discussed with Christian religious leaders', he opened the door for dialogue with representatives of other religions.[23]

A dialogue that starts with controversial topics ends as soon as it begins. In this respect, Said Nursi revealed his outstanding wisdom that should guide all those involved in interreligious dialogue. This approach has been expressed in many rules concerning dialogue, such as 'Let's focus on what we have in common, not what divides us', formulated by the leaders of the particular religions, their experts, i.e. theologians, as well as those who conduct the so-called dialogue of life (in their neighborhood, place of work or place of study). The dialogue of everyday life does not touch upon controversial theological subjects. If they are mentioned

---

23 M.F. Gülen, *Education from Cradle...*, *op. cit.*, p. 87.

at all, it is only in order to acknowledge the existence of these difficult themes. The rules formulated by Said Nursi were closely followed by John Paul II, who, in dialogue with Islam, never raised the issue of one God in Trinity, a subject that is controversial to Muslims.

Gülen's conviction about the necessity of dialogue between people of various religions has surely been strengthened by another spiritual master, Sufi Jalaluddin Rumi (d. 1273). This is how Gülen summarised Rumi's ideas about dialogue:

> Jalaluddin Rumi said: 'Like a compass, I have one foot in the center and the other in the seventy-two kingdoms [all nations – E.S.]', and he drew a large circle encompassing all monotheistic religions. Assuming that the days of raw power will end, he added: 'Victory over the civilized people will be attained through persuasion'. Thus he indicated that dialogue, persuasion and discussion based on proofs are of fundamental importance to those of us who want to serve religion.[24]

It is worth noting that Rumi lived and worked in the 13th century, which witnessed dramatic events and developments including a serious crisis in the Catholic Church, the emergence of several unorthodox dissenting movements and the continuation of the Crusades that sought to liberate the Holy Land from the rule of Islam. On the other hand, the 13th century also saw clear signs of dialogue on the Christian side, namely St. Francis of Assisi (d. 1226) and Raimundus Lullus (Ramon LLull), a Franciscan tertiary from Majorca (d. ca. 1315). Their involvement in dialogue was without precedence. John Paul II certainly took lessons from these holy men of dialogue.

Hodjaefendi knows full well that the dialogue is the only effective remedy to violence. True, talking to a terrorist will not make a big difference in the worldview of the individual whose one and only imperative is to kill people so as to paralyse and terrorise everyone, particularly politicians. However, engaging children – the young generation in its formative years – in the dialogue can make a huge difference. 'Pedagogical miracles' are not spectacular achievements that would fill everyone with awe. They are religious signs that take into account the well-being and happiness of man. This is what Gülen aims at when he draws up the Islamic educational project whose main component is the affirmation of dialogue meeting the demands of the 21st century.[25]

When analysing Gülen's idea of dialogue, Carroll points out man's innate value and dignity, and the ideal of freedom. He also indicates interhuman dialogue as the starting point for any kind of understanding. Education plays a significant role in paving the way for dialogue. According to Carroll,

---

24 *Ibid.*
25 J.B. Carroll, *Dialog według koncepcji Fethullaha Gülena*, [in:] M. Lewicka, Cz. Łapicz (eds.), *Dialog chrześcijańsko-muzułmański...*, *op. cit.*, p. 75.

Gülen makes a categorical statement that man needs education that enables the protection and maintenance of human values in various communities around the world. Because nobody is strong enough to impose their will and change the lives of all people on the earth.[26]

Dialogue makes sense only if words are translated into actions. The most elevated verbal declarations are void if they are not fulfilled. Gülen's words have been verified by the works of those who listen to him and follow his teachings.

In the model of interreligious dialogue, Kardaş takes note of Gülen's intellectual activity, political views, reference to the law (shariah), focus on education, understanding of spirituality and approach to media and business. As Gülen teaches, 'ignorance can be overcome through education; poverty through work and accumulation of capital; internal divisions and separatism through unity, dialogue and tolerance'.[27]

Politics – legislation – peace

Gülen's great concern is about establishing peace between all nations and countries that are not at peace, and about strengthening and developing existing peace where it is under constant threat. Peace, in all its dimensions, is most effectively strengthened by factors associated with religion. The human attitude towards God brings about and multiplies peace. In its most profound dimension, peace is a matter of human heart and conscience.

Hodjaefendi asserts that he is not a politician. Reportedly, he has cast his vote in elections, but only once has he not revealed who he had voted for. Nor has he persuaded his supporters and sympathisers to favour a particular political party. Over the years, Gülen has been aware that if he supported any particular political faction, his message might not reach those sections of the society where different views on the State and government prevail. He has strived to work for unity so as to reach all kinds of people, whether they belong to a minority or majority. Gülen has made it the goal of his life to solve conflicts and build unity.[28]

Gülen has distanced himself from all parties because of the way he understands the essence of Islam. He claims that 'Islam is a religion, not a political agenda or constitution. 95% of Qur'an law is of personal nature and does not require the existence of administrative apparatus'. Furthermore, Hodjaefendi believes democracy to be 'the best method of governing society. After all, democracy requires continual efforts to satisfy spiritual needs'.

---

26   J.B. Carroll, *Dialog według koncepcji...*, *op. cit.*
27   M.F. Gülen, *Education from Cradle...*, *op. cit.*, p. 88.
28   A. Kardaş, *Praktyczny wymiar...*, *op. cit.*, p. 85.

'People of non-Muslim religions'[29] experience fear of Islam's sharia law. They know that sharia is the foundation of social order in Islam, as well as among the diaspora living in Europe. The fear of Islam and its law not only stems from deep-seated, century-old anxieties but also from ignorance and unfamiliarity with the basic facts about this religion. The Western world's dread of Islam was born primarily due to the very birth of Islam, followed by its expansion, the fall of Constantinople (1453) and events associated with the Battle of Vienna (1683) that had a paralysing effect on the Europeans despite their victory. This fear not only results from the lack of knowledge about Islam but also from general ignorance in religious matters. John Paul II tirelessly appealed to Christians and people of good will to break free from the destructive fear and become more familiar with each other.

Although Gülen is regarded by certain opinion centers as an Islamic traditionalist (or even fundamentalist, according to some), his attitude and teaching can effectively dispel the erroneous view on Islamic law and Islamophobia. The Turkish intellectual has never propagated sharia law in the legislative sense. Centuries ago, Islam adopted a division of the world, or rather, the countries making up the world, into *darul islam* (house of Islam) and *darul harb* (house of war). The house of Islam is essentially one state in which peace, consent, social harmony, justice, and well-being should prevail. On the other hand, chaos and evil will prevail in the house of war as long as it is not under the rule of Islam. The appearance of Islam is supposed to replace war with peace. Nowadays, this line of argument has been adopted by fundamentalist groups that not only distance themselves from all things Western but also want to convert the West to Islam. Gülen, on the other hand, has never intended to convert any country to Islam, although on many occasions he has stressed the exceptional value and importance of his religion.

In the recent history of Islam, Hodjaefendi stands out as the one who has the courage to replace previous theological and legal concepts with new ones. He identifies countries that constitute *darul islam* but also recognises those that belong to *darul hidmah*, i.e. the house of service. Kardaş concludes that 'the replacement itself can be considered revolutionary in Islamic jurisprudence'.[30]

---

29 *Ibid.*, p. 90.
30 *Ibid.*, p. 85.

Forgiveness and tolerance

In Gülen's educational vision of solving conflicts and building unity, a key role is played by forgiveness, tolerance and openness.

Muslims praise and worship the Merciful God. Faith in Allah, who shows merciful love and takes pity on humanity, presupposes faith in forgiveness. God worshipped by Muslims forgives human beings for their sins and evil in general as long as they demonstrate contrition and repentance.

Islam is a religion of memory. Before the holy book of Islam, the Qur'an, was written down, it existed in the memory of many consecutive generations of believers. Muslims' memories, however, were not limited to what God wanted and what was a manifestation of obeying God's will. Muslim families also remembered the wrongs they had suffered. In the not-so-distant past, there was a custom of family revenge, i.e. retribution for the disgraceful acts committed against a member of a particular family. The accounts would sometimes be settled by paying back with evil instead of with forgiveness. It has to be stressed, however, that such revenge has never been widespread in Islam.

The Qur'an conveys a very meaningful message of forgiveness:

> So whatever thing you have been given – it is but [for] enjoyment of the worldly life. But what is with Allah is better and more lasting for those who have believed and upon their Lord rely, And those who avoid the major sins and immoralities, and when they are angry, they forgive (Surah 42: 36–37);

> And whoever is patient and forgives – indeed, that is an exercise of resolution in the conduct of affairs (Surah 42:43).]

The Qur'an warns against cheating one another:

> Oh you who have believed, indeed, among your wives and your children are enemies to you, so beware of them. But if you pardon and overlook and forgive – then indeed, Allah is Forgiving and Merciful (Surah 64:14).

God is generous and forgiving, as the following passage of the Qur'an indicates:

> When the victory of Allah has come and the conquest, And you see the people entering into the religion of Allah in multitudes, Then exalt [Him] with praise of your Lord and ask forgiveness of Him. Indeed, He is ever Accepting of repentance (Surah 110:1–3).

In an essay entitled *Forgiveness*, published on Gülen's website, we can read:

> Humans are creatures with both exceptional qualities and faults. Until the first human appeared, no living creature carried such opposites within its nature. At the same time as humans beat their wings in the firmaments of heaven, they can, with

sudden deviation, become monsters that descend to the pits of Hell. It is futile to look for any relationship between these frightening descents and ascents; these are extremes because their cause and effect take place on very different planes. At times humans are like a field of wheat bending in the wind; at other times, although they appear as dignified as a plane tree, they can topple over, not to rise again. Just as the times that the angels envy them are not few, neither are the times when even the devils are shocked by their behavior. For humans, whose natures contain so many highs and lows, even if committing evil is not essential to their nature, it is inevitable. Even if becoming sullied is accidental, it is likely. For a creature which is going to spoil his good name, forgiveness is paramount.[31]

A plea for forgiveness addressed to a person one has wronged (and expecting that forgiveness) is morally valuable. According to Gülen, forgiving is 'much greater an attribute and virtue'. Forgiveness is not separate from virtue, which is a permanent human inclination to do specific good. Both are interrelated. When explaining the 'methodology' of forgiving, Gülen quotes the well-known adage (also known in the Christian world): 'To err is human, to forgive divine'. When we receive forgiveness, we ultimately become a new being, a new person. We repair our life and revise our past ignoble behaviour. What is more, we return to our essence and find ourselves again.

God, the Infinite Mercy, appreciates every effort humans make to forgive. Gülen observes that God 'put the beauty of forgiveness into the human heart'. Then he adds:

> While the first man dealt a blow to his essence through his fall, something which was almost a requirement of his human nature, forgiveness came from the heavens because of the remorse he felt in his conscience and because of his sincere pleas.[32]

Humans frequently err in their lives, which is a reflection of the human condition: weak, susceptible to falls and sins, an imperfect creature. In his essay *Forgiveness*, Gülen thus continues his reflections:

> Whenever people err, by boarding the magical transport of seeking forgiveness and by surmounting the shame caused by their sins and the despair caused by their actions, they are able to attain infinite mercy and are shown the generosity that is involved in veiling their eyes to the sins of others.

Humans guided by hope for forgiveness rise towards the light. Forgiveness carries them up, as if on wings, towards the truth about themselves and other

---

31 M.F. Gülen, *Forgiveness*, available at: http://fgulen.com/en/fethullah-gulens-works/toward-a-global-civilization-of-love-and-tolerance/forgiveness-tolerance-and-dialogue/25214-forgiveness61 (accessed: 2.07.2012).

32 *Ibid.*

people. In this context, Gülen makes this lofty remark about forgiving: 'Those who forgive are honored with forgiveness. One who does not know how to pardon cannot hope to be pardoned.' However, he does not avoid frank, straightforward language:

> Those who close the road to tolerance for humanity are monsters that have lost their humanity. These brutes that have never once been inclined to take themselves to task for their sins will never experience the high solace of forgiveness.[33]

Gülen makes a statement without precedence when he refers to the words spoken by Jesus Christ (recorded in the Gospel) about the profound meaning of forgiving:

> Jesus Christ said to a crowd that was waiting rocks in hand to stone a sinner: 'If anyone of you is without sin let him be the first to throw a stone' [John 8:7]. Can anyone with a sin on their conscience still be inclined to stone another if they truly understand this idea? If only those unfortunate ones of today who spend their lives putting the lives of others to the litmus test could understand this! In fact, if the reason for stoning a person is our malice and hatred, if this is the reason why we have passed judgment on them, then it is not possible to pass this sentence on them.[34]

The lack of forgiveness is an act of idolatry. Gülen appeals to 'destroy the idols in our ego as courageously as Abraham destroyed the idols'. Overcoming idolatry in our own conscience is the surest path towards forgiving others. Forgiving is as ancient as humanity. The greatest figures in the history of the world, those who have determined its fate have been guided in their lives by the spirit of forgiveness and tolerance. Gülen remarks that

> [...] malice and hatred are the seeds of Hell that have been scattered among humans by evil spirits. Unlike those who encourage malice and hatred and turn the Earth into a pit of Hell, we should take this forgiveness, and run to the rescue of our people who are confronted by countless troubles and who are being continually pushed toward the abyss. The past few centuries have been turned into the most unpleasant and foul years by the excesses of those who do not know forgiveness or recognize tolerance. It is impossible not to be chilled by the thought that these unfortunate ones could rule the future.[35]

Each case of a plea for forgiveness and the response to such a plea requires an examination of the injustice and harm done to the aggrieved party. Gülen views forgiveness as a key that opens people's hearts in which there is fear and suffering, bad memories, thirst for revenge, moral chaos, and disorientation. We have to forgive ourselves and others in order to understand ourselves and others. As

---

33 M.F. Gülen, *Forgiveness, op. cit.*
34 *Ibid.*
35 *Ibid.*

postulated by John Paul II, forgiveness holds an important place in the process of purifying memory. Inspiration to forgive should be drawn from the adoration of God whose Mercy manifests itself in forgiving humans their sins.

Another important element of Gülen's pedagogical vision is tolerance, which means being receptive not only to the 'People of the Book', i.e. Jews, Christians and Zoroastrians (as stated by the Islamic tradition 1,500 years ago), but also to people of other religions and world views, including non-believers. According to Gülen's teaching, people should be receptive to contemporary philosophical trends, empirical sciences and democracy. This receptiveness is not tantamount to losing one's identity. Quite the contrary, it is about discovering the treasures of one's religious and cultural tradition. It is about recognising and appreciating one's identity against the background of other identities. Being receptive is not about tolerating evil occurring in the life of individuals, entire nations, countries or even religions. Tolerance has nothing to do with allowing human dignity to be trampled upon, or with promoting immorality as obligatory lifestyle.

Keeping Gülen's discourse in mind, we can and should pose the following question: if in certain countries there exists political approval for the promotion of immorality, why is there no consent to opposing such promotion? The ruthless and brutal dictate of any minority over each majority is nothing but totalitarianism! Receptiveness does not mean giving consent to the propagation of immorality. In the name of openness, we should firmly oppose ethical chaos, working together with people of various religions and world views. Such conclusions are supported not only by the writings of Hodjaefendi but also the teachings of John Paul II and Benedict XVI.

It is worth mentioning that openness and receptiveness go hand in hand with the affirmation of otherness. This affirmation is a manifestation of love, which is far from sentimentality, pomposity and unnaturalness. Love is the acceptance of another person not for their individual qualities but for the supreme value, i.e. existence, life that they owe to God. According to Gülen, forgiveness and tolerance, along with love and compassion, are the cornerstones of dialogue. They all play a key role in his concept of the pedagogy of dialogue. As Kardaş notes, 'Gülen's idea of openness is clearly visible in the institutions of the Gülen Movement'.[36]

Tolerance is a manifestation of openness to the otherness of another individual and group, including the adherents of other religions. This openness should not imply rejecting one's own creed and ethos of one's own group. Someone who is truly tolerant is aware of their identity and value, and is not susceptible to manipulation.

In his propagation of forgiveness, tolerance and openness, Gülen clearly emerges as a religious teacher and educator. While elaborating on the valuable

---

36 A. Kardaş, *Praktyczny wymiar...*, *op. cit.*, p. 87.

intuitions of Islam, his proposal of the Islamic educational project is wholly original. This project should be implemented throughout the life of any individual. He who studies life should teach life to others. Someone involved in dialogue should get others involved in dialogue as well. 'We can be truly human', Gülen claims, 'only when we learn, teach others and give others an inspiration'.[37]

'Gülen's Path' is the path of John Paul II and Benedict XVI

'Gülen's Path' – the path of respect for universal human values, religious freedom, truth, good and beauty, forgiveness and tolerance – is the same path that was followed by John Paul II and Benedict XVI. The problems in education appearing in Gülen's teaching, as discussed above, coincide with the subjects taken up primarily by John Paul II, but also by Benedict XVI. The interfaith and intercultural work of these three men of God, representing two sisterly religions, Islam and Christianity, is truly impressive. Gülen emphasizes the existential dimension of education. The existential, personal dimension was characteristic of the teachings of John Paul II and Benedict XVI. Hodjaefendi indicated the tasks fulfilled by education for the reconciliation of science and religion. The teachings of the two pontiffs were similar.[38]

Karol Wojtyła, a philosopher and ethicist, and Joseph Ratzinger, a theologian and polymath, had a very serious approach to studies on the relationship between science and religion, and indicated their complementary character. John Paul II even published a special encyclical letter dedicated to the 'wings of life' [E.S.] thanks to which humans can rise towards God. *Fides et ratio: Encyclical Letter to the Bishops of the Catholic Church on the Relationship Between Faith and Reason* begins with these meaningful words:

> Faith and reason are like two wings on which the human spirit rises to the contemplation of truth; and God has placed in the human heart a desire to know the truth – in a word, to know himself – so that, by knowing and loving God, men and women may also come to the fullness of truth about themselves.

The teachings of Benedict XVI follow similar lines.

---

37 Th. Michel, *Gülen jako wychowawca i nauczyciel religijny*, available at: http://pl.fgulen.com/content/view/ 18/5/ (accessed: 13.10.2013).

38 See E. Sakowicz, *Dialog Kościoła...*, op. cit.; id., *Pryncypia dialogu Kościoła z religiami Dalekiego Wschodu i Indii w świetle nauczania Soboru Watykańskiego II oraz dokumentów posoborowych*, UKSW Press, Warsaw 2006; id. (ed.), *Jan Paweł II. Encyklopedia dialogu i ekumenizmu*, Polwen, Radom 2006; id., *Kontynuacja czy innowacja? Benedykt XVI wobec dialogu międzyreligijnego*, [w:] R. Bartnicki, W. Kawecki (eds.), *Chrześcijaństwo a kultura*, UKSW Press, Warsaw 2006, pp. 211–229.

Dialogue, in various forms, manifestations and dimensions, is a priority in Gülen's work. Intercultural and interreligious dialogue has been close to the heart of Hodjaefendi; it was equally important to John Paul II (Benedict XVI showed less dedication and commitment).

Dialogue plays a key role in the resolution of conflicts and building unity among people around the world, as well as at the interpersonal level. It requires effort and courage to turn towards another person in order to understand them better. Dialogue involves thinking, speech, intellect and emotions. John Paul II defined dialogue as the entirety of positive, constructive relationships primarily with individuals, though with large human communities as well. Dialogue is not limited to a mere communication of specific information. It is more than conversation even though it is usually associated with the notion of 'dialogue'. Dialogue is more than verbal communication of views and opinions. For sure, it is not about confrontation and polemics. Those who consciously accept the challenge of dialogue primarily want to overcome the limitations to understanding other persons belonging to a different religion or culture.

The unwillingness to undertake dialogue reveals a deep complex and unhealed inner wounds. The absence of dialogue between cultures and religions is the hallmark of arrogance, excessive pride, even contempt and hatred among people. At the root of all wars lies cultural hatred and arrogance, the desire for power – to put it simply, anti-dialogue. Understanding oneself opens up the mind, heart and spirit to another person and community. Participation in dialogue teaches people to understand others and themselves. Those who avoid or reject dialogue will never understand themselves or another human being, and will never develop a sense of empathy, compassion and solidarity.

According to John Paul II, dialogue helps overcome all difficulties of an external nature (arising from processes taking place in societies) and internal nature (arising from the internal 'disintegration' of an individual who is often unable to open up to another human being, is distrustful and immersed in resentment and memories). Hodjaefendi shares the same vision of dialogue.

In the speeches and sermons by John Paul II, we come across the term 'friends' applied to the adherents of non-Christian religions, including Muslims. Calling non-Christians friends was not merely a manifestation of the pontiff's courtesy. It reflected the attitude of openness, readiness to share experiences and do good deeds as well as willingness to joyfully share spiritual gifts and receive them. The historical, geographical, cultural, spiritual and religious distance is of no importance here. Friendship removes obstacles placed on the paths of mutual communication. Partners in dialogue are close or distant friends with each other.

The goal of dialogue, instructed by John Paul II and Benedict XVI, is to overcome divisions that have usually been created artificially and handed down from generation to generation. Harmony can be achieved by rejecting the egoistical lifestyle. Consensus can be built based on unrestrained service, that is full of love and offered to everyone without exception. Given the realities of life in the modern multicultural and multireligious world, there are many opportunities for that.

Those participating in dialogue know that courage is a prerequisite for overcoming the lack of understanding, the suspicions, and the prejudices that obstruct the creation of a harmonious community. Gülen, John Paul II and Benedict XVI were all men of God characterised by such uncompromising courage. Encounters of religions in various environments and contexts contribute to the 'improvement of the world'. On many occasions during his pontificate, John Paul II pointed out that all people, both believers and non-believers, have to unite and work together for the betterment of the world in which they all live in. The most recognisable and meaningful proof of that were the World Day of Prayer for Peace in Assisi organised by John Paul II in 1986 and 2002.

Adherents of various religions should meet as often as possible in order to serve one another as well as the other people who are not involved in dialogue. According to John Paul II, 'dialogue is the result of an inner impulse of love' and, as such, is a 'powerful tool of cooperation between people' who jointly undertake the effort to remove the evil affecting the individual and the community. Dialogue should contribute to the introduction and strengthening of the appropriate social order, and to the spiritual growth of all people. Dialogue should reassure the adherents of various religions in their belief that they have a shared responsibility for the public good and the country in which they live as well as for the good of all humanity. As John Paul II observed, this joint responsibility of various religions for the fate of the world 'is a key prerequisite for the globalisation of solidarity that has to be attained to ensure the safe future of the world'.

Dialogue depends on the deep and genuine respect for other religious traditions as well as those who do not believe in God. This attitude, which constitutes a starting point and stimulates the continuation of dialogue, has nothing to do with false irenicism rooted in religious indifferentism. The method of conducting dialogue is in opposition to the destructive indifferentism that promotes cognitive chaos. Benedict XVI was particularly sensitive to that.

A partner in dialogue, even if they live 'nearby', always 'comes from afar' in a certain sense, as John Paul II used to say. Therefore, dialogue requires respect for the guest who is exhausted and needs to rest and regain strength after the journey. Dialogue is a recognition of the status of the guest. As such, it is never a 'one-way movement'. 'A friend who comes from afar' also pays a visit to faraway friends. The starting point meets the destination. The motivation for dialogue is intertwined with its objective. A friendly meeting, the sharing of thoughts and joint reflection make up an effective dialogue method.

The pontiffs John Paul II and Benedict XVI should be admired for their involvement in conducting policies 'with a human face', the promotion of legislation that respects natural law as well as their actions supporting world peace. One could present thousands of pages discussing the teachings and initiatives of the Supreme Shepherds of the Church with regard to politics and peace, including jurisprudence seeking the well-being of man in the contemporary and future world.

There is no doubt that Gülen, John Paul II and Benedict XVI followed the same path of respect for every individual and the entire humanity. Finally, it should be noted that the Holy Books of their religions, i.e. the Qur'an and the Bible, the adherents of these religions, i.e. Muslims and Christians, as well as all people of 'good will' living 'here and now', have met in their persons.

Bibliography

Akmman N., *W prawdziwym islamie terroryzm nie istnieje. Wywiad z Fethullahem Gülenem*, [in:] E. Çapan (ed.), *Terroryzm i zamachy samobójcze. Muzułmański punkt widzenia*, trans. from English J. Sander, Dialog, Warsaw 2007.

Albayrak I., *Islam and Terror: From the Perspective of Fethullah Gülen*, available at: http://www.Gülen.org (accessed: 10.06.2006).

Carroll B.J., *Dialog cywilizacji. Muzułmańskie ideały Gülena a dyskurs humanistyczny*, trans. from English J. Surdel, Dunaj Instytut Dialogu, [Warsaw], [s.a].

Carroll J.B., *Dialog według koncepcji Fethullaha Gülena*, [in:] M. Lewicka, Cz. Łapicz (eds.), *Dialog chrześcijańsko-muzułmański. Historia i współczesność, zagrożenia i wyzwania*, Nicolaus Copernicus University Press, Toruń 2011.

Działalność międzywyznaniowa i międzykulturowa, available at: http://pl.fgulen.com/content/view/3/2/ (accessed: 10.08.2012).

Gülen M.F., *Education from Cradle to Grave*, [in:] M.F. Gülen, *Essays – Perspectives – Opinions*, The Light, Somerset, New York 2007.

Gülen M.F., *Forgiveness*, http://fgulen.com/en/fethullah-gulens-works/toward-a-global-civilization-of-love-and-tolerance/forgiveness-tolerance-and-dialogue/25214-forgiveness61.

Kardaş A., *Praktyczny wymiar dialogu w nauczaniu Fethullaha Gülena*, [in:] M. Lewicka, Cz. Łapicz (eds.), *Dialog chrześcijańsko-muzułmański. Historia i współczesność, zagrożenia i wyzwania*, Nicolaus Copernicus University Press, Toruń 2011.

Michel Th., *Fethullah Gülen as Educator*, available at: http://www.thomasmichel.us/gulen-educator.html (accessed: 2.07.2012).

Michel Th., *Gülen jako wychowawca i nauczyciel religijny*, available at: http://pl.fgulen.com/content/view/18/5/ (accessed: 13.10.2013).

Musiałek A., *Dialog religijny w Republice Południowej Afryki*, 'Collectanea Theologica' 2009, 79, 3.

Sakowicz E., *Dialog Kościoła z islamem według dokumentów soborowych i posoborowych (1963–1999)*, UKSW Press, Warsaw 2000.

Sakowicz E. (ed.), *Jan Paweł II. Encyklopedia dialogu i ekumenizmu*, Polwen, Radom 2006.

Sakowicz E., *Kontynuacja czy innowacja? Benedykt XVI wobec dialogu międzyreligijnego*, [w:] R. Bartnicki, W. Kawecki (eds.), *Chrześcijaństwo a kultura*, UKSW Press, Warsaw 2006.

Sakowicz E., *Pryncypia dialogu Kościoła z religiami Dalekiego Wschodu i Indii w świetle nauczania Soboru Watykańskiego II oraz dokumentów posoborowych*, UKSW Press, Warsaw 2006.

The Journalists and Writers Foundation. Towards Universal Peace, Istanbul 2011.

NAZILA ISGANDAROVA
Wilfrid Laurier University
Waterloo (Canada)

Critical Analysis of Feminist Movements of Azerbaijani Muslim Women during Russian Colonialism

The deteriorating conditions of the Azerbaijani Muslim women in the Russian Empire, since the occupation of Azerbaijan in 1812 until 1918, overwhelmed the nationalist, secular, liberal, and social-democratic men and women in their response to the systematic problems, including discrimination, identity crisis, etc., of women. The 'woman question' became the priority on the social, political, and religious agenda of the emerging feminist and pro-feminist movements in Azerbaijan during that time, and affected diverse strata of the society, which represented different aspects of cultural and political views of the world, of Azerbaijan's Muslim women.

The word 'feminism' emerged in 1837 with the works of the French philosopher and a utopian socialist Charles Fourier.[1] As a mindset or perspective on the role of women that aimed to enable them to participate in the political, economic and social life of the society, the feminist movements first appeared in France and the Netherlands in 1872, in the UK in the 1890s and in the United States in 1910s. These movements mainly advocated suffrage for women, thus promoting women's right to vote. If we take into the consideration the influence of the European Enlightenment on the Russian tsarist upper- and upper-middle-class intellectuals and the feminist ideas on the feminist movements in Russia, we can predict that the feminist thinking in Azerbaijan was influenced by the European intellectuals through the works of Russian intellectuals. Due to the severe class tensions during the tsarist rule, the feminist ideals in Russia and Azerbaijan were constituted by social and political goals of the revolutionary and social-democratic movements.

---

1 L. Goldstein, *Early Feminist Themes in French Utopian Socialism: The St.-Simonians and Fourier*, 'Journal of the History of Ideas' 1982, 43, 1.

As an extension of the community activities of the Muslim women, the feminist movements in Azerbaijan sought to achieve equal power relations between men and women. Within this time frame, the principle of EQUALITY OF ALL CITIZENS became the dominant discourse of the feminist movements in Azerbaijan. Nevertheless, for the Azerbaijani feminists, the core principles of feminism did not conflict with the traditions and religion; otherwise, it could have been more harmful to the Azerbaijani culture. Moreover, the feminist movements in Azerbaijan also represented the unique cultural, religious and social aspects of the Azerbaijani society. What made them unique and different from the Russian feminist movements was their support for the nationalist struggle against the Russian colonialism.

This paper presents a brief historical narrative of the secular Muslim feminist movements in Azerbaijan in order to examine the effects of patriarchy and colonisation on the status of women and the emergence of Muslim feminist movements in Azerbaijan. I argue that the understanding of the theological and ideological positions of Muslim feminist movements during the Russian colonisation is important for comprehending the historical emergence of feminism in Azerbaijan. Resources have been taken from the writings of the Muslim men and women in Azerbaijan. The paper provides a general background on the secular feminist movements of the Muslim women and their struggle for equality in Azerbaijan in order to answer the question: what role did the struggles of particular women (e.g. the struggles against colonialism and patriarchy) play in the emergence of the feminist movements in Azerbaijan? The paper also deals with the emergence of the feminist movements and provides examples of the achievements and struggles of the Azerbaijani feminists, especially in terms of women's right to education.

Colonialism and colonial patriarchy

Azerbaijan, located between Russia and the Middle East, Europe and central Asia, had been the crossroads of the 'great powers' since the ancient times. The rich and beautiful landscape of this southern Caucasus state lied on the

> [...] margins of what is now the most turbulent area of the world: the crescent land running from central Asia through Afghanistan and Iran to the Mediterranean.[2]

The rich oil resources and trade routes, which had been developed tremendously during the tsarist Russia, added more to the polarised policy of the colonial West, Russia, the Qajar Iran and the Ottoman Empire in the 19th and the beginning of the 20th century. In the midst of the historical tension of Azerbaijan, as newly

---

2   T. de Waal, *Reinventing the Caucasus*, 'World Policy Journal' 2002, 19, 1, p. 51.

divided between the Qajars and Russia with the Gulustan Treaty in 1812 and finally with the Turkmenchay Treaty in 1828, the Azerbaijani women suffered from Russian colonialism alongside the unjust patriarchal oppression. Moreover, the Russian tsarist regime established a special brand of patriarchy – colonial tsarist patriarchy – for colonialism needed patriarchy to be successful in Azerbaijan. As Kwok Pui-lan points out, colonialism involved 'the contest of male power,' and 'patriarchal ideology,' and was 'constantly reshaped and reformulated in the colonial process,'[3] Russian colonialism, therefore, reinforced the already established patriarchies in Azerbaijan and strengthened unequal gender relationships in the society. The racial politics of colonialism led to more injustices toward the Muslim women and resulted in the double colonisation of women by both the patriarchal and imperial forces. In addition, the colonial tsarist regime depicted the Azerbaijani Muslim women as nameless and nationless, and ignored them under colonial patriarchy. The term 'tatars' was used by the tsarist regime as a derogatory name and indicated that the Russians viewed the ethnic identity of the Azerbaijani women – and the Azerbaijanis in general – as lower in status, in comparison with that of the Russians. The similar tactic was employed in other Muslim countries as well. In Egypt, for example, the term 'native' was used by the British ruler of Egypt, Sir Evelyn Baring – Lord Cromer and other colonizers to describe Egyptians; therefore, the differences between indigenous cultures were lost in the anonymity of the terms used by the colonisers.[4]

Cultural and religious practices of the Azerbaijani women, including their position on the equality, veil, etc., established the Russian perception of the dissimilarity and inferiority of the Azerbaijanis, their religion and culture, in comparison with the 'superiority' of the Russian Empire over non-Russians. Such approach of the colonial powers was employed in order to justify the colonial domination over other nations.[5] As Leila Ahmed points out, the colonial powers usually presented the European (in this case, Russian) women as an 'ideal' and as civilised, in comparison with the Muslim women. For colonizers, Christianity as a civilised religion preached respect for women, therefore the European men 'elevated' women, following a 'commandment' of their religion; on the other hand, the Muslim men degraded their women because of the teachings of their religion. They presented the plight of Muslim women as a consequence of the nature of their religion, which gave licence to 'lewdness' against women. Marriage in Islam was accepted as a union 'not founded on love but on sensuality' and a Muslim

---

3   Kwok Pui-lan, *Postcolonial Imagination and Feminist Theology*, Westminster John Knox Press, Louisville 2005, p. 81.
4   M. Badran, *Feminists, Islam, and Nation*, Princeton University Press, Princeton 1996, p. 12.
5   L. Ahmed, *Women and Gender in Islam: Historical Roots of a Modern Debate*, Yale University Press, New Haven – London 1992, p. 152.

wife, 'buried alive behind [the] veil', was therefore regarded as a 'prisoner and slave' rather than an equal partner and companion to her husband.[6] Veiling was presented as the most visible marker of the dissimilarity and inferiority of Muslim women and Islamic societies in general. It

> [...] became the symbol now of both the oppression of women (or, in the language of the day, Islam's degradation of women) and the backwardness of Islam.

Cromer, the 19th century British administrator in Egypt, for example, blamed Islam for its failure as a social system and [for] its treatment of women.[7] Nevertheless, Cromer and the like-minded colonial powers themselves did not attempt – or even halted the progress of – the 'woman question' in their territories.

The Western narratives of women in Islam were usually drawn from male-dominated sources, which mainly relied on the seventeenth-century Western ideas about Islam, the tales of travelers and crusaders, and the readings of Arabic texts poorly understood by Christian priests.[8] Therefore, the colonizers, including some missionary women and Western feminists, attempted to 'rescue' the Muslim women from the 'ignorance and degradation' in which they existed, and attempted to convert them to Christianity. For these colonial Western feminists, there was

> [...] an intrinsic connection [that] existed between the issue of culture and the status of women, and [...] progress for women could be achieved only through abandoning the native culture.[9]

Furthermore, colonial feminism as a kind of Western colonial ideology supported the Western dominance over non-Western nations and was used against the indigenous cultures in the service of colonialism, assigning a false mission of 'redeemer' to colonial regimes.[10] These 'colonial feminists' strongly believed that, because of the implied cultural lack of the third-world women, they [third-world women] [could not] represent themselves; they [had to] be represented.[11]

---

6   L. Ahmed, *Women and Gender...*, op. cit., p. 154.
7   *Ibid.*, p. 152–153.
8   According to Leila Ahmed, these sources are: Annie [sic!] van Sommer and Samuel M. Zwemer (eds.), *Our Moslem Sisters. A Cry of Need from Lands of Darkness Interpreted by Those Who Heard It*, F.H. Revell, New York 1907; A. van Sommer, S.M. Zwemer (eds.), *Daylight in the Harem*, Oliphant, Anderson & Ferrier, Edinburgh – London 1911; Earl of Cromer, *Modern Egypt*, 2 vols., Macmillan, New York 1908; *Cromer Papers*, [cit. in:] J.E. Tucker, *Women in Nineteenth-Century Egypt*, Cambridge University Press, Cambridge 1985; A.B. de Guerville, *New Egypt*, William Heinemann, London 1906.
9   L. Ahmed, *Women and Gender...*, op. cit., p. 244.
10   *Ibid.*, p. 151.
11   L. Gandhi, *Postcolonial Theory: A Critical Introduction*, Allen & Unwin, St. Leonards 1998, p. 86.

The 'redeemer' mission of colonial feminists toward the Muslim women was to abolish the practices of the Muslim women because they believed that those practices prevented the Muslim women from following the path of civilisation. The Russian tsarist colonisers, for example, started to remove the *qadis* (the Muslim judges who ruled by the sharia) from the realm of civil and criminal law; they were allowed only to record births, deaths, and marriages. However, the tsarist regime was aware that a strict and radical attack on the Muslim judges and *ulema* (Muslim religious scholars) would cause an uprising against the tsar. Therefore, this class of society was granted certain power, including some privileges, such as land, titles, or tax exemptions.[12]

Thus, colonial tsarist understanding and perception of the status of the Azerbaijani Muslim women failed to grasp the specific content and meaning of their customs and the influence of patriarchy on their conditions. Therefore, many Azerbaijani Muslim women rejected colonial 'redeemers' and did not believe in the sincerity of colonial tsarist powers with their attempts to 'save them.' Furthermore, they witnessed further marginalisation of the working class and the poor in the colonized Muslim lands and blamed the tsarist regime for the bad condition of the nation in general.

Emergence of Muslim feminism in Azerbaijan

The critical perspective of the Muslims and Islam in general on the colonialists, with regard to the status of the Muslim women in the society, had found a new voice in the writings of the early Azerbaijani feminist and pro-feminist male writers of the 19th – 20th centuries, such as Mirze Fatali Akhundov (1812–1878), Alakbar Zeynalabdin oglu Tahirzadeh, also known as Mirza Elekber Sabir (1862–1911), Hasan bey Melikov (Zardabi) (1837–1907) and his wife Hanifa Malikova-Abayeva (1856–1929), Mirza Jalil Mammed-Quluzadeh (1866–1932), his wife Hamideh Javanshir (1873–1955), Khadija Alibeyova (1884–1961), an oil baron Haji Zeynalabidin Taghiyev (1823–1924) and his second wife Sona Arablinsky (1881–1932), Alimardan bey Topchubashov (1862–1934), Sakina Akhundzadeh (1865–1927), Gevhar Gayibova (1885–1944), Khurshud Vazirova (1863–1913), Abbas Sahhat (1874–1918), Mahmud bey Mahmudbeyov (1863–1923), and others. The early Muslim feminists in Azerbaijan started to reflect the lives of the Muslim women under patriarchy and argued how to liberate the Muslim women from the patriarchal bondage in order to modernise the Muslim nations. A higher level

---

12 N. Tohidi, *Azerbaijan: Islamic Feminism and the Soviet Legacy of Modernization*, [in:] A. Samiuddin, R. Khanam (eds.), *Muslim Feminism and Feminist Movement: Central Asia*, Global Vision Publishing House, Delhi 2002, pp. 99, 81–114.

of industrialisation and modernisation contributed to the primary role of early feminists in opposing the colonisation.[13] Nevertheless, the religious and spiritual heritage of the Azerbaijanis was also an integral item on the political and social agenda of the nationalists and the Muslim reformers.

The feminist movements of the Azerbaijani men and women existed side by side as secular[14] and religious during the Russian colonialism. The Azerbaijani feminists never based their feminist activism on purely secular foundations or acted outside the bounds of Islam: they belonged to the *Jadid* (renewal of Muslim societies) movement, which sought to reform, and modernize the nation, particularly with regard to the women's status.[15] At the same time, some of the feminist and pro-feminist men belonged to various ideological and political groups and parties, including the secular-nationalist, social-democratic and Muslim modernist groups that were inspired by a Crimean Tatar journalist Ismail Gaspirinski (1851–1914) and Mirze Feteli Akhundov, an Azerbaijani philosopher known as the 'Molière of the Orient.'[16] Some other prominent feminist men and women belonged to the famous Pan-Turkist movement[17] in the Ottoman Empire and wrote in the newly emerged Ottoman Turkish, for example Ismail Gaspirinski and Mirze Feteli Akhundov, both of whom promoted theTurkish nationalism in the Ottoman and Russian empires.[18] In general, the feminist and pro-feminist

---

13   N. Tohidi, *Azerbaijan...*, *op. cit.*, p. 99.

14   According to Seyyed Hossein Nasr, secularism or *'al-almaniyya* (Arabic term for 'secularism' and 'atheism'), *dahriyya* or *zamani* ('temporal' as supposed to 'eternal'), *dunyawi* ('this-worldly' in contrast to 'other-worldly'), *ladini* ('nonreligious') and so on, have various meanings and definitions in the Islamic lexicon, yet these words do not convey the exact meaning of secularism. See Nasr, *Islamic Life and Thought*, State University of New York Press, Albany 1981, p. 14. The word *'al-almaniyya*, for example, is derived from the word *alam* ('the world') and refers to people who adhere to the worldly life in contrast to being *dini* ('religious'). Very recently, *madaniyya* ('civilisation') emerged in the post-Mubarak era in Egypt to support the civil society in opposition to the military rule and to demonstrate the compatibility of Islam with democracy and civil society. Nader Hashemi points out that, regardless of the emerging new terms and definitions of secularism across the Muslim world, the highly politicized concept of secularism 'has been discredited and its image severely tarnished'. See N. Hashemi, *Islam, Secularism, and Liberal Democracy: Toward a Democratic Theory for Muslim Societies*, Oxford Unvieristy Press, New York 2009, p. 138.

15   N. Tohidi, *Azerbaijan...*, *op. cit.*, p. 99.

16   Ismail Gaspirinski used the Islamic framework to revive Islam. However, Akhundov, who converted to Christianity, used the arguments of materialism and atheism to advance the society. Moreover, Akhundov became known as the founder of the atheist movement in Azerbaijan.

17   As a cultural and political movement of all Turkic ethnicities and nations, Pan-Turkism emerged in the 1880s among the Turkic intellectuals of the tsarist Russia and Ottoman Empire. In Azerbaijan, Ahmed bey Aghaogly, Memmed Emin Rasulzade and others were the active members of this political movement.

18   R.G. Suny, *Looking Toward Ararat: Armenia in Modern History*, Indiana University Press, Bloomington – Indianapolis 1993, p. 25.

Azerbaijani intellectuals targeted the emancipation of women as a prerequisite for the revival of Muslim civilisation and Azerbaijan's economic, social, and cultural development in the late 19th and early 20th centuries[19]. Below, a few examples from the writers of the Molla Nasreddin magazine (1906–1930) and other intellectuals describe the development of the feminist discourse on the Azerbaijani women.

'Molla Nasreddin' magazine

Since the first issue of the magazine by Mirza Jalil Mammamquluzadeh on 7 April 1906 in Tiflis at the Geyrat Publishing House, the writers of this journal used powerful satire and cartoons, especially in criticising the establishment of corrupt colonial rule and their local supporters, such as the religious conservatives and *mullahs* who advocated compulsory veiling and seclusion of women, polygyny, wife beating, violence and other oppressive practices against women. For example, Mirze Alakbar Sabir was merciless in his criticism about the arbitrariness of the colonial tsarist officials, landowners, *qochus* ('bouncers') and *beys* ('nobles') who were insensitive to the needs of their people. He also criticised the backwardness of the *mullahs* who ignited the sectarian tension in the Muslim world and caused the status of women to degrade by misinterpreting the key sources of Islam. He drew attention to the low social situation of *fahle* ('working people') and *kendchi* ('peasants').

Mirza Jalil Mammadquluzadeh wrote numerous articles, e.g. *Xanimlara* (*To the Women*), *Mirt-Mirt* (*Chit-Chat*), *Anam-bajim* (*My mother, My Sister*), *Dord Yuz Qiz* (*Four Hundred Girls*), *Nishanli bir Qiz* (*Engaged Girl*), *Qiz terbiyesi* (*Education of Girl*), *Ovret Meselesi* (*Women's Problem*), etc. discussing the dramatic conditions of Muslim women and girls, their slavery and unbearable tragedy, as a national issue. In general, almost all the writers of Molla Nasreddin launched a war against the backward *mullah*, resulting from their negative attitude towards women, the advocacy to marry young girls rather than sending them to school, and called for liberating women from the houses of 'detention'. For them, education of women was an important prescription for the emancipation of the nation: they pointed out that the uneducated women gave birth to ignorant generations, which in turn dragged the society into an ongoing cycle of decline. Such fierce criticism against those who prevented the Muslim women benefiting from the achievements of the society demanded enormous courage. The founder of the magazine, Jalil Mammadguluzadeh had already experienced

---

19   T. Swietochowski, *Russian Azerbaijan, 1905–1920: The Shaping of National Identity in a Muslim Community*, Cambridge University Press, Cambridge 1985, pp. 30–35.

the danger from the radical elements of the society before. In one of his articles, *Sharqi Rus* (*The Eastern Russia*) (1903–1905), he described the discussions with and the threats of Mehemmed agha Shahtakhtinsky (1848–1931) to the newspaper for using the words 'freedom of women' and advocating women's rights. The threats to the feminist women and pro-feminist male writers forced them to hide their true identity. Sabir, for example, used the pseudo names such as 'Hophop', 'Aghlar guleyen', 'Abunasr Sheybani', 'Jingoz bey' and Jalil Mammadquluzadeh used the pseudo names 'Laghlaghi', 'Deli', 'Demdemeki', 'Jirjirama', 'Herdemkheyal', etc. In his *Qanli Fajie* (*Black Tragedy*) (1910), Mammadquluzadeh also described the tragedy of thousands of little girls who were forced to marry older men: he wrote that the tears of those little girls were enough to create the oceans. In his *Kohne Derdim* (*My Old Wound*) (1924), Mammadquluzadeh acknowledged that he had dedicated a considerable part of his career to the freedom of the Muslim (Eastern) women.

Taghiyev school

The struggle of the Azerbaijani intellectuals for women's right to education resulted in developing various beneficial projects at the beginning of the 20th century. Probably, the most outstanding of them was the school project of the famous Azerbaijani oil baron and philanthropist, Haji Zeynalabidin Taghiyev who was one of the fiercest and most dedicated fighters for women's rights in Azerbaijan. Taghiyev belonged to the first generation of Azerbaijani noblemen, who sent their daughters to the famous Smolny Lyceum in St. Petersburg. However, he realized that not many people had the financial means and social support to educate their daughters outside Azerbaijan and they had to send their daughters to the schools that operated only in private houses. An example of such schools was the home schooling for girls established by Hanifa Malikova-Abayeva, the wife of Hasan bey Zardabi and Hamideh Javanshir in Garabagh. Therefore, Taghiyev used his connections with high-ranking colonial officials to realise his dream of girls' school in Azerbaijan. For example, he wrote a letter to Kirill Yanovky, who was in charge of schools in the Caucasus, in which he mentioned:

> The isolation of the Muslims [...] is supported by some dogmatic religious principles [...]. What constitutes the very stronghold of these pseudo-religious is seclusion of the Muslim woman and her unawareness of her human rights [...]. What is needed is to bring to a Muslim woman a comprehension of her inalienable human rights through secular education.[20]

---

20 H.Z. Taghiyev, cit. in: F. Akhundov, *Educating Women to Educate a Nation: The Taghiyev School for Girls in Baku*, UN Development Programme and UN Population Fund, 2007, p. 50.

Sona Arablinhky, Taghiyev's wife, also played an important role in the development of the school projects and also in other charity projects of Taghiyev. As a result of their dedication, the first secular boarding school for girls, which was named Alexandrian Russian-Muslim Boarding School for Girls, later Taghiyev Secular School for Muslim Girls (after Taghiyev[21]), was welcomed on 9 October 1901. The school was the only existing one for the non-Russian Muslim girls in the Caucasus. At the inauguration of the school, 58 students (35 of them belonged to the lower classes and were sponsored by Taghiyev) represented almost all regions of Azerbaijan and the Caucasus.[22] The school applied a secular and liberal education framework to train the generation of female teachers and educators; subjects such as theology, drawing, technical sketching, calligraphy and needlework were also taught.[23] The main language of instruction was Russian and the primary curriculum was based on that of the Russian schools for girls in Caucasus. Due to the shortage of the Azerbaijani female teachers, Taghiyev invited Muslim teachers Rahilya Teregulova-Hajibababeyova, Maryam Sulkevich and Maryam Gembitskaya from Tbilisi (Georgia), Kazan (Tatarstan), Lithuania and Poland.[24]

The leading members of the Muslim reformist movements in Azerbaijan, such as Hasan bey Zardabi, the founder of the first Azerbaijani newspaper 'Ekinchi' ('Ploughman') and educator, and his son-in-law, Alimardan bey Topchubashov, Mirze Jalil Javanshir and his wife Hamida Javanshir were among many other most supportive proponents of Taghiyev school. Topchubahsov, for example, considered the inauguration of Taghiyev school

> [...] the beginning of a new epoch of revival for the Muslim woman, this wonderful creature standing at the very core of the family in any society and giving birth to the public, national and international associations.[25]

The 'Kavkaz' ('Caucasus') newspaper in Tbilisi, which also represented the Muslim reformers in the Caucasus, considered the school

---

21 Haji Zeynalabidin Taghiyev was a former illiterate construction worker and a latter rich oil baron who understood the importance of education of women in order to empower the Azerbaijani nation. He also funded the construction of the first European theatre (Tahgiyev's Theatre, which is now called Shikhali Qurbanov Musical Comedy Theatre) in 1883 in Baku. The first opera which was performed in January 1908 in Taghiyev's Theatre was *Leyli and Majnun* by a famous composer and reformist Uzeyir Hajibeyov. Taghiyev also supported the Baku School of Commerce, the Baku Mechanical and Technical College, and St. Mary's High School for Girls. See F. Akhundov, *Educating Women...*, *op. cit.*, p. 20. See N. Tohidi, *Azerbaijan...*, *op. cit.*
22 F. Akhundov, *Educating Women...*, *op. cit.*, p. 72.
23 *Ibid.*, pp. 20, 80.
24 *Ibid.*, p. 82.
25 Alimardan bey Topchubashov, cit. in: *ibid.*, p. 72.

[...] the first educational center aiming at [...] the destruction of the Chinese Wall which was fervently protecting Muslim women up to now from any impacts of our time.[26]

Thus, the Muslim reformers in Azerbaijan and all over the Russian Empire valued the Taghiyev school as the access point of the Muslim girls to the Western civilisation and acquiring knowledge of human rights and values alongside the sharia rules.[27]

Hamida Javanshir

The Azerbaijani women were also active in demanding the equality of educational rights for themselves. Hamida Javanshir, for example, who was trained in ballroom dance lessons and studied German, Polish, Russian (which were very rare practices among the Muslim women in Azerbaijan at that time), and wanted to study medicine in Moscow (a dream which she could not realize due to the death of her first husband, lieutenant Colonel Ibrahim bey Davatdarov), founded the first Azerbaijani school where boys and girls could study in the same classroom. The school opened in 1908 in her estate at Kahrizli village near Aghjabedi, where her daughter Mina Davatdarova (1895–1923) also volunteered until her death. Hamida was also famous for her social support for the poor and established the Muslim Women's Caucasian Benevolent Society, together with other female members of the Azerbaijani nobility.[28] As a famous businesswoman, she organized employment opportunities for women at a cotton processing plant that she had established in Azerbaijan in 1912, and participated in the 13th Congress of the Cotton Producers of the Transcaucasus.[29] Hamideh was concerned with the condition of the Azerbaijani women and reflected on the poverty issues among other nations as well. In her famous *Memoirs of Iran*, she mentions:

> The Kurds were very poor. The women and children were dressed in rags. They spoke Turkish with us, but Kurdish amongst themselves. The poor Kurdish women worked both at home and in the fields.

---

26 'Kavkaz', cit. in: F. Akhundov, *Educating Women...*, *op. cit.*, p. 74.
27 See the letter of the leaders of the Muslim community in Kazan (Tatarstan), a center of the Jadid movement in the Russian Empire (*ibid.*, pp. 7–75).
28 *Megastar and Her Light*, an interview with Hamideh Javanshir's granddaughter, Dr. Mina Davatdarova, available at: http://gender-az.org (accessed: 26.02.2014).
29 F. Heyat, *Azeri Women in Transition: Women in Soviet and Post-Soviet Azerbaijan*, RoutledgeCurzon, London – New York 2002, p. 68.

The reflections on the poverty of women revealed her genuine spirit of sympathy for social injustice in Azerbaijan and other countries. She was concerned with the double burden of women, in comparison with men: women who worked outside their homes also cared for their families at homes. When describing the anger of one particular refugee woman from the Caucasus in Iran at the foolish custom of pinching women in public, Hamideh quoted her:

> You made these Iranian women miserable and wretched and intimidated. You use this to pinch them in public where ever they were. In order to protect their honor, they don't go out. Aren't you angry at this? Do you think Caucasian women will also shut up and not speak out? Next time, I'll come to the bazaar with a pistol. Let someone be so bold as to offend me. I'll shoot him.[30]

Publication of 'Ishiq' by Azerbaijani women

The emergence of early secular Muslim feminism in Azerbaijan occured due to an increasing literacy rate among the upper- and middle-class Azerbaijani women: since the beginning of colonialism, one of the opportunities for the Muslim women was to study in colonial tsarist schools and become the 'early voices' of feminism during the colonial regime in Azerbaijan. Through literary works of these women during colonialism, which Badran calls 'early unveiling of women's voices'[31] when she writes about the first generation of feminists in Egypt, the educated women all over the Muslim world, including Azerbaijan, attempted and managed to overcome a domestic confinement and acquired a public presence. The powerful voices of these early feminist Muslim women rendered them the early founders of secular Muslim feminism. However, their feminist ideology was compatible with Islam in Azerbaijan.

The increasing rate of literacy among the Azerbaijani women reflected itself in the emergence of the publications for women, for example *Ishiq* (Light), the first newspaper for and by women, edited by Khadija Alibeyova in 1911–1912 in Baku. *Ishiq* played a significant role in developing the feminist discourse in Azerbaijan and used the religious traditions of the Azerbaijani women, such as deconstructing the patriarchal readings of the Qur'an and *hadith*, to enlighten the Azerbaijani women regarding their right to education and employment.[32]

Despite the caution and indirect criticism of many Muslim reformers against the conservative *mullahs* in Azerbaijan, the reformist ideas of 'Ishiq', including the women's right to education and employment, were severely attacked by the

---

30 H. Javanshir, *Memoirs of Iran*, pp. 279–280.
31 M. Badran, *Feminists, Islam..., op. cit.*, p. 16.
32 N. Tohidi, *Azerbaijan..., op. cit.*, p. 84.

qadimists (old thinkers), who used patriarchal understanding of Islam to resist changes, such as the emancipation of women. The opposition affected the financial support for the journal, which resulted in the cessation of publishing after one year.

Challenges of feminist discourse of Azerbaijani intellectuals

The advancement of the feminist discourse of the Azerbaijani intellectuals, both men and women, is due to several factors. First of all, either the Russian colonizers or the fundamentalist Muslim *mullahs* were not interested in the development of Taghiyev school or the improvement in women's status at all and presented a real danger for the feminist projects in Azerbaijan during the tsarist times. The colonist and fundamentalist threat was one of the main reasons why the Taghiyev school was overcrowded and expensive.

Secondly, the radical class and ideological stances in the Russian society affected the status of the feminists in Azerbaijan. Regardless of the clear position of the prominent feminist and nationalist figures in Azerbaijan concerning the respect of the cultural and religious values of the Azerbaijani people, they faced severe opposition from the reactionaries and traditionalists. Even the oil baron, Taghiyev was not spared the strict opposition from the *qadimists* who were not ready to overcome their sexist bias against women.

However, the struggle for the rights of women was an irreversible movement: the upper, upper-middle as well as the lower class of the society contributed their efforts to the advancement of women's rights. While the upper-class Azerbaijani men and women saw the emancipation of women as the prescription for the building and modernisation of the Azerbaijani nation, the lower class mobilised women for setting the more revolutionary agenda, such as demand for maternity leave for women, on-the-job time for nursing unweaned children, and medical benefits for all workers.[33] Simultaneously, an advancement of the 'woman question' among the Azerbaijani intellectuals could be seen. Some of them even used the veil argument in order to establish another girls' school in Baku and called for improving the status of the Muslim women and for abolishing the veiling practice.[34] Mirza Feteli Akhundov, an Azerbaijani reformer and intellectual who converted to Christianity and supported the Russian Empire, advocated a complete Europeanisation (including the dress code) in order to achieve the full emancipation of women. The front cover of the 'Ishiq' newspaper symbolically pictured a woman

33 A. Altstadt, *The Azerbaijani Turks: Power and Identity Under Russian Rule*, Hoover Institutions Press, Stanford 1992, p. 56.
34 *Ibid.*, p. 64.

wearing a black *yashmak* (traditional face cover), holding a child's hand and showing the rising sun. Jalil Mammadquluzadeh compared the black face veiling of the Muslim women with the black clouds of the Muslim women's lamentations. This and the other attempts and arguments indicated that the Muslim reformers saw the unveiling[35] as a significant step toward the improvement in the status of the Azerbaijani women. However, it would also represent one of the most controversial subjects in any discussion about the status of Muslim women in general.[36]

Nevertheless, I argue that criticism against the Islamic cultural and religious practices of Muslim women was a general trend in many colonial feminist movements, and this extreme criticism isolated the Azerbaijani women from their economic and colonial tsarist context. The colonial feminists and some pro-feminist Muslim men, including Akhundov, failed to see that the established economic and political tsarist order in Azerbaijan widened the gap between classes and ethnic groups, supported the power of the upper class over the lower class, the dominance of men over women, Christians over Muslims, Russians over non-Russians, and prevented a progressive cultural and social transformation in Azerbaijan. Furthermore, the assault on the face veiling and other local practices of the Azerbaijani women reflected, what Leila Ahmed calls 'the internalisation and replication of the colonialist perception'[37] when referring to the similar trend in Egypt, in terms of the 'superiority' of the European civilisation over local civilisations.

Nevertheless, the supporters of the school projects for the Azerbaijani girls had to take a fierce and courageous action and ask the tsarist colonial officials to allocate funds for the expansion of the projects. Their main argument was the need for education to make women good citizens of the Russian Empire, and good mothers. As a consequence of those efforts, the number of the schools for girls

---

35 We learn from *Memoirs of Iran* of Hamideh Javanshir that women usually wore traditional chadors with a black face covering of thick gauze, which obscured the entire face.

36 The similar line of discussions also occurred in other parts of the Muslim world. In Egypt, for example, Qasim Amin, an Egyptian lawyer, advocated the adoption of the Western style of clothing. However, some feminist women, including Malak Hifni Nassef, a strong advocate of women's rights in Egypt, refused to affiliate themselves with the Westernisation. Nassef especially criticised male arrogance 'in dictating what women ought to do' and provided a critical reflection on 'the issue of adopting Western customs'. She opposed the Westernisation, because she saw it represent a new brand of male dominance over women through the contemporary male discourse on the veil. Some of those women did not believe that the Western style of clothing made women more modern and progressive; they even accused the upper- and middle-class women of being preoccupied with fashion rather than being motivated by a desire for liberty and knowledge. See L. Ahmed, *Women and Gender...*, *op. cit.*, pp. 80, 173.

37 *Ibid.*, p. 160.

increased gradually. In 1913 there were 8 Russian-Azerbaijani schools for girls and 337 female students, in comparison with 2249 male students.

The nationalization of education was also an important item on the agenda of the Muslim reformers and nationalists who realised that most Azerbaijanis refused to send their children to schools, as an attempt to avoid the adoption of the Russian cultural identity. The refusal also reflected their resentment at the Russian discrimination against the Muslims in Azerbaijan and their ongoing support for the Armenians who shared religious heritage with the Russians. The demand for the nationalisation of education by the Muslim reformers was also a priority for the social-democratic men and women in Azerbaijan who mainly represented the low and middle class and established their own movement *Himmat* ('Endevour') together with a women's wing of *Himmat*.[38] In July 1913 they demanded the establishment of the Azerbaijani-language school.[39] Both groups also dedicated themselves to the Akhundov's desire to change the Azerbaijani Perso-Arabic alphabet for the modified Latin alphabet.

Thus, we may draw some conclusions about the nature of the early narrative of the Azerbaijani Muslim feminist movements. First of all, many members of feminist movements belonged to the nationalist or social-democratic movements. They resented the Russian discrimination against the Azerbaijani women as if ignorant, uneducated, anti-modern and domesticated. In the second place, the Muslim secular feminist and nationalist movements did not articulate their ideas exclusively within a religious discourse. The feminists talked about the Islamic modernism in a general way and usually organised campaigns to reform the religion-based Muslim personal status code. They were dedicated to reforming the sharia and did not oppose the application of the basic principles of Islam. Some of them did not even abandon their *hijab* (head covering) even though they also adopted the European style of head covering, e.g. hats.

The implications of the feminist discourse in Azerbaijan during the tsarist regime influenced the later generations, especially the founders of the Azerbaijan Democratic Republic (1918–1920). Despite the short life of the independent ADR, the most crucial steps, such as the extension of suffrage to include women, were taken for the first time in the Muslim world, making Azerbaijan the first Muslim nation to grant women equal political rights with men.[40] Had it not been killed in its infancy by the Red Army of the Bolsheviks, the ADR and its progressive citizens and supporters who lost their lives during the 'Red Terror' (Nasib bey

---

38 Sabirmamedoc, *Put k progrecu*, Azerbaijan Dovlat Nashriyat Komitesi, Baku 1986, p. 4.

39 B. Schaffer, *Borders and Brethren: Iran and the Challenge of Azerbaijani Identity*, Harvard University Press, Cambridge 2002.

40 F. Kazemzadeh, *The Struggle for Transcaucasia: 1917–1921*, Philosophical Library, New York 1951, pp. 124, 222, 229, 269–270.

Nasibeyli, Huseyn Javid, Mikayil Mushfig, Ahmed Javad, Salman Mumtaz, Ali Nazmi, Tagi Shahbazi and other intellectuals) and their killed or exiled wives, daughters and sisters would have advanced the cause of the Azerbaijani women, while respecting their cultural and religious tradition.

Conclusion

The Azerbaijani feminists and pro-feminist men were under the influence of the European and Russian feminist movements. However, they did not only aim to achieve equal power relations between men and women, but also supported the nationalist struggle against the Russian tsarist colonialism. Furthermore, the Azerbaijani feminists reconciled the core principles of feminism with their traditions and religion. They also fought against the Russian representation of the Azerbaijani women as ignorant, uneducated, anti-modern and domesticated, and wanted to advance the Islamic modernism in a general way. The increased literacy rate among the Azerbaijani men and women and the emerging schools, newspapers and magazines were used as a means to spread the feminist message across the masses.

Bibliography

Ahmed L., *Women and Gender in Islam: Historical Roots of a Modern Debate*, Yale University Press, New Haven – London 1992.

Akhundov F., *Educating Women to Educate a Nation: The Taghiyev School for Girls in Baku*, UN Development Programme and UN Population Fund, 2007.

Altstadt A., *The Azerbaijani Turks: Power and Identity Under Russian Rule*, Hoover Institutions Press, Stanford 1992.

Badran M., *Feminists, Islam, and Nation*, Princeton University Press, Princeton 1996.

Earl of Cromer, *Modern Egypt*, 2 vols., Macmillan, New York 1908.

Gandhi L., *Postcolonial Theory: A Critical Introduction*, Allen & Unwin, St. Leonards 1998.

Goldstein L., *Early Feminist Themes in French Utopian Socialism: The St.-Simonians and Fourier*, 'Journal of the History of Ideas' 1982, 43, 1.

Guerville A.B. de, *New Egypt*, William Heinemann, London 1906.

Hashemi N., *Islam, Secularism, and Liberal Democracy: Toward a Democratic Theory for Muslim Societies*, Oxford University Press, New York 2009.

Heyat F., *Azeri Women in Transition: Women in Soviet and Post-Soviet Azerbaijan*, RoutledgeCurzon, London – New York 2002.

Javanshir H.K., *Memoirs of Iran*.

Kazemzadeh F., *The Struggle for Transcaucasia: 1917-1921*, Philosophical Library, New York 1951.

Kwok Pui-lan, *Postcolonial Imagination and Feminist Theology*, Westminster John Knox Press, Louisville 2005.

Nasr, *Islamic Life and Thought*, State University of New York Press, Albany 1981.

Sabirmamedoc, *Put k progrecu*, Azerbaijan Dovlat Nashriyat Komitesi, Baku 1986.

Schaffer B., *Borders and Brethren: Iran and the Challenge of Azerbaijani Identity*, Harvard University Press, Cambridge 2002.

Sommer A. van, Zwemer S.M. (eds.), *Daylight in the Harem*, Oliphant, Anderson & Ferrier, Edinburgh – London 1911.

Sommer A. van, Zwemer S.M. (eds.), *Our Moslem Sisters. A Cry of Need from Lands of Darkness Interpreted by Those Who Heard It*, F.H. Revell, New York 1907.

Suny R.G., *Looking Toward Ararat: Armenia in Modern History*, Indiana University Press, Bloomington and Indianapolis 1993.

Swietochowski T., *Russian Azerbaijan, 1905–1920: The Shaping of National Identity in a Muslim Community*, Cambridge University Press, Cambridge 1985.

Tohidi N., *Azerbaijan: Islamic Feminism and the Soviet Legacy of Modernization*, [in:] A. Samiuddin, R. Khanam (eds.), *Muslim Feminism and Feminist Movement: Central Asia*, Global Vision Publishing House, Delhi 2002

Tucker J.E., *Women in Nineteenth-Century Egypt*, Cambridge University Press, Cambridge 1985.

Waal T. de, *Reinventing the Caucasus*, 'World Policy Journal' 2002, 19, 1.

Ewa Teodorowicz-Hellman
Stockholm University
Stockholm (Sweden)

The Place of Christianity in Swedish Primary Schools: Historical Outline and Contemporary Social Discourse

Introduction

Sweden is regarded as one of the most secularised nations in Western Europe. It adopted Christianity in the 11th century, but as a result of Reformation, it broke off ties with the Holy See and proclaimed its own monarch – Gustav Vasa – as the new head of church. His coronation (1523) marked the beginning of a centuries-long period of close relations between the State and the Church of Sweden. Each successive monarch had to be a follower of Lutheranism and a member of the Church of Sweden. The Evangelical Lutheran faith was both the national and State religion: by virtue of the *Uppsala lagen 1593* (Uppsala Law of 1593), every Swede was born and died a member of the Church of Sweden on the principle of 'one state, one nation, one religion'.

Tangible and symbolic evidence of the mutual relations between the State, monarchy and the Church of Sweden exists to this day. The Swedish Parliament's annual autumn sessions open with a service at the Stockholm Cathedral (*Storkyrkan*). Nowadays, the service has an ecumenical character (formerly it was a Lutheran service) and is usually conducted by the Archbishop of Uppsala or the Bishop of Stockholm in the presence of the king, queen, members of parliament and numerous representatives of political parties. It is an old tradition, which has lately been criticised as a manifestation of the Church's influence over the State and its administrative structures. The separation of Church and State took place in the year 2000.[1] All religions were declared equal under the Swedish law, and

---

1 *Lag om Svenska kyrkan*, available at: http://www.riksdagen.se/sv/Dokument-Lagar/Lagar/Svensk-forfattningssamling/Lag-19981591-om-Svenska-kyr_sfs-1998-1591/ (accessed: 14.05.2013).

the financial support received from the State became dependent on the revenues from taxes paid by the members of the religious denominations. It was then that the Catholic Church became officially recognised and, thanks to large numbers of emigrants from Central Europe, Africa, Asia and Latin America, it became the second largest Christian church in Sweden (after the Church of Sweden).[2]

For centuries, the Evangelical Lutheran Church influenced Swedish culture, tradition and customs. It also contributed to the development of reading habits among the society. The annual so-called interrogations, during which pastors examined members of the congregation on their knowledge of the Bible and the teachings of Luther, resulted in the fact that, in times when illiteracy was widespread in Europe, the average Swedish peasant possessed good reading skills. In order to see Christianity's impact on Sweden's culture, all one needs to do is look at the calendar: Swedes celebrate Christmas, Good Friday, Easter, Pentecost, Ascension Day, All Saints' Day. The local church is still quite frequently the place where students of Swedish elementary schools traditionally celebrate the end of the school year, St Lucia's Day, and put on nativity plays. At least this is how things were up until recently, as the situation is currently changing.

Every week, Swedish daily papers print the Church of Sweden's news bulletin, which contains information regarding where masses and services will be held on the upcoming Sunday and, quite often, also the name of the pastor who will be delivering the sermon. Similar bulletins appear in local papers. On Saturday evening, Swedish television and radio broadcast the evening service (*helgmålsbön*[3]) and on Sunday, Channel 2 of Swedish national public television broadcasts a church service at 10 a.m., usually from the Church of Sweden, though sometimes from other churches, e.g. the Catholic Church or one of the so-called Christian Free Churches.[4] On Christmas Eve, the Midnight Mass from the Vatican is broadcast, though not so much for religious reasons as simply because it is a grand spectacle.[5]

At present, only a small portion of the Swedish society have a deeper bond with religion and the Church; the number of baptisms, church weddings and even funerals is steadily declining; however, the fall is not as dramatic as it is in relation to the confirmation of teenagers. Obituaries published in Sweden's largest daily paper 'Dagens Nyheter', more and more often contain a picture of the deceased person's favorite flower, pet or hobby rather than the symbol of the cross.

---

2 M. Chamarczuk, *Problematyka integracji imigrantów w Kościele katolickim w Szwecji*, Francis de Sales Scientific Society, Warsaw 2013.

3 All translations from Swedish have been made by the author of the paper.

4 *Frikyrkor* are the so-called Christian free churches which evolved from religious revival movements. An element which plays an important role in these churches is the personal experience of transcendence.

5 J. Kubicki, *Alfabet szwedzki*, Difin, Warsaw 2011, p. 63.

The selected information referring to the presence of the Church of Sweden in contemporary Swedish society presented in the paper could at least partly contradict the statement made in the first sentence of the article about Sweden being the most secularised country in Europe. Nevertheless, it is a fact that in this atheistic and at the same time materialistic and pragmatic country, religious behaviour is an expression of culture rather than of faith.

Christian religion in Swedish schools[6]

In 1842, the Swedish Parliament decided to introduce a four-year elementary school (*folkskola*). Since then, religious education has been included in the curricula for elementary schools.[7] In the 19th century, the schools' objective was to provide students with education in the Evangelical-Lutheran faith. Religious education, like school education in general, was confessional in character and included religious instruction, reading texts from the Bible, and the history of the Church of Sweden. Religion lessons, which constituted the main pillar of education, were compulsory until 1873, when a directive was issued stating that children belonging to different denominations could be exempted from them. In 1911, the school textbook entitled *Luthers lilla katekes* (*Luther's Small Catechism*) was replaced by a new one entitled *Vår kristna tro* (*Our Christian Faith*), which focused on issues relating to faith and morality.

In 1917, Minister of Education Värner Rydén, with the support of the *Socialdemokraterna* (Social Democrats) party, took firm action against confessional teaching in Swedish schools. Soon the number of religious education classes was reduced and the name of the subject was changed to *Kristendomskunskap* (Christian Studies), which allowed for extending the syllabus to content beyond Lutheran Christian denominations. Such changes met with a strong reaction from the Church of Sweden. In 1927 the government received a petition signed by

---

6 Elementary schools in Sweden are divided into three stages: 1–3 (*lågstadiet*), 4–6 (*mellanstadiet*), 7–9 (*högstadiet*). In referring to these stages, the author of the paper uses the common term 'elementary school'. However, the paper deals mainly with education in grades 4–9. Lower grade students are taught natural religions, they become familiarised with legends and myths and the most important traditions during the year.

7 *Folkskola* consisted of 6 grades in 1882, 7 grades in 1936, 8 grades in 1950 and has consisted of 9 grades since 1972. *Cf.* K.-G. Algotsson, *Från katekesundervisning till religionsfrihet. Debatten om religionsundervisning i skolan under 1900-talet*, Rabén & Sjögren, Uppsala 1975; E. Almén, R. Furenhed, S.G. Hartman, B. Skogar, *Livstolkningar och värdegrund. Att undervisa om religion, livsfrågor och etik*, Skapande vetande, Uppsala 1975; G. Gustavsson, *Tro, samfund och samhälle*, Libris, Örebro 1997; S.G. Hartman, *Lärarens kunskap. Traditioner och ideér i svensk undervisningshistoria*, Skapande vetande, Linköpings Universitet, Linköping 1995; S.-Å. Selander, *Undervisa i religionskunskap*, Studentlitteratur, Lund 1993.

350,000 members of the society demanding that Luther's catechism be reinstated in elementary schools. The government reacted to the demands with reproof. From that moment on the Church's influence on school education began to diminish and *de facto* the process of secularization of Swedish education became a fact.

After World War II, the *Socialdemokrater* (Social Democrats) was the ruling party of Sweden. The period was characterized by a strong secularization and dechristianization of society. In 1955 curriculum[8] the subject treating about religion continued to be called *Kristendomskunskap*. In accordance with the *Sveriges religionsfrihetslag* (Religious Freedom Act) introduced as part of an education reform, it was no longer obligatory for a teacher of religious education to be a pastor and teachers were no longer required to be members of the Church of Sweden. Religious education lessons were to be taught in an objective manner.[9] In 1956, bishops were deprived of their right to conduct school inspections.

In the subsequent curriculum, published in 1962, emphasis was placed on the important role of the student in the education process.[10] Religious education retained its name *Kristendomskunskap* (Christian Studies), but the focus shifted from the history of the Church towards contemporary times. Objectives specified in the document included familiarising students with the major religions in the world and stressing the link between religion and other subjects, though it was clearly stated that they needed to retain their integrity as well as identity. The number of lessons dedicated to religious education was further reduced, and the requirement for 'teaching objectively' was upheld.

The year 1964 marked the foundation of the *Kristen Demokratisk Samling* (Christian Democratic Unity),[11] an organisation which spoke out against the decline in morality, stressed the need for a personalistic upbringing, and promoted Christian ideas in family and social life. The party had considerable influence on the shape of the discourse on the teaching contents and objectives of religious education in Swedish schools. It was responsible for social protests against reducing the number of religious education classes in schools. Within a short period of time, the citizens of the small country collected over two million signatures to show their opposition to changes in school study programs which ran against religious education. However, the government dismissed the voices, stating the

---

8   Kungliga Skolöverstyrelsen, *Undervisningsplan för rikets folkskolor,* Svenska Bokförlagat Norstedts, Stockholm 1955.

9   G. Richardsson, *Svensk utbildningshistoria,* Studentlitteratur, Lund 1999, p. 88.

10 Kungliga Skolöverstyrelsen, *Läroplan för grundskolan. Lgr 1962,* Stockholm 1962.

11 In later years, *Kristen Demokratisk Samling* evolved into *Kristdemokraterna* (Christian Democrats) and in their political program they called for education in the spirit of Christianity, training in the name of personalism, and preserving the Christian system of values and moral norms in the society. *Cf.* http://www.kristdemokraterna.se.

public opinion should not influence education policy. In the course of discourse, the governing parties – the Social Democrats and the left-wing parties – more and more often began to issue demands for the separation of church and State, and for making religion a private matter.

In 1969 religious education changed its name in the school study programs (*The 1969 Curriculum for Elementary Schools*[12]) from *Kristendomskunskap (Christian Studies)* to *Religionskunskap (Religious Studies)*. The syllabus for the subject reflected changes that had taken place in the homogenous Swedish society, which, due to an influx of emigrants, had been transformed in a short period of time into a society of cultural, ethnic and linguistic diversity. The subject's teaching objectives included: becoming familiarised with not just Christian denominations but also with Judaism, Buddhism, Islam, Hinduism, primitive religions, and mythology. Teachers were to discuss the students' contemporary moral and ethical issues not just from the point of view of Christianity. Teaching retained its objective character while one of the schools' main objectives at the time was developing critical thinking skills in students.

The next curriculum, published in 1980 (*The 1980 Curriculum for Elementary Schools*[13]), put an even greater emphasis on the student as the key element in the education process. Religion classes changed their name to *Religionskunskap, människans frågor inför livet och tillvaron (Religious Studies, Issues of Human Life and Existence)*. The syllabus for the subject was clearly in step with the continuing changes in the ethnic and religious structure of Swedish society, caused by great waves of immigration, not only from Europe but also from very distant countries and cultures. Special importance was attached to democratic education, respect for human dignity, and tolerance. As it was stated in the curriculum:

> Even if Christianity is the key to understanding our culture, Christian heritage should be compared with other outlooks on life. The religious heritage of foreigners is a valuable contribution to understanding many problems.[14]

In terms of the teaching goals set for religion classes, the biggest emphasis continued to be placed on faith and worldview related issues, knowledge about Christianity and other religions, as well as various outlooks on life and ideologies, e.g. humanism and Marxism.[15] Probably for the first time, the curriculum also mentioned the Catholic Church, most likely in response to the large numbers of immigrants from Central Europe, Africa, Asia and Latin America.

---

12   Skolöverstyrelsen, *Läroplan för grundskolan. Lgr 1969*, Utbildningsförlaget, Stockholm 1969.
13   Skolöverstyrelsen, *Läroplan för grundskolan. Lgr 1980*, Liber, Läromedel/Utbildningsförlaget, Stockholm 1980.
14   *Ibid.*, p. 119.
15   *Ibid.*, p. 128.

The 1994 curriculum (*The 1994 Curriculum for the Compulsory School System*[16]) was actually only a general framework and did not explicitly state the contents of teaching for the particular subjects. It was rather a set of guidelines pointing to the direction in which school education should be heading. The curriculum was prepared when Sweden was ruled by a coalition formed by the *Moderaterna* (Moderate Party), *Folkpartiet* (Liberal People's Party) and *Kristdemokraterna* (Christian Democrats). During that period of time, Christian Democrats gained a greater influence on the shape of school education. This was reflected in the syllabus for religious education. Special emphasis was placed on the role of Christianity in school education. The curriculum mentioned human value and dignity, gender equality and solidarity with others. Religious education comprised three basic topic areas: *Livsfrågor och livstolkning, etik samt tro och tradition* (*Life problems and their interpretation, ethics, and faith and tradition*). Education in school retained its nondenominational character. Issues related to ethics and morality were to be explored from the perspective of *kristen tradition och västerländsk humanism*, i.e. 'Christian tradition and Western humanism'.[17] The notion of 'Western humanism' provoked an animated discussion on the relationship between humanism and Christianity, a discussion which continues to determine the course of discourse on the place of Christianity classes in Swedish elementary schools.

The present curriculum, approved in 2011,[18] has returned to the previously used name for religious classes *Religionskunskap* (*Religious Studies*). Work on the curriculum lasted a few years and its endorsement caused numerous protests and discussions. *Skolverket* (The Swedish National Agency for Education) prepared a curriculum in which all the major world religions – Christianity, Islam, Judaism, Buddhism and Hinduism – were given equal status in school education. Jan Björklund, a representative of the *Folkpartiet* (Liberal People's Party), one of the parties in power, strongly criticized this approach, stating that the aim of teaching religion in school should be to

> [...] provide students with the knowledge and understanding of how Christian traditions influenced the Swedish society and its system of values [...]. It is obvious that students will be taught about all the major religions in the world, but it is equally obvious that Christianity will have a special status in the Swedish school, also in the

---

16   Skolverket. Utbildningsdepartementet, *1994 års läroplan för det obligatoriska skolväsendet. Lpo 94*, Stockholm 1994.

17   *Ibid.*, p. 3.

18   Skolverket (The Swedish National Agency for Education), available at: http://www.skolverket. se/om-skolverket/visa-enskild publikation?_xurl_=http%3A%2F%2Fwww5.skolverket.se%2F wtpub%2Fws%2Fskolbok%2Fwpubext%2Ftrycksak%2FRecord%3Fk%3D2575 (accessed: 17.08. 2014).

future. This has definitely been the dominant religion in our country, it has shaped our way of life in a completely different manner than, for example, Hinduism [...].[19]

In an interview he gave to *Svenska Dagbladet*, Jan Björklund maintained that his decision to give precedence to Christianity in school education did not stem from the fact

> [...] that the Christian religion is better than any other, it has rather to do with the enormous influence Christianity has had in our country, and still does have in our part of the world.[20]

The minister of education's arguments and critical remarks proved effective. The 2011 curriculum (*Curriculum for Elementary Schools, Preschools and School Common Rooms, 2011*) emphasises the influence of Christianity on the Swedish society and the unique role it has played in the development of Swedish culture. In the syllabus for religious education for grades 7–9 we read, for instance, that the student should become familiar with:

> [...] the main ideas of Christianity and the typical features of its three major denominations: Protestantism, Catholicism and the Orthodox Church [...]. Moreover, the student is to acquire knowledge about the history of Christianity in Sweden, from the time of the unity of the church until the period of religious diversity and secularism.[21]

The student is also to become acquainted with other world religions as well as secular worldviews, such as secular humanism, in order to understand their influence on the development of society, the moral and ethical issues of contemporary man and on his identity. School education has retained its nondenominational character, students are to choose (on their own, without the teacher's assistance) a worldview (religion) that is agreeable to them, but the position of Christianity as far as religious education is concerned has been strengthened.

The 2011 curriculum has provoked numerous and lively discussions in the media, where the main focus has been on the following issues: assigning Christian churches a special role in education and in the school reality, comparing secular Western European humanism with Christian values and the right to religious freedom in the democratic Swedish state. Let us now take a closer look at those discussions.

---

19 J. Björklund, *Kristendomen ska prioriteras i skolan*, 'Svenska Dagbladet' 10.10.2010, available at: http://www.svd.se/nyheter/inrikes/kristendomen-ska-prioriteras-i-skolan_5483341.svd (accessed: 13.06.2013).
20 *Ibid.*
21 Skolverket, *Läroplan för grundskolan, förskoleklassen och fritidshemmet*, Stockholm 2011, p. 189.

Christian religion in contemporary social discourse

The Swedish school has maintained relations with the Church of Sweden for centuries. That is why even today the ceremony at the end of the school year is often held in church, where the students and the teachers sing psalms, listen to the pastor's words, accept wishes for a good summer vacation and sometimes even receive the blessing. Over the past few years, the approaching summer holidays have served as a pretext for animated discussions in the daily papers, as atheist parties and unions claim that the tradition of students visiting a church is at odds with the 'Swedish Education Act' (*Skollagen*), which guarantees the non-confessional character of education in Swedish schools.

Under pressure from *Förbundet. Humanisterna* (The Swedish Humanist Association)[22] and other secular organisations the debate has recently become much more heated. It turns out that the problem lies not just in the fact of students and teachers visiting a church but also in the 17th century psalm *Den blomstertid nu kommer... (The blooming period is nearing...* own translation – E.T.-H.[23]), sung for centuries during the ceremony marking the end of the school year. In 1973 Sweden's most outstanding writer of children's books, Astrid Lindgren, wrote a paraphrase of the psalm. Her song, *Idas sommarvisa (Ida's Summer Song)*, is one of the most beloved children's songs in Sweden. Both the psalm and the song, performed during the celebrations marking the end of the school year, include, apart from suggestive descriptions of nature coming to life, existential issues raised from the perspective of an adult in the psalm and from the perspective of a child in the song. Both compositions talk indirectly about a greater force (God) and thanks to such simple yet deep content they appeal to believers and atheists. Despite all this, the performance of the best loved of all Swedish psalms at the end of the school year ceremony has raised numerous objections.

The animated discussion forced *Skolverket* (The Swedish National Agency for Education) to take a stance on the matter. In October 2012 the agency published a special legal handbook (*Juridisk vägledning*) related to school activities involving religion and cultural tradition. In the guide we read, for example, that:

---

22 Humanisterna (förbund), home page: http://www.humanisterna.se; E. Teodorowicz-Hellman, *Nowy humanizm* (lecture), University of Warsaw, 20.05.2010.

23 *Den blomstertid nu kommer (The blooming period is nearing...* [own translation – E.T.-H.]) is Psalm 474 in the Church of Sweden's psalm book *Den svenska psalmboken*, Nacka 1977, whereas in the psalm book of the Catholic Church, *Cecilia. Katolsk Psalmbok*, 1986, it is Psalm 199. *Idas sommarvisa* was written by Astrid Lindgren for the movie *Emil och grise-knoen* in 1973. The song became very popular and is regarded as an alternative to the psalm *Den blomstertid nu kommer* during celebrations marking the end of the school year, cf. A.J. Evertsson, '*Den blomstertid du kommer' utan 'Du ska inte tro det blir sommar'*, 'Religionsvetenskaplig InternetTidskrift' 2001, 1, available at: http://www.teol.lu.se/fileadmin/user_upload/ctr/pdf/rit/1/evertsson.pdf (accessed: 16.06.2013).

School education must be non-denominational and cannot include religious elements. [...]. Religious holidays are to be discussed in elementary schools (or other types of schools where education is compulsory) just like traditions connected with the liturgical year [...]. The end of the school year ceremony may be held in church on the condition that it is prepared in such a way that emphasis is placed on traditions, the ceremony itself, on being together and that it does not include religious elements such as prayer, blessing or creed [...]. Singing *Den blomstertid nu kommer*, which is a hymn, but one deeply rooted in the tradition of celebrating the end of the school year, is permissible.[24]

Therefore, schools are allowed to visit a church and uphold Swedish Christian traditions and customs related to observing religious holidays, but the pastor present at the church may not say anything about God, pray with the students, or administer the blessing. It is the responsibility of the head of the school to make sure there are no religious elements during the ceremony marking the end of the school year if it is held at church. At this point, it is worth stressing that due to these circumstances, Swedish bishops are looking for new forms of cooperation between schools and the church. For example, they have suggested preparing non-mandatory religious services to celebrate the end of the school year.[25] One matter that everyone agrees on is that all children, including the children of non-Christian emigrants, should be allowed to celebrate the end of the school year together and no one should be excluded from the celebrations.[26] Thus, in the name of tolerance for other faiths, to avoid any feelings of religious discrimination, Swedes are willing to break off with their own, age-old cultural tradition. However, it should also be pointed out that those accusing the school of not being nondenominational and of giving precedence to Christianity in teaching and school reality are not the representatives of other faiths but various secular organisations.

Henrik G. Ehrenberg of the 'Civitas' Institute writes that with such a stand on the matter on the part of the Swedish National Agency for Education, it will be impossible to celebrate Advent, St. Lucia's Day or put on nativity plays in church. After all, their link with religion, specifically Christianity, is undeniable. The

---

24 Skolverket, *Juridisk vägledning. Mer om... Skol- och förskoleverksamhet i kyrkan eller annan religiös lokal*, available at: http://www.skolverket.se/polopoly_fs/1.162944!/Menu/article/attachment/Skolan%20och%20kyrkan%20121016_granskad121018.pdf (accessed: 12.04.2013).

25 Two books have been published on various forms of cooperation between schools and the church. They have the telling title *Den blomstertid nu kommer* and have been prepared by the *Sveriges kristna råd* (Christian Council of Sweden). *Cf.* E.E. Lindblom (ed.), *Den blomstertid nu kommer*, Sveriges kristna råd, Sundbyberg 2007; P. Ekman, D. Ekh (eds.), *Den blomstertid nu kommer*, Sveriges kristna råd, Sundbyberg 2010.

26 R. Persenius, Bishop of Uppsala, *Dags att sluta skolavslutningar i kyrkan*, 'Dagens Nyheter' 11.01.2007, available at: http://www.dn.se/debatt/dags-att-sluta-fira-skolavslutningen-i-kyrkan/ (accessed: 10.04.2013).

author of the article states that the decision made by the agency in the name of tolerance for other-than-Christian denominations and worldviews, not only leads to breaking with the school and religious tradition in Sweden, but is also an act of severance of ties with native Swedish culture. It is necessary at this point to quote the author's words:

> Puritan atheism like the one advocated by the Swedish National Agency for Education is reflected in the school law, which means in practice that the state is conducting a cultural revolution. However, it is impossible to understand culture, society and its system of values, legislation and history without understanding where the ideas, views and traditions derive from. And in the future schools will either gather on account of various religious holidays, [...] and traditions will be upheld, or in the worst-case scenario, they will be filled with content, which will change Swedish cultural traditions beyond recognition. Religious symbols, texts and figures are *de facto* also representatives of the religion and values they illustrate [...]. One cannot forget that in eliminating them, we are committing an act of violence on our own culture, which is irreplaceable. We should put a stop to this terrible debate by changing the law.[27]

Ehrenberg's words take on a deeper sense: they shift the main focus of the debate from religion classes to preserving one's cultural roots, upholding Swedish traditions, customs and practices connected with the church year. Severing one's ties with Christianity means cutting oneself off from one's past, history, and in result one's tradition and even... identity. At this point however, it needs to be said that over the last 50 years the Swedish society has undergone profound changes, which have transformed it into a society of ethnic, linguistic and religious diversity, while the former system of values based on tradition has given way to pluralism of norms and principles.

Teachers have also voiced their opinions in the debate on the place and contents of religious education classes on Christianity in Swedish schools. These are the words with which Metta Fjelkner, president of the *Lärarnas Riksförbund* (National Union of Teachers in Sweden), concluded her article *Kristendomen en grund som behövs i skolan, men inte för trons skull* (*Foundations of Christianity Needed in Schools, but Not for the Sake of Preserving Faith*), published in the *Svenska Dagbladet*:

> We are doing the right thing in Sweden by focusing on the religion that has influenced us more than the other denominations. However, we teachers want to stand up for the secular, non-confessional character of schools. Teaching should be based on knowledge and acquired experience. It must be convincing and logical and

---

27 H.G. Ehrenberg, *Skolverket och den puritanska ateismen*, 26.11.2012, available at: http://www.civitas.net/skolverket-och-den-puritanska-ateismen (accessed: 10.04.2013). Also a published text entitled *Ska eleverna ha lussetåg utan Lucia?*, 'Aftonbladet' 9.06.2013.

provide students with information which they will need in their future jobs and in life. I believe that – faith – is and should remain a private matter in a modern and tolerant society.[28]

Representatives of the secular *Förbund. Humanisterna*[29] (The Swedish Humanist Association) go much further, demanding the removal of all religious elements present in the school reality and in Swedish society. The association's goal is to create a modern secular atheist society in Sweden, one based on the achievements of empirical scientific, and humanist ideals. In their debates, Christianity is seen as anachronistic, old-fashioned, conservative, and lacking scientific rigor. That is why instead of Christianity, the Humanists recommend a secular worldview called *västeuropeiska humanismen*, i.e. Western European humanism (mentioned in the syllabi for 2011), which regards the human being and his/her needs as the greatest and most important value. Taking such an approach allows one not to link ethics and morality with any religion, which is extremely significant considering the diversity of denominations in present-day Sweden and the fact that they are sometimes at odds with Swedish legislation. By citing the words of the Swedish National Agency for Education that school education must be non-denominational, the Humanists claim that the Swedish state is constantly breaking the law by continuing to give precedence to Christianity in school teaching. Moreover, the Humanists believe that the views they present are a worldview and as such should, in a democratic society and state, enjoy the same rights as religions.[30] The debate on the system of values of Western European humanism and Christianity is present on Swedish radio, television and the Internet.[31]

Among others who have expressed their point of view in connection with the ongoing debate on the subject of religion in Swedish schools are the *Folkhögskolor* (Folk Universities), which offer education to teenagers and adults. Their

---

28 M. Fjelkner, *Kristendomen en grund som behövs i skolan, men inte för trons skull*, 'Svenska Dagbladet' 13.10.2010, available at: http://www.svd.se/opinion/brannpunkt/kristendomen-en-grund-som-behovs-i-skolan-men-inte-for-trons-skull_5496203.svd (accessed: 1206.2013).

29 Humanisterna, *Välkommen till Humanisterna!*, available on: http://www.humanisterna.se (accessed: 12.04.2013).

30 So far the petitions submitted to parliament calling for acknowledging humanism as a religion have been rejected, but humanists in Iceland have been recognised as a religious association, which entitles them to receive funding from the state for further activity: *Island erkänner humanismen som livsåskådning*, 5.05.2013, available at: http://www.humanisterna.se/news/island-erkanner-humanismen-som-livsaskadning/ (accessed: 14.05.2013).

31 *Cf.* programs on YouTube: *Moral utan Gud? Debatt*, available at: http://www.youtube.com/watch?v=wtZUwWCmi_c (accessed: 14.05.2013); *Moral med eller utan Gud*, available at: http://www.youtube.com/watch?v=wtZUwWCmi_c (accessed: 14.05.2013); *Religionskunskap i skolan och religiösa friskolor (2010)*, available at: http://www.youtube.com/watch?v=PKoagevpe8c (accessed: 14.07.2013); *Ateism eller kristen tro – vad är rationellt?*, available at: http://www.youtube.com/watch?v=sSDyqagqc9s (accessed: 14.07.2013).

representatives have suggested a way of getting out of the complicated student-school-religion-faith-State situation. The daily paper *Dagens Nyheter* recently published an article entitled *Sverige behöver fler religiösa folkhögskolor* (*Sweden in Need of More Confessional Universities*[32]), signed by representatives of Judaism, Islam, the Orthodox Churches and heads of folk universities. Its authors propose drawing a clear distinction between religious studies (*religionskunskap*) and religious education (*religiös utbildning*), which usually takes place within the framework of a church or mission. They also propose that religious education be handed over to them, as this will make it easier for the Swedish State to bring the right to religious freedom (*religionsfrighet*) into effect. Therefore, education at folk universities would supplement the general system of education: in school students would learn about various denominations, whereas religious education would focus on spiritual development and issues of faith in correspondence with the religion of the particular students. Faith would become every individual's personal matter.

As the authors of the article propose, folk universities could, with the course of time, also become cultural centers where national minorities would be able to satisfy their spiritual needs. Such centers could also, in cooperation with the state, train imams, priests and rabbis. This would result in a Swedish society and state characterized by cultural and religious diversity and an equal status for all religions in the face of law. The article ends with the telling words:

> Let's strive together to build a strong Sweden for the future Europe, in which religious freedom will not just mean freedom from religion, but also freedom of religion.[33]

Instead of a conclusion

Over the last 100 years, religious education classes in Swedish elementary schools have been subjected to significant changes with regard to terminology used to denote the subject, content of teaching as well as methods of working with the student. The process of radical secularisation of Swedish schools began when the Social Democrats were in power. After a period of confessional teaching about Lutheranism, religion classes began opening up first to other Christian denominations, then to different world religions evolving more into lessons on various worldviews, where much time was devoted to ethical issues. Moreover, religious education was combined with other subjects (history, civics, geography) and as a result it faced the risk of losing its identity and integrity. Various trends

---

32   Y. Aydin *et al.*, *Sverige behöver fler religiösa folkhögskolor*, 'Dagens Nyheter' 9.10.2012, p. 14.
33   *Ibid.*

in education[34] caused that the role of the student changed from that of the object of teaching to that of the subject of an education process. The governments of the Social Democrats and 'the Moderates' and the coalition parties had an impact on the place of religions, especially the Christian religion in the Swedish elementary school. This is particularly noticeable in the 2011 curriculum, where precedence was given to Christian religion.

In the present-day debate on the role of Christianity in Swedish schools a lot is being said and written about religious traditions connected with the church year. However, these traditions are being stripped of their 'religiousness' and instead emphasis is being placed on their cultural significance. The Swedish state built its culture first on Catholicism, then on Protestantism. That is why it is impossible to separate the cultural elements from the religious ones. In the name of democracy and tolerance for other faiths and also in line with the new integration policy[35] calling on Swedes to integrate, the Swedish National Agency for Education was prepared to give all the world religions equal status during religious education classes. These plans were not implemented due to the policy of the present government. The Moderates and the coalition parties regard Christianity not only as a significant, but even integral part of Swedish cultural heritage.

Pursuant to the Education Act, Swedish schools are to conduct educational activity in a non-confessional manner, teach critical thinking and present the so called 'Swedish table' (*svenska smörgåsbordet*) of different religions and systems of values, expecting the student to make the choice himself/herself – there are no bad choices to make.[36] The *Kristdemokrater* (Christian Democrats) oppose this way of thinking and call for personalism in the education process of young people. They also demand that schools educate students, paying regard to the development of their system of values based on Christian ideals.

It is worth mentioning at this point, in the form of a brief reflection, that Pope John Paul II in his speeches and works on the relationship between faith and culture called for an immanent dialog between the two and believed that patterns of behavior could not be replaced by an objective transfer of information which excluded evaluation. 'A human being shaped in this manner would, with time, fall into relativism, into radical pragmatism, and live according to the dictates of passing fashion'.[37]

---

34 The pedagogical theories of educationalists John Dewey, Burrhus Fredric Skinner, Lev Semyonovich Vygotsky influenced education in Swedish schools after 1945.

35 Regeringskansliet, *Integration*, available at: http://www.regeringen.se/sb/d/2279 (accessed: 14.05.2013); cf. J. Kubicki, *Alfabet szwedzki, op. cit.*

36 *Cf.* fn.42 and J.-O. Hellsten's *Sagan om det stora smörgåsbordet* at the end of the article.

37 J. Król, *Ku nawróceniu. Jan Paweł II*, Wydawnictwo Diecezjalne, Sandomierz 2005, p. 202; J. Życiński, *Wiara chrześcijańska w dialogu z kulturą współczesną wg Jana Pawła II*, 'Ethos' 1988, 41/42, pp. 134–137.

Christian values, especially Catholic values, are often discredited in the Swedish debate and willingly replaced with the ideas of Western European humanism; this is often accompanied by remarks stressing the superiority of this worldview. Those taking part in the discussion point out the universality of humanism in the globalized world, refer to the United Nation's declaration of human rights, reproach Christianity for causing religious wars, and for its non-scientific backbone, lack of tolerance, and conservatism. The problem has recently become the subject of research carried out by Swedish scholars, resulting in an extensive research project entitled *'Den katolska faran'. Antikatolicismen som en identitesformande kraft i Norden 1815–1965* (*'The Danger of Catholicism'. Anti-Catholicism as an Identity Shaping Force in Scandinavian Countries in the Years 1815–1965* [own translation – E.T.-H.]). The project was launched in 2011. It is supervised by Professor Yvonne Maria Werner from Lund University. Research will be conducted until 2016).[38]

Let us return to religion lessons. They have changed over the years because Sweden has changed. It has evolved from an agricultural country into a highly developed and industrialised country, in which a consumerist society plays an important role. Moreover, Swedish schools have undergone a process of secularisation and de-Christianisation. The once homogenous Swedish society has changed into a society of great ethnic, linguistic and religious diversity.

The paper on the place of the Christian religion in Swedish schools being placed in the hands of the readers does not, of course, exhaust the subject due to the limited length of the article as well as the complexity of the presented matter. Nevertheless, it attempts to signal a few issues worth pondering. One should, for instance, ask why the Christians lost the debate held in the 1960s, despite having collected over two million signatures. How did they manage to strengthen the position of Christianity in schools, which was reflected in the 1994 and 2011 curricula? Was this the result of the political climate or the *Sveriges kristna råd* (Christian Council of Sweden) and its influence on Swedish offices and institutions?[39] And finally, one more important question: Is the 2011 curriculum for religious education classes an authentic victory or just a partial win with regard to the place of Christianity in Swedish schools?

Lessons on Christianity in Swedish schools do not deal with religious matter *sensu stricto*. Religious issues have started shifting towards the spheres of culture, tradition and ethics. And perhaps what has been lost in this extremely heated

---

38 Y.M. Werner, *'Den katolska faran'. Antikatolicismen som en identitetsformande kraft i Norden 1815–1965*, available at: http://www.kultur.lu.se/o.o.i.s?id=21349&p=443 (accessed: 12.05. 2013).

39 *Sveriges kristna råd* is a council of 25 Christian Churches in Sweden. Its primary goal is ecumenic cooperation. The council represents Christian churches in talks with representatives of political parties, the government and various institutions.

debate is the most important issue of all – the issue of faith – which cannot be substituted by bare facts about Christian Churches simply because it's impossible. It seems that the problem has recently been noticed by representatives of folk universities and certain religious groups, who talk about two separate goals of education: teaching about religion(s) and religious education. In the secularised Swedish State only the first task can be the responsibility of the school. In the past, religious education was provided by confessional schools, e.g. Catholic confessional schools, which are held in high regard in Sweden.[40] But they too are obliged to comply with the norms of objective teaching based solely on experience and scientific knowledge.

We do not know what the future holds for religious education classes in Sweden or what place Christianity will have in Swedish school education, but it will certainly continue to be a topic readily discussed in the media, in politics, in religious and educational institutions, by members of the society, the government and maybe parliament. Will Christian Churches be able to defend their position in school education? Will secular humanism, religious syncretism, atheism and the New Age movement – which regard Christian religion only as an outdated element of Swedish culture – fail in their attempts to remove them from school and social environments? The questions are endless. Nevertheless, the need for spirituality seems to be an inherent part of the history of mankind and the situation is no different today. Contemporary people, perhaps more than ever before, are searching for the sense of their existence. Looking for answers, some turn towards primitive and natural religions, others towards Islam, Buddhism, Hinduism and various forms of New Age, even occultism, and still others turn towards secular humanism. There are also those who remain loyal to the values, principles and norms of Christianity, which is noticeable among present-day Swedish society.

Jesusmanifestationen (Manifestation in the Name of Jesus)[41] is an event that has been organised in Sweden for the past six years. Followers of Christian faiths march through the streets of many Swedish cities and towns praying, singing religious songs and raising crosses. In 2013, over 10,000 people took part in the march in Stockholm; it was not an event organised by the Church of Sweden, but an ecumenical manifestation of Christians: Protestants, Catholics, members of the Orthodox Church, Pentecostals as well as others for whom Jesus is a role model. The Manifestation in the Name of Jesus takes place on Pentecost, commemorating the descent of the Holy Spirit upon the Apostles, when Christ's church began its activity. At present, this church has a unique place in the curricula for elementary

---

40 M. Chamarczuk, *Problematyka integracji imigrantów...*, op. cit., pp. 78–88.
41 J. Augustin, *Jesus kom till Stockholm*, 'Dagens Nyheter' 19.05 2013, p. 14.

schools (1994, 2011) though not as an expression of faith or religiousness but an important element of Swedish history and culture – Swedish heritage.

I would like to conclude with a short story by Jan-Olof Hellsten entitled *Sagan om det stora smörgåsbordet* (*The Story of the Great Swedish Table*[42]), on the topic of teaching religion in Swedish schools:

> Once upon a time there was a small country located almost on the edge of the world. It had a well-developed education system thanks to which students learned a variety of useful things like reading, writing, mathematics and computer literacy. When their knowledge and skills were measured on an international scale, they always achieved very good results. In this country, people talked a lot [...] about the school's core values, such as gender equality, the equal value of all people and the individual's right to choose his/her own beliefs regarding politics, faith and lifestyle. In practice this meant that schools taught about different ideologies, religions and value systems, but they were on no condition permitted to influence the students in their choices regarding particular worldviews. Schools were not allowed to evaluate [...]. Education was to be objective. This was interpreted in the following way: the teacher's role was to discuss different worldviews without expressing his or her opinion about them. The different worldviews were represented as various dishes set out buffet-style on a large table and one was free to pick and choose among them. Schools were not allowed to influence the students' choices, but could only present to them everything that was laid out. The students were to take a stance and choose themselves (it is not known when exactly the students were to make their choice, most probably once all the meals had been presented). The reason why any religious elements were forbidden in school education was that religion was the most private of all human matters. However, to enable parents to familiarise their children with their faith – pursuant to the UN's declaration of human rights – the state permitted setting up confessional schools on the condition that their teaching would be objective as well. After some time however, many began to question these schools claiming they got in the way of their children freely choosing from among the wide range of worldviews available. Or even worse: such schools could potentially become a breeding ground for intolerance.[43]

Bibliography

Algotsson K.-G., *Från katekesundervisning till Religionsfrihet. Debatten om religionsundervisning i skolan under 1900-talet*, Rabén & Sjögren, Uppsala 1975.

Almén E., Furenhed R., Hartman S.G., Skogar B., *Livstolkningar och värdegrund. Att undervisa om religion, livsfrågor och etik*, Skapande vetande, Uppsala 1975.

---

42   *Svenska smörgåsbordet*, i.e 'Swedish table' – in other words a *buffé* – means a table full of multiple cold dishes of various foods to which guests can help themselves.

43   J.-O. Hellsten, *Sagan om det stora smörgåsbordet*, 'Signum' 2006, 8, available at: http://www.signum.se/archive/read.php?id=3112 (accessed: 15.05.2013). Trans. from Polish by A. Ryłek-Kostowska.

Ateism eller kristen tro – vad är rationellt?, available at: http://www.youtube.com/watch?v=sSDyqagqc9s (accessed: 14.07.2013).

Augustin J., *Jesus kom till Stockholm*, 'Dagens Nyheter' 19.05 2013.

Aydin Y. *et al.*, *Sverige behöver fler religiösa folkhögskolor*, 'Dagens Nyheter' 9.10.2012.

Björklund J., *Kristendomen ska prioriteras i skolan*, 'Svenska Dagbladet' 10.10.2010, available at: http://www.svd.se/nyheter/inrikes/kristendomen-ska-prioriteras-i-skolan_5483341.svd (accessed: 13.06.2013).

Chamarczuk M., *Problematyka integracji imigrantów w Kościele katolickim w Szwecji*, Francis de Sales Scientific Society, Warsaw 2013.

Ehrenberg H.G., *Skolverket och den puritanska ateismen*, 26.11.2012, available at: http://www.civitas.net/skolverket-och-den-puritanska-ateismen (accessed: 10.04.2013).

Ekman P., Ekh D. (eds.), *Den blomstertid nu kommer*, Sveriges kristna råd, Sundbyberg 2010.

Evertsson A.J., *'Den blomstertid du kommer' utan 'Du ska inte tro det blir sommar'*, 'Religionsvetenskaplig InternetTidskrift' 2001, 1, available at: http://www.teol.lu.se/fileadmin/user_upload/ctr/pdf/rit/1/evertsson.pdf (accessed: 16.07.2013).

Fjelkner M., *Kristendomen en grund som behövs i skolan, men inte för trons skull*, 'Svenska Dagbladet' 13.09.2010, available at: http://www.svd.se/opinion/brannpunkt/kristendomen-en-grund-som-behovs-i-skolan-men-inte-for-trons-skull_5496203.svd (accessed: 12.06.2013).

Gustavsson G., *Tro, samfund och samhälle*, Libris, Örebro 1997.

Hartman S.G., *Lärarens kunskap. Traditioner och ideér i svensk undervisningshistoria*, Skapande Vetande, Linköping Univ. 1995.

Hellsten J.-O., *Sagan om det stora smörgåsbordet*, 'Signum' 2006, 8, available at: http://www.signum.se/archive/read.php?id=3112 (accessed: 15.05.2013).

Humanisterna (förbund), home page: http://www.humanisterna.se.

Humanisterna, *Välkommen till Humanisterna!*, available on: http://www.humanisterna.se (accessed: 12.04.2013).

Island erkänner humanismen som livsåskådning, 5.05.2013, available at: http://www.humanisterna.se/news/island-erkanner-humanismen-som-livsaskadning/ (accessed: 14.05.2013).

Kristdemokraterna, home page: http://www.kristdemokraterna.se.

Król J., *Ku nawróceniu. Jan Paweł II*, Wydawnictwo Diecezjalne, Sandomierz 2005.

Kubicki J., *Alfabet szwedzki*, Difin, Warsaw 2011.

Kungliga Skolöverstyrelsen, *Undervisningsplan för rikets folkskolor*, Svenska Bokförlaget Norstedts, Stockholm 1955.

Kungliga Skolöverstyrelsen, *Läroplan för grundskolan, Lgr 1962*, Stockholm 1962.

Lag om Svenska kyrkan, available at: http://www.riksdagen.se/sv/Dokument-Lagar/Lagar/Svenskforfattningssamling/Lag-19981591-om-Svenska-kyr_sfs-1998-1591/ (accessed: 14.05. 2013).

Lindblom E.E. (ed.), *Den blomstertid nu kommer*, Sveriges kristna råd, Sundbyberg 2007.

Moral med eller utan Gud, available at: http://www.youtube.com/watch?v=wtZUwWCmi_c (accessed: 14.05.2013).

Moral utan Gud? Debatt, available at: http://www.youtube.com/watch?v=wtZUwWCmi_c (accessed: 14.05.2013).

Persenius R., Bishop of Uppsala, *Dags att sluta skolavslutningar i kyrkan*, 'Dagens Nyheter' 11.01.2007, available at: http://www.dn.se/debatt/dags-att-sluta-fira-skolavslutningen-i-kyrkan/ (accessed: 10.04.2013).

Regeringskansliet, *Integration*, http://www.regeringen.se/sb/d/2279 (accessed: 14.05.2013).

Religionskunskap i skolan och religiösa friskolor (2010), available at: http://www.youtube.com/watch?v=PK0agevpe8c (accessed: 14.07.2013).

Richardsson G., *Svensk utbildningshistoria*, Studentlitteratur, Lund 1999.

Selander S.-Å., *Undervisa i religionskunskap*, Studentlitteratur, Lund 1993.

Ska eleverna ha lussetåg utan Lucia?, 'Aftonbladet' 9.06.2013.

Skolöverstyrelsen, *Läroplan för grundskolan, Lgr 1969*, Liber, Utbildningsförlaget, Stockholm 1969.

Skolöverstyrelsen, *Läroplan för grundskolan, Lgr 1980*, Liber, Läromedel/Utbildningsförlaget, Stockholm 1980.

Skolverket (The Swedish National Agency for Education), available at: http://www.skolverket.se/om-skolverket/visa-enskildpublikation?_xurl_=http%3A%2F%2Fwww5.skolverket.se%2Fwtpub%2Fws%2Fskolbok%2Fwpubext%2Ftrycksak%2FRecord%3Fk%3D2575 (accessed: 17.08.2014).

Skolverket, *Juridisk vägledning. Mer om... Skol- och förskoleverksamhet i kyrkan eller annan religiös lokal*, available at: http://www.skolverket.se/polopoly_fs/1.162944!/Menu/article/attachment/Skolan%20och%20kyrkan%20121016_granskad121018.pdf (accessed: 12.04.2013).

Skolverket, *Läroplan för grundskolan, förskoleklassen och fritidshemmet*, Stockholm 2011.

Skolverket. Utbildningsdepartementet, *1994 års läroplan för det obligatoriska skolväsendet, Lpo 94*, Stockholm 1994.

Teodorowicz-Hellman E., *Nowy humanizm* (lecture), University of Warsaw, 20.05.2010.

Werner Y.M., *'Den katolska faran'. Antikatolicismen som en identitetsformande kraft i Norden 1815–1965*, available at: http://www.kultur.lu.se/o.o.i.s?id=21349&p=443 (accessed: 12.05.2013).

Życiński J., *Wiara chrześcijańska w dialogu z kulturą współczesną wg Jana Pawła II*, 'Ethos' 1988, 41/42.

Zuzana Svobodová
Charles University
Prague (Czech Republic)

Paideia as Care of the Soul – the Potentials of Contemporary School

Paideia in classical antiquity

Ancient Greeks associated the education process with the term PAIDEIA; only later was this term also used to refer to the contents of education ('education' in the sense of gaining knowledge, skills and attitudes), exactly as the German term *Bildung* or the Latin word *cultura* with the same meaning have objectivised.[1]

Allegedly, the first time the word PAIDEIA appears in Aeschylus' work *Seven Against Thebes* (467 BC); its meaning is similar to TROFÉ ('nurture, nourishment, behaviour, educating'; TROFEION – 'educational, nurturing'; TROFEUS, TROFOS – 'educator, foster parent').[2]

From the very beginning, the word PAIDEIA has also been close to ARETÉ,[3] as it was already in Homer in his *Iliad*[4] and *Odyssey*. In the 5th century BC we also often find the word PAIDEIA in the 'lower' sense, i.e. approximately in the sense of nurture, care (of a child). When Aristophanes uses the expression 'old paideia'

---

1 W. Jaeger, Paideia: *Die Formung des Griechischen Menschen*, Walter de Gruyter, Berlin 1959, p. 384.
2 Aeschylus, *Seven Against Thebes*, Harvard University Press – William Heinemann, Cambridge – London 1926, available at: http://data.perseus.org/citations/urn:cts:greekLit:tlg0085.tlg004.perseus-grc1:1 (accessed: 25.10.2013).
3 The term ARETÉ is derived from ARESKÓ – 'to be pleasing'.
4 Homer, *Iliad* 443, 784, 315–322, quotes Cicero De or. III, 57–v. 443; see M. Tullius Cicero, *M. Tulli Ciceronis Rhetorica*, A.S. Wilkins (ed.), 1902, available at: http://data.perseus.org/texts/urn:cts:latinLit:phi0474.phi037.perseus-lat1 (accessed: 26.10.2013).

in his satire entitled *Clouds* (418 BC),[5] he means the Athenian education approximately in early 5th century BC, which was also special beginning in the mid-6th century BC – typical of its newly non-military character. From the 4th century BC, a 'new paideia' was known, as it was born from a crisis and fall and therefore clinged to the heights; now it is about education level in the sense of striving for nobility, integrity. New PAIDEIA expresses its essence in the phrase 'care of the soul', which will later be called *cultura animi* and *philosophia* by Cicero or *humanita* by Cicero and Varro,[6] i.e. striving for humanity, a culture itself. Therefore, Werner Jaeger can write that the history of Greek *paideia* is the history of Greek literature, expressing the very essence of Greek history, the process of shaping of the Greek character. Those who participate in Greek *paideia*, not necessarily those who share Greek nationality, are the real Greeks, as Isocrates reminds us.

Nevertheless, in his treatise *Against the Sophists*, Isocrates speaks against those who – according to his words – only pretend to be looking for the truth and consider this search for the truth the most important thing, but in fact – according to Isocrates – it is a lie from the very beginning. It is most probably an attack against the followers of Socrates, in particular against Antisthenes who at the time already had a significant reputation as an educator in Athens focusing only on the most important element in *paideia* – search for the truth, essence, name.[7] Antisthenes was, according to some in ancient times, considered the most faithful disciple of Socrates. Diogenes Laertius, however, also speaks about a situation where Antisthenes showed off a torn coat and Socrates, seeing it, said: 'Through the coat I see your pride.'[8] Antisthenes was also Plato's opponent; he especially rejected his theory of ideas.[9] While Isocrates calls the search for the criterion of truth a lie, Antisthenes believed it was of utmost importance to find such criterion through philosophising in order to gain EPISTÉMÉ (by logical-dialectical examination). This would further determine every *paideia* whose objective, in his

---

5   Aristophanes, *Aristophanes Comoediae*, vol. 2, F.W. Hall, W.M. Geldart (eds.), Clarendon Press, Oxford 1907, v. 961, available at: http://data.perseus.org/citations/urn:cts:greekLit:tlg0019. tlg003.perseus-grc1:961 (accessed: 26.10.2013).

6   '"Humanitatem" appellaverunt id propemodum, quod Graeci paideian vocant, nos "eruditionem institutionemque in bohas artes" dicimus. Quas qui sinceriter percupiunt adpetuntque, hi sunt vel maxime humanissimi. Huius enim scientiae cura et disciplina ex universis animantibus uni homini data est idcircoque "humanitas" appellata est. Sic igitur eo verbo veteres esse usos, et cumprimis M. Varronem Marcumque Tulllium, omnes ferme libri declarant' – Aulus Gellius, *Noctes Atticae* XIII, 17, 1, [in:] *id.*, *The Attic Nights of Aulus Gellius*, trans. J.C. Rolfe, William Heinemann, London 1927, available at: http://data.perseus.org/citations/urn:cts:latinLit:phi1254.phi001.perseus-lat1:13.17 (accessed: 27.10.2013).

7   One of his most extensive works was entitled 'PERI PAIDEIAS É PERI ONOMATÓN' – DL VI 15–18.

8   DL VI 8–9.

9   DL VI 7–8.

opinion, was ethical conduct, in a capable, honourable life (ARETÉ); unlike Plato, not metaphysically. According to Stobaeus, it was Antisthenes who answered the question to whom he would entrust his son for education, using the words: 'If he wants to live with gods let him become a philosopher; if with people let him become an orator.'[10]

The polysemy of what is referred to as PAIDEIA is manifested quite soon. The view of the dual paideia is particularly famous in this polysemy: one paideia which is later described by Dio Chrysostom as divine education (DAIMONIOS, THEIA), which is great, strong and easy, and the other human *paideia* (ANTHRÓPINÉ), which is small, weak, long, and involves many risks.

It is not necessary to demonstrate extensively how Plato's PAIDEIA is connected with godliness. The true godliness is a manifestation of the true *paideia*. God is the educator of the whole world.[11] Therefore, later many Christian thinkers could accept much of Plato without major corrections. Diogenes Laertius interprets that for Plato, the human objective is to try to model god.[12] According to Jaeger's research, the norms of human and social behaviour in Greek *paideia* have always been derived from sacred norms of the world which were called PHYSIS – natural (*natura*).[13] It is also the fundamental and characteristic manifestation of the entire Greek philosophy, that all breathes together (PANTA SYMPNEI), all shares the common spirit (PNEUMA, *spiritus*) or soul (PSYCHÉ, *anima*) which brings everything to life – the thought of one spirit spreading through the whole organism comes from Greek medicine from which it made it to stoic philosophy.[14]

Jan Patočka, when interpreting Plato's role in history, speaks about Plato's transformation of the myth into religion, i.e. transformation from the passive fantasy (which does not know that it is fantasy, which is substantially practical) into a reality which requires personal activity, personal interest and faith. Patočka calls it the first purely moral religion.[15] Therefore Plato's care of the soul, breaking free from the sphere of APEIRON (from the sphere of indulging in desires which are capable of growing without limits, from the principle of multiplicity and uncertainty[16]), to a higher, graduated, concentrated, definite and formed up being that does not dissolve, but is. It is the essence of probably the most famous story wherein the essence and structure of paideia is shown: the story by Plato about

10 STOB. II 31, 76: *Cf.* V A 173: Giannantoni, *Socratis et Socraticorum Reliquiae*, available at: http://ancientsource.daphnet.org/texts/Socratics/V-A,173 (accessed: 28.10.2013).

11 See Dio Chrysostom, *Dionis Prusaensis quem vocant Chrysostomum quae exstant omnia*, vol. 1–2, J. de Arnim (ed.), available at: http://data.perseus.org/citations/urn:cts:greek Lit:tlg0612.tlg001.perseus-grc1:4.29 (accessed: 28.10.2013).

12 DL III, 1, 78.

13 W. Jaeger, *Early Christianity and Greek* Paideia, Belknap Press of Harvard University Press, Cambridge 1985, c 1961, p. 18.

14 *Ibid.*, p. 22.

15 J. Patočka, *Péče o duši: [soubor statí a přednášek o postavení člověka ve světě a v dějinách] II*, I. Chvatík, P. Kouba (eds.), Oikoymenh, Prague 1999, p. 257.

16 *Ibid.*, p. 259.

the difference between the educated and uneducated soul.[17] 'PAIDEIA is above all PERIAGÓGÉ, conversion of the soul. [...] PAIDEIA as movement aims at shaping up the soul [...]'.[18] PAIDEIA is therefore a movement to find the form, direction and purpose of the soul; therefore, it is possible to refer to *paideia* as religion (Plato describes a soul which sees the essence of existence as circling in the traces of the gods[19]). A soul that does not pursue *paideia* is not idle but is in motion – if it is a soul, it is always in motion – but this is an aperatic loss of appearance, a form of blurring in an uncertain illusion where the soul is diffused in diverse desires up to superficial oscillation in multiplicity. It is therefore possible to call this state a passive fantasy, which is the opposite of a definite religion or spirituality.

PAIDEIA as an essential, deliberate and oriented care of the soul establishes a new concept of a citizen's task. The ruler in his *Constitution* is the most excellent result of education, and his task is to be the greatest educator. He who cares the most about the education of the soul (PSYCHÉS PAIDEUSIS) is the one who really loves. The objective of Plato is also 'conversion' – in the sense of turning to the light of the true Being. If Plato speaks about god in this context, there is a great difference from the traditional Olympic gods; therefore, for his followers the philosophical system of the Hellenist period was a way of 'spiritual refuge'. For Plato, god is the world's educator,[20] god is the measure of everything (as opposed to Protagoras' understanding that man is the measure of existence of all things). The objective of the true education is true justice. The true education corresponds with the process of building the state. Therefore, Henri Irene Marrou can speak in his work *Histoire de l'éducation dans l'antiquité,* about the PAIDEIA civilisation which he sees between the civilisations POLIS and THEÓPOLIS.[21]

At the same time, when Plato or Isocrates, who elevate the expression PAIDEIA to 'unprecedentedly spiritual meaning', is active, this concept is trivialised in other

---

17 Plato, *Resp.* 514–520: 'TÉN HÉMETERAN FYSIN PAIDEIAS TE PERI KAI APAIDEUSIAS' – Plato, *Platonis Opera*, J. Burnet (ed.), Oxford University Press, Oxford 1903, available at: http://data.perseus.org/citations/urn:cts:greekLit:tlg0059.tlg030.perseus-grc1:7.514a (accessed: 29.10.2013).

18 J. Patočka, *Péče II, op. cit.,* p. 374.

19 Plato, *Faidros,* 246a.

20 Plato, *Leg.* 897b: '[...] THEON ORTHÓS THEOIS, ORTHA KAI EUDAIMONA PAIDAGÓGEI PANTA [...]'. Plato, *Platonis Opera*, J. Burnet (ed.), Oxford University Press, Oxford 1903, available at: http://data.perseus.org/citations/urn:cts:greekLit:tlg0059.tlg034.perseus-grc1:10.897b (accessed: 29.10.2013).

21 H.-I. Marrou, *Histoire de l'éducation dans l'Antiquité.* Éd. du Seuil, Paris 1981, p. 152.

circles. It is used, for example, by Xenophon in his work *Oeconomicus*, 22 or in verb form in *On Horsemanship*.[23]

When Aristotle, knowing Homer, searches for the term to describe the essence of education, the focus of his efforts, he finds an example in an old term describing the noble morality,[24] in ARETÉ in its highest meaning. In *Politics* Aristotle mostly deals with education in connection with the antique ideal of an educated, versed and mature man: KALOKAGATHOS.[25] Aristotle considered all of ethics to be a part of political science because for him, man was directly defined by the definiteness of his life for life in a community (then, of course, ethics was also a matter of the community).[26] The community precedes an individual, just as the whole precedes the part.[27] Also, according to *Nicomachean Ethics*, man is intended for life in a community (in the sense of purpose).[28]

When Alexander the Great initiated the establishment of a cosmopolitan city bearing his name, Alexandria, its citizens also included Diaspora Jews, who were granted as a reward for the alliance the same rights as the Hellenists. Jews in Alexandria spoke Greek and at some point starting in the 3rd century BC they started using the Greek translation of the Law (*Torah*) – *Pentateuch*, subsequently followed by translations of other books of the Old Testament. Thus, gradually until the 1st century BC the Greek set of Jewish writings called *Septuagint* was written. This text also contains the concept of PAIDEIA. In most places, the word is used in the sense of 'rebuke', 'punishment', 'teaching' and 'instruction', but PAIDEIA is used also with the sovereign meaning – the 'LORD's PAIDEIA' – which plays a fundamental role in the relationship of man and his capacity to live from and in connection with God.

With Philo of Alexandria, who addresses his writings to educated Hellenised Jews, the concept of paideia summarizes the contents of Jewish tradition. We can therefore read in his work, for example: 'the light of the soul is PAIDEIA', or he uses also the phrase 'ENKYKLIOS PAIDEIA' (general education).[29] Hellenised Jews used

---

22   Xenofon, *Oikonomikós* 13,9 – Xenophon, *Xenophontis opera omnia*, vol. 2, Clarendon Press, Oxford 1921 (repr. 1971), available at: http://data.perseus.org/citations/urn:cts:greekLit:tlg0032. tlg003.perseus-grc1:13.9 (accessed: 30.10.2013).

23   Xenofon, *Peri ippikés* 5,1.

24   *Ethica Nic.* 1104b, [in:] *Aristotle's Ethica Nicomachea*, J. Bywater (ed.), Clarendon Press, Oxford 1894, available at: http://data.perseus.org/citations/urn:cts:greekLit:tlg0086.tlg010. perseus-grc1:1104b (accessed: 30.10.2013).

25   Aristotle, *Politics* 1293b 39ff; *Ethica Nic.* 1249a.

26   Aristotle, *Politics* 1278 b 19: 'estin anthrópos zóon politikon'. *Cf.* Aristotle, *Politics* 1253a 2. 9: 'ho anthrópos fysei politikon zóon', 'politikon ho anthrópos zóon'.

27   Aristotle, *Politics* 1253 a 19.

28   Aristotle, *Ethica Nic.* 1097b 11: 'fysei polikon ho anthrópos'.

29   Philo, *Legum allegoriae* III, 58 – FÓS DE PSYCHÉS ESTI PAIDEIA; *Phil. Iub. lib. de cherub.* § 2; *Cf.* P. Milko, *Úvod do byzantské filosofie: se studií Michala Řoutila Na východ od Antiochie:*

the word PAIDEIA to approach Greek culture, education level, and their own tradition of divine revelation as well.

The later Christian acceptance of the high value of paideia was also facilitated by the Septuagint text (early Christians used the Old Testament in the version of the Septuagint). This is especially the case when it speaks of *paideia* in the sovereign sense. Despite the fact that this term was important in Greek thinking, it is used in the Septuagint not in the sense of Greek philosophy, but according to the usage of the common Hellenic language and, in this broad sense, as the fruit of Hellenic culture.

Paideia in Christianity

Although many Christians in the patristic period will perceive adoption of the essence of Greek culture as 'blinding by Hellenic *paideia*',[30] in the New Testament the word PAIDEIA is only encountered six times,[31] of which four occur in the Book of Hebrews. It is possible to state several reasons for this. The most frequent reason would probably be a reference to Paul's rejection of the worldly wisdom and the path to the discovery of the soul through internal thought view. Yet the most important change in the Christian view of the soul is the rejection of the essence of the soul in looking at the truth in favour of the concept of a soul which is exposed to the truth of its own source, the truth associated with eternal responsibility. This opening up to the immenseness of divinity and humanity causes such intensification of the soul that Jan Patočka considers Christianity the greatest and insurmountable leap forward. However, it cannot be thought through entirely and it empowers man in his fight against decadence.[32] It is a drama in which the life of the soul is decided, where the soul can choose, and (perhaps) arrive at the purpose, i.e. its cause, through this assumption of responsibility in facing death, in anxiety and hope through choice.

The apocryphal narrative of the *Acts of Philip* describes the performance of the apostle Philip in Athens (in front of the same audience and with the same questions as the canonical book of *Acts* describes Paul's acts), who says: 'I came to

---

řecké myšlení za hranicemi Byzance, 2.–8. století: syrská traduce, P. Mervart, Červený Kostelec 2009.

30   Epiphanius, *Ancoratus und Panarion II*, K. Holl, Leipzig 1922 (GCS XXXI), p. 523, 14–18: 'ÓRÍGENES, APO TÉS PROEIRÉMENÉS HELLÉNIKÉS PAIDEÍAS TYFLÓTHEÍS...'

31   For example, contrary to a different expression for the content and process of teaching – DIDACHÉ: 'teaching', 'study', 'instruction', 'tutoring' – which is encountered thirty times in the New Testament.

32   J. Patočka, *Péče o duši III*, I. Chvatík, P. Kouba (eds.), Oikoymenh, Prague 2002, pp. 107 ff.

Athens to reveal Christ's *paideia* to you.'[33] If Christianity is called Christ's *paideia* here, it emphasises the intention to show Christianity in continuity with the classical Greek *paideia* (and Greek PAIDEIA has become the tool of the author of this apocryphal narrative).

In the canonical Letter to the Ephesians, written sometime after 75 AD, we find the phrase 'PAIDEIA KAI NOUTHESIA KYRIOU' (6:4). In the *First letter of the Clement of Rome to Corinth*, which is dated approximately 96 AD, the term PAIDEIA is used often (in particular in section 56) in the sense of rebuke, punishment, but it also contains the phrase 'PAIDEIA TOU THEOU' (62,3), where PAIDEIA is already in the sovereign sense.

Clement of Alexandria and Origen are considered founders of Christian philosophy. Both build upon the sovereign concept of *paideia* in Plato. In the fight against the proliferating teachings of the Gnostics, they have promoted the concept of Christianity as the true gnosis. Christian Platonians were convinced that they can confront different mystifications like Plato with their more scientific approach, in which the view and exoteric approach was emphasised with focus on the concept of ALÉTHEIA as opposed to the more mythical approach where the focus was impression – DOXA – and esoteric approach. Clement of Alexandria dedicated his work PROTREPTIKOS PROS HELLÉNAS (*Exhortation to the Greeks*) to the Greeks, but soon in his work PAIDAGÓGOS aimed directly at the centre of Greek culture, at the Hellenic paideia, because Christ is called the true PAIDAGÓGOS. It is not rejection of the previous great Greek tradition but rather a conviction that in Christ all PAIDEIA finds its intensification. At this point Christianity aspires to realize the entire Christian civilisation to which all previous great cultures were *propaideia*, but Christian religion is the true PAIDEIA – Christianity in its theological form, as Christian gnosis, which also implies that Christianity is the divine *paideia*. In Origen, the concept of PAIDEIA had always anagogic (uplifting, educational, noble, festive) character,[34] i.e. in the sense of THEIA PAIDEIA. Christianity has now become a new *paideia* as opposed to the Greek idea of uniform culture in the Hellenic *paideia*, whose source is the divine *Logos*, the Word which creates the world. Christian PAIDEIA, unlike other concepts of paideia with human teachers, differs particularly in the concept of Jesus as the embodied divine Word – Logos.

The later times will assign a task to the Christian *paideia* to show a formative strength of its intellectual work – in particular in the intellectual and artistic domain. Only Cappadocian Fathers – Basil of Caesarea, Gregory of Nazianzus

---

33   W. Jaeger, *Early Christianity...*, *op. cit.*, p. 12. Acta Philippi c. 8 (3).

34   H. Chadwick, *Early Christian Thought and the Classical Tradition: Studies in Justin, Clement, and Origen*, repr. Clarendon Press, Oxford [Oxfordshire] 1984, p. 75 ff.

and Gregory of Nyssa – created a new culture for which they used both the art of rhetoric as well as philosophy.

In his work *Life of Moses* Gregory of Nyssa focuses on the narration of Moses' life as an example of virtuous life and also spiritual life,[35] through which Gregory answers the question what comprises perfect life, thus providing an interpretation of Christian spirituality, using an example of the man whom also Philo of Alexandria shows as a role model of perfection and greatness. It is in *Life of Moses* where we encounter Gregory's thought about eternity as a measure of virtue. God alone is the perfect virtue. A man is called to search for the good: 'Human perfection is probably characterised as desire to have ever fuller good.'[36] According to Gregory, every man is called to choose an image which he will model (although from the point of view of the Biblical story of creation, man is made in God's image). In this sense, everybody is a father to himself. Wise parents (i.e. true view of the image, 'foresighted thought') will of course equip a newborn child for the journey through the stream of the world with a basket made of various sticks, i.e. with education (PAIDEUSIS) in various disciplines. This is the way Gregory allegorically interprets the Biblical story of little Moses being put in a basket and allowed to float on the Nile. Also, the writing *On Perfection* includes a warning against stopping on the journey of increasing in virtue:

> Because the true perfection means never stopping in the growth toward the ever greater and never limiting perfection with any boundary.[37]

Gregory of Nyssa contributes to the concept of *paideia* here in particular by his emphasis on the eternal process of education – maturing as a journey to virtue and perfection – and Plato's idea of education as a movement toward perfection, to the highest virtue, to good, is also apparent here. If, however, virtue is eternal, then this way of *paideia* is also never ending and its purpose lies in searching, in PERIAGÓGÉ, conversion, in the very movement of the soul.

The concept of PAIDEIA has therefore acquired a broad semantic field in the way from Aeschylus to Gregory of Nyssa, in which the most important element for the practice of education which would want to draw on this concept is perhaps the reference to the orientation to the essence of life. This may be called, according to different concepts, generally virtue or, more specifically, goodness or God. At any rate, PAIDEIA is thus associated with that which represents the highest

---

35   This also corresponds with the name of the work according to the major manuscripts: *On Virtue or the Interpretation of the Life of Moses*. In the construction of the second part of Gregory's book we see 'an elaborate plan of spiritual life' – see L. Karfíková, *Řehoř z Nyssy: Boží a lidská nekonečnost*, Oikoymenh, Prague 1999, p. 201.

36   *Vita Moysis* I / GNO VII/1,5,2 ff.

37   GNO VIII/1,214,4 ff.

value for the given system. The second important characteristic of *paideia* is dynamism, continuity, variability and fundamental incompleteness.

Education retains this characteristic also in the thinking of other great figures of the philosophy of education, such as Saint Augustine, John Amos Comenius and, most recently the Czech philosopher Jan Patočka. For them, humanity is not a hereditary reality but rather a reality assigned to us as a task to be realised, therefore humanity is acquired as an option.

Paideia in the present day Europe

It is possible to derive by analysis from the current European Union documents concerning education that the highest values toward which education should be directed are: employability, high level of sustainable growth, self-realisation (the source of which is identified as creativity), social cohesion, and active citizenship (which includes, for example, capability of positive communication with those who come from different environments, sense of initiative and entrepreneurship, cultural and intercultural competence, promotion of democratic values, and respect for fundamental rights and the environment). It is obvious that these fundamental values of education define the civil focus of the school system – or, more generally, perception of the human task (as understood by the documents of the European Union) to become a quality (employed) citizen. Therefore, education is principally perceived as the education of a citizen, i.e. civic education.

We can see the source for this perception of education in the enlightenment of the 18th century, which was perhaps most strongly manifested in France when it comes to the school system.

The roots of education of citizens in France's state schools

From 1791 to 1792, Marquise de Condorcet wrote *Cinq Mémoires sur l'instruction publique* (*Five memoires on public instruction*), and has been considered the 'founder of citizenship' ever since. Condorcet set a number of objectives to which instruction should lead. For example, instruction should contribute to moral and spiritual progress of mankind and should

> [...] fill the political equality recognised by the *Declaration of the Rights Man and of the Citizen* with realistic content by providing everybody, regardless of the environment in which he was born, with an opportunity to develop all talent in its fullness.[38]

---

38   F. Furet, *Člověk romantismu a jeho svět*, Vyšehrad, Prague 2010, p. 133 (orig. F. Furet, *L'uomo romantico*, Laterza 1995).

For others, school instruction means the foundation of humanity or a chance to form a new generation.

Until then, the schools that had been initiated by Reformation or Counter--Reformation were designed to raise good Christians or to educate against the 'other' form of Christianity, but these objectives cannot be compared with the post-Revolution objectives.

Jean-Paul Rabaut Saint-Étienne was a Calvinist pastor. Shortly before his execution, he published in 1793 in a magazine called 'La Feuille villageoise' the Table des devoirs de l'homme et du citoyen (which is symmetrical to the Table de droits – Table of the Rights Man and of the Citizen). It is one of the founding texts of lay morality. The obligations listed here as inalienable are submission, kindness, righteousness and obedience of the laws.

Until the 19th century, a school was not yet 'school institution' in France; many times schools were established in improvised conditions, by an agreement between the teacher and a community of citizens; often it was 'funded' from donations or inheritance. The school was often in one of a rectory's rooms, in a teacher's house, in an attic, or in a stable. Although the 18th century brought along new knowledge in pedagogical theory, the practice was far behind: use of a switch, birch sticks and scourges were common. Specialised education for teachers was nonexistent. Teachers were trained as sub-teachers, working together with more experienced colleagues. Early as in this period, young people, parents and other adults went to school in evenings to expand their knowledge. A teacher had a prophylactic function: evening education courses for adults became in this period more popular than visiting cabarets.

It was often enough for parents when the children only could read (this made catechism instruction and observance of the mass easier); many parents did not require the more expensive instruction of writing and mathematics.

The French Revolution meant a significant material loss for schools: confiscation of church property; civil constitution of the clergy was enforced; church orders were dissolved; and many elementary schools were closed (on at some locations) for some time.

In 1870, when – after the defeat in the Franco-Prussian war – Louis Napoleon was captured and the Third Republic began. At that time, the 'divinisation of teacher' occurred in France; the work of a teacher was in the 'age of maturity'. Many school laws were written, yet because they were hindered by people's resistance and a lack of money, they therefore had little effect. The main change since the declaration of the Third Republic was free, obligatory and lay education, which became the subject of discussion.

The expression 'modern man' meant man mastering writing. This was true after the Reformation, as it was possible for a literate man to access the Bible – both the Reformation and Counter-Reformation, of course, agreed on this. The school institution became the heir of such sanctification of writing. The teacher was an apostle of civilisation.

After a survey of the republican school, it was revealed that at some places school was nonexistent or it was facing such difficulties that its survival was not certain. On the other hand, non-public school, which was attended by the highest number of pupils, was winning everywhere. This also meant victory for parents and local communities over the state. As opposed to schools having the immature values of the Revolution, a school of classical values, where reading, 'good manners' and religion were taught, was preferred. The most successful teachers were those who abandoned republican speeches to go back to catechism, mass songs and the role of sacristans. Future lawmakers and governments learned from this discovery that a school cannot be introduced if there is no support from the parents. This was also used in Austria-Hungary.

Objectives of schools in the 19th century included: literacy, enhancement of the morality and national cohesion, and maintenance of social order. Countries where the Industrial Revolution had started also had common pedagogical resources. The school regulations of the Prussian or Saxo-Weimar elementary schools were very similar to the statutes of French elementary schools of 1834; Greek and Italian school legislation were similar as well. In terms of education, France was a centre between the more advanced Northern and Eastern Europe and the relatively underdeveloped southern countries.

There was an intensive discussion that the teacher office is critical for the development of democratic ideas. According to the act of 1882, education is free, obligatory, neutral and secular.

Historically, the separation of the church and State in France occurred on 9 December 1905, resulting in the separation of the church and school as well. Elementary schools started teaching ethics and lay ethical education – or moral education, to be more specific. It represented, for example, the following topics: body, virtues, courage, kindness, benevolent activity, nobility, thriftiness, diligence, temperance and moderation, patience, honesty, righteousness, tolerance, conscience and patriotism. Special chapters were dedicated to the good characteristics of a woman, in particular, diligence, complaisance and thriftiness. Another way was the concept of *la morale* ('ethics', 'morality') as *la science des devoirs* ('science of duties'). It was divided into duties to others (family, friends, other people) and duties to self (care of the body – hygiene; character education – order, training, firm character, control of emotions, providing the mind with inspiration; strengthening of will – success and work, conscience and judgment, pride and modesty). What was very common was the transfer of lessons in the form of citations, e.g. using the notable figures Epictetus, Tacitus, Cicero, Seneca, Victor Hugo, Montaigne, Tocqueville, Rousseau, Romain Rolland and Pascal.

For decades, the study of great moral values was at the heart of the instruction in republican schools. This included humanistic foundation, appealing to reason, without looking for any religious support. For example, the meanings and values of courage, reasonability, decency, justice and thankfulness were taught. Lay morality or also lay catechism, as the sum of values was called, was also pictured as two columns, of which one consisted of the values – or, more precisely, valuable environments which needed to be taken care of: family – school – country; the second column consisted of society – revolution – rights of the people. It is obvious that there is a reference to the sources on which the world of values of the lay morality draws and from which it grows.[39]

Since 1968, ethical education (*la morale*) in France has been dropped as a result of the student rebellions. Moral education is disappearing because it is considered overly strict, overly anxious, overly bookish, overly dogmatic and overly simplifying: there is an abundance of criticism.

But after forty years – in 2008 – a few lines in support of ethical education appeared in official instructions. French president Nicolas Sarcozy himself promoted *la morale* again. The centre of his presidential election campaign was *l'identité, la morale* and *les valeurs* (identity, morality / ethics, and values). Discussions and debates have begun about ethical education, and they still persist. There are also new books for ethical education. They are to be used, for the time being, within the civic education (*l'instruction civique*), for example, which recommends new values which should be conveyed within ethics instruction: courage, responsibility, politeness, tolerance, justice and solidarity.[40]

Education for values in the system of European schools

The objectives of education today can be specifically analysed, for example, from the program of instruction of the subject of non-confessional ethics, which is taught in alternation with religion (which is taught confessionally) in the system of European schools (Schola Europaea; first established in 1953 for the children of members and officials of the institutions of the European Union[41]).

---

39 *Carnet de Morale*, Paris 2007; C. Hernandez, J. Gougaud, *La morale à l'école 1905–1950*, Berg International, Paris 2009; M. Jeury, J.-D. Baltassat, *Petite histoire de l'enseignement de la morale à l'école*, Robert Laffont, Paris 2000; *Les livres de Morale de nos grands-mères*, Archives & Culture, Paris 2006.

40 For example: H. Caudron, *Oser à nouveau enseigner la morale à l'école*, Hachette Education, Paris 2007; L. Loeffel (ed.), *École, morale laïque et citoyenneté aujourd'hui*, Presses Universitaires du Septentrion, Villeneuve d'Ascq 2009.

41 Official website of European schools available at: http://www.eursc.eu/.

Non-confessional ethics classes are therefore attended by all students who do not attend religion. The same structured selection of competencies which the students should gain – and which are used to grade the students in the subjects – is important for the concept of values which the school should develop.

In the subject of non-confessional ethics, the pedagogical domain should lead to discovery of positive behaviour and positive values; application of democratic principles and measures ensuring respect to the rights belonging to every living being; participation in humanitarian and environmental activities related to current events; realisation of the sense of belonging to communities in which the student lives an whose opinions he shares; discovery of the meaning of holidays, their rituals, and their symbolism; interest in traditions and beliefs of other communities and cultures; formation of personality through everything that makes life meaningful; the search for answers to existential questions with which man deals for his whole life.

The subject is based on four needs or wishes which affect the behaviour of every human being: the desire to be, to have, to do, and to say. The student should turn away from the primary egocentrism to ever more generous forms of behaviour toward people with which he comes in contact, then toward society in general, which leads to personality development. For problem situations, ever broader social groups are considered: house, street, class, then school, city, nature, up to society, Europe, world. It is obvious that it is based on the principles of the moral development of a personality as discovered by Kohlberg.

Examples of topics[42]: in the third year it is recommended to talk about the topics of protection of the nature but also own use of free time; in the fourth year students learn about the Convention on the Rights of the Child; and in the fifth year they learn about the principles of the Declaration of Human Rights. It is obvious that the texts are very difficult, but this corresponds with the critical reading capability which is developed by such method of instruction.

The below competencies are listed on the report card and the teacher grades them on a four-level scale:

– 1st year: positively integrates with the group, observes the surrounding world and starts asking questions, is able to recognise good and bad behaviour in stories;
– 2nd year: listens to others carefully and with respect, understands the rules of everyday life, listens to stories and compares them with real life situations;

---

42 More details in: Z. Svobodová, P. Jandejsek, H. Martinek, R. Milfait, *Důstojně a radostně: příspěvek k lidskoprávnímu, občanskému a etickému vzdělávání*, Z. Svobodová (ed.), Susa, Středokluky 2012; Z. Svobodová (ed.), *K etické výchově*, Karez, Prague 2011; Z. Svobodová, *Etická výchova jako cesta z omezené každodennosti*, 'Paideia: Philosophical E-Journal of Charles University' 2011, 8, 1, available at: http://userweb.pedf.cuni.cz/paideia/index.php?sid=2&lng=cs&lsn=10&jiid=24&jcid=189 (accessed: 17.08.2014).

- 3rd year: can identify with others, understands the reasons for respecting life, perceives the hidden meaning of stories, pictures and characters, understands the meaning of celebrations and traditions;
- 4th year: expresses opinions tolerantly and constructively, assess behaviour according to the accepted standards; understands how celebrations remind of the key moments within a community, starts thinking about the basic aspects of life;
- 5th year: acknowledges the right of everybody to free speech, conduct and conscience, analyses current events according to the accepted standards, analyses the deeper meaning of the prescribed text, accepts responsibility for his behaviour.

On the secondary level (from the 6th year of school attendance up to the graduation; 7 years in total) the objective of the subject of non-confessional ethics is to teach students to use an open discussion to search for complete and clear answers, while strictly adhering to the facts and rational thinking; it should also lead students to assume a personal, responsible attitude, to be self-sufficient and perceptive, and finally to help create a real moral code based on tolerance which includes the ability to shape oneself.

The contents of the subject are divided into two main directions: social development and personality development. Examples of the topics: authority, health and happiness, rights and obligations, maturation, right to be different, rational and critical, communication and exclusion, forms of communication, democracy and citizenship, freedom and responsibility, science, technology and ethics.

Conclusion

The above implies that, even today, education includes teaching of values which were discovered by philosophers as substantial as early as in the classical antiquity – may it be the finding of the right relationship to other people or own body and health. At the same time it is necessary to emphasise that many types of programs of secular schools now also include information on the major religions, their celebrations and rituals and also the values which are manifested in religious traditions. It is not possible, however, to overlook how the technical language of the basic documents of the European Union is shown also in the current document on the strategic framework of European cooperation in the area of education in which the education objective is defined by the vision of Europe as the most competitive and dynamic knowledge economy in the world. If the meaning of the term 'knowledge economy' was understood in the sense of 'house – *oikos*, which takes its responsibility for *paideia* seriously', if such important task of paideia was supported including openness to the values and traditions of religious systems, there is hope that man can develop in such a house toward the fullness of his humanity and will be able to co-form and further communicate this *paideia*.

From its foundations, the concept of *paideia* is conditional upon the twofold possibility of radical openness – openness of the educator – teacher and the person educated as well as their ability to listen dialogically to what makes the dialog possible at all. Therefore, an essential part of the professional training of educators and teachers is the learning of the basics of philosophy of education, i.e. philosophy which either is education at the same time (using the words from an antique source: philosophy which is the care of the soul), or which is no philosophy at all.

Bibliography

Aeschylus, *Seven Against Thebes*, Harvard University Press – William Heinemann, Cambridge – London 1926, available at: http://data.perseus.org/citations/urn:cts:greekLit:tlg0085.tlg004.perseus-grc1:1 (accessed: 25.10.2013).

Aristophanes, *Aristophanes Comoediae*, vol. 2, F.W. Hall, W.M. Geldart (eds.), Clarendon Press, Oxford 1907, available at: http://data.perseus.org/citations/urn:cts:greek Lit:tlg0019.tlg003.perseus-grc1:961 (accessed: 26.10.2013).

Aristotle's Ethica Nicomachea, J. Bywater (ed.), Clarendon Press, Oxford 1894, available at: http://data.perseus.org/citations/urn:cts:greekLit:tlg0086.tlg010.perseus-grc1:1104b (accessed: 30.10.2013).

Carnet de Morale, Paris 2007.

Caudron H., *Oser à nouveau enseigner la morale à l'école*, Hachette Education, Paris 2007.

Chadwick H., *Early Christian Thought and the Classical Tradition: Studies in Justin, Clement, and Origen*, repr. Clarendon Press, Oxford [Oxfordshire] 1984.

Cicero M. Tullius, *M. Tulli Ciceronis Rhetorica*, A.S. Wilkins (ed.), 1902, available at: http://data.perseus.org/texts/urn:cts:latinLit:phi0474.phi037.perseus-lat1 (accessed: 26.10.2013).

Dio Chrysostom, *Dionis Prusaensis quem vocant Chrysostomum quae exstant omnia*, vol 1–2, J. de Arnim (ed.), available at: http://data.perseus.org/citations/urn:cts:greek Lit:tlg0612.tlg001.perseus-grc1:4.29 (accessed: 28.10.2013).

Furet F., *Člověk romantismu a jeho svět*, Vyšehrad, Prague 2010.

Gellius A., *The Attic Nights of Aulus Gellius*, trans. J.C. Rolfe, William Heinemann, London 1927, available at: http://data.perseus.org/citations/urn:cts:latinLit:phi1254.phi001.perseus-lat1:13.17 (accessed: 27.10.2013).

Giannantoni, *Socratis et Socraticorum Reliquiae*, available at: http://ancientsource.daphnet.org/texts/Socratics/V-A,173 (accessed: 28.10.2013).

Hernandez C., Gougaud J., *La morale à l'école 1905–1950*, Berg International, Paris 2009.

http://www.eursc.eu/.

Jaeger W., *Early Christianity and Greek* Paideia, Belknap Press of Harvard University Press, Cambridge 1985.

Jaeger W., Paideia: *Die Formung des Griechischen Menschen*, Walter de Gruyter, Berlin 1959.

Jeury M., Baltassat J.-D., *Petite histoire de l'enseignement de la morale à l'école*, Robert Laffont, Paris 2000.

Karfíková L., *Řehoř z Nyssy: Boží a lidská nekonečnost*, Oikoymenh, Prague 1999.

Les livres de Morale de nos grands-mères, Archives & Culture, Paris 2006.

Loeffel L. (ed.), *École, morale laïque et citoyenneté aujourd'hui*, Presses Universitaires du Septentrion, Villeneuve d'Ascq 2009.

Marrou H.-I., *Histoire de l'éducation dans l'Antiquité*, Éd. du Seuil, Paris 1981.

Milko P., *Úvod do byzantské filosofie: se studií Michala Řoutila Na východ od Antiochie: řecké myšlení za hranicemi Byzance, 2.–8. století: syrská traduce*, P. Mervart, Červený Kostelec 2009.

Patočka J., *Péče o duši: [soubor statí a přednášek o postavení člověka ve světě a v dějinách] II*, I. Chvatík, P. Kouba (eds.), Oikoymenh, Prague 1999.

Patočka J., *Péče o duši III*, I. Chvatík, P. Kouba (eds.), Oikoymenh, Prague 2002.

Plato, *Platonis Opera*, J. Burnet (ed.), Oxford University Press, Oxford 1903, available at: http://data.perseus.org/citations/urn:cts:greekLit:tlg0059.tlg030.perseus-grc1: 7.514a (accessed: 29.10.2013).

Svobodová Z., *Etická výchova jako cesta z omezené každodennosti*, 'Paideia: Philosophical E-Journal of Charles University' 2011, 8, 1, available at: http://userweb.pedf. cuni.cz/paideia/index.php?sid=2&lng=cs&lsn=10&jiid=24&jcid=189 (accessed: 17.08.2014).

Svobodová Z. (ed.), *K etické výchově*, Karez, Prague 2011.

Svobodová Z., Jandejsek P., Martinek M., Milfait R., *Důstojně a radostně: příspěvek k lidskoprávnímu, občanskému a etickému vzdělávání*, Z. Svobodová (ed.), Susa, Středokluky 2012.

Xenophon, *Xenophontis opera omnia*, vol. 2, Clarendon Press, Oxford 1921 (repr. 1971), available at: http://data.perseus.org/citations/urn:cts:greekLit:tlg0032.tlg003.perseus- grc1:13.9 (accessed: 30.10.2013).

KATARZYNA WROŃSKA
Jagiellonian University
Cracow (Poland)

The Polish Family in View of the Idea of a Civil Society[1]

A separation and comparison of family and civil society spheres is neither an easy task nor a problem-free task. The family is described as the homestead, a habitat for human life and development, a place where one's own privacy is protected from the prying eyes of others and the interference of authority. Civil society, on the other hand, is seen as the sphere of attitudes and actions of citizens which extend beyond the confines of the four walls, and thus beyond the private zone, constituting the public sphere in the form of a network of associations, movements, groups and societies that are open for other participants, observers and critics, as well as politicians and authorities, to see and to assess. Nonetheless, it remains autonomous and independent in relation to the State. Despite the spheres being distinct, this text will consider their interdependencies stemming from the assumption that the level of social commitment is closely associated with none other than the family culture. Introducing this assumption into the analysis of Polish society, we are faced with a number of questions which are worth pondering. Firstly, to what extent is the idea of civil society a Polish reality, consolidated by experience, to which one may refer and relate rather than being an idea brought in from the outside, alien to indigenous thought and tradition? Secondly, if one assumes that it is necessary to learn how to be a citizen, and to practice this role, then how is the Polish family coping with this task? Thus, are family culture, behavioural models, attitudes, beliefs and values – which are drummed into Polish citizens and which characterise Polish society – conducive to the propagation of civil virtues? Furthermore, are they convergent? Do moral and social values cultivated within Polish families provide opportunities to furnish our children with

---

1 This is an amended version of the text published in Polish in 'Paedagogia Christiana' 2010, 2(26).

the social capital that will empower them to be active and responsible citizens? How able and willing are individuals to cross the boundaries of zones delineated by the interests and needs of the family, and to voluntarily enter into relations broader that those based on kinship? How important are public matters within Polish families? What is the effect of the components of family culture on the level of public trust in our society, and what are the reasons for the connection between Polish religiousness and attitudes lacking in public trust as well as the low levels of social and civil commitment? In what way and which entities are able to and should support families when taking into consideration their significant environmental variations and the divergence of cultivated traditions in the social/civil commitment of their members and, predominantly, the younger generation? How may one help invigorate the potential held in Polish families and how to make it up where it is lacking? What role may the Catholic Church assume in this scope?

This text attempts to answer, at least partially, the questions and problems raised above. Its primary purpose is to describe the state of the Polish family in terms of the development of civil solidarity, treating civic virtue (civil attitude) as a positive distinguishing feature of both individuals and the society, remembering the triple ideological heritage of citizenship (republican, liberal and socio-democratic). Despite the politicising of the concept of citizenship in Poland, perhaps constituting one of the causes stifling social involvement of Poles, the author will pay due care herein to treat it independently of the divisions as an idea symbolising individual and civil Self in a democratic society.

The idea of a civil society set in the Polish reality

Many researchers of civil society assume that the idea itself, the beginnings of which may be sought as far back as in the ancient political concepts of Aristotle and Cicero, developed most vigorously in the modern era, to dim slightly after Hegel and Marx halfway through the 19th century in Europe and then to reawaken there again in the 20th century. In Poland, as well as the other countries in Eastern Central Europe, the idea clearly made its presence felt in 1980 and then at the end of the 1980s, as caused by Soviet bloc societies breaking free of the communist system shackles by self-organisation and by civil mass initiatives. The upheaval of the multimillion 'Solidarity' movement was described in terms of a civil movement with significant public trust capital, bringing together various social groups and strata. Are we able to, aside from the 'Solidarity' movement in Poland, find and refer to other historic traces of the existence of civil tradition?

In my opinion, interwar Poland was an example of attitudes of social involvement and self-governance that were invigorated by the patriotic wave sweeping the country after independence was regained and the country returned to the political maps of Europe as an independent and sovereign Republic of Poland. This was preceded by an enduring, century-and-a-half period of dependence and denationalisation. Despite the oft-turbulent political moments, the interwar period stands for a time of social invigoration, reawakening of various traditions of cooperation, associating, neighbourly assistance, self-assistance and local self-governance. At the same time, it was the heyday of social thought, of various orientations, within the scope of social pedagogy significantly influenced by the works of Helena Radlińska and Stanisław Karpowicz, as well as progressive authors, scholars and activists such as Edward Abramowski, Stanisław Brzozowski, Janusz Korczak, Stefania Sempołowska, Jan Władysław Dawid, Izabela Moszczeńska or those creating the state-supporting civil trend like S. Czerwiński, Kazimierz Sośnicki and Zygmunt Mysłakowski.[2] Maria Ossowska's work from 1946 entitled *Wzór obywatela w ustroju demokratycznym* can undoubtedly be cited as a manifest of civil-democratic attitude and thought.

One would be hard pushed to call the earlier period of the Partitions conducive to the propagation of civil virtues, as it was more suitable for the practice of adaptive strategies. On the other hand, resistance to foreign domination gave socially active Poles a stimulant to combine their efforts to free themselves from the authoritarian foreign rule and to find or win areas of unobstructed activity. The most spectacular examples of such actions were the uprisings, national freedom fighting, which united people in common actions against the invaders. Each of the Partitions also constituted an arena for groups of opposing activists to spring up, getting together in the name of progress, proliferation of education, elimination of inequalities stemming from the remains of the feudal system still seen in the balance of social and economic powers. Activists included: Galician democrats, Warsaw's positivists, Poznań's constitutionals, and progressives from the Kingdom of Poland in the early 20th century.[3] One of the characteristics of civil society is its independence from the State, sometimes exhibiting itself in the act of civil unrest. Polish society had many an opportunities to 'practice' the act of countering the State/authority, less frequently as a force independent of the State; resistance constituted social forces. However, maybe there was another form in which the social spirit manifested itself?

After World War II, the reality of Polska Rzeczpospolita Ludowa (PRL – People's Republic of Poland) provided another opportunity to master the skills of, on the one hand, building adaptive structures, and on the other hand, resistance. Yet

---

2 See S. Wołoszyn, *Nauki o wychowaniu w Polsce w XX wieku*, Strzelec, Kielce 1998, pp. 155–162, or for a broader view, see A. Mencwel, *Etos lewicy. Esej o narodzinach kulturalizmu polskiego*, PIW, Warsaw 1990.

3 For a broader take see: M. Janowski, *Polska myśl liberalna do 1918 roku*, Znak – Fundacja imienia S. Batorego, Cracow – Warsaw 1998, pp. 257–281.

Poles were devoid of the opportunity to build bottom-up organisational struc-tures, voluntary associations and societies around freely chosen spheres of activ-ity. This was a time of civil mourning, lasting twice as long as the patriotic wave after 1918. It is no wonder then that it became more rooted and present in social attitudes and habits; as a way of life, it was recreated and presented to the next generation. The prewar generation of patriots and social activists did not have the opportunity to disseminate its ideals and wisdom among the postwar generation. Many thinkers and progressive activists, as long as they survived the nightmare of the war, were subject to repressions and persecutions by the authorities; many were forced to emigrate. A large part of the society learned how to resist based on internal emigration and passed this skill on to the next generation.

Generally speaking, the tradition of social movement in Polish history was most profoundly represented amongst leftists, socialist camp activists, predomi-nantly of Polska Partia Socjalistyczna (PPS – Polish Socialist Party), with repre-sentatives and followers of the liberal thought in second place. The republican inspiration was mainly focused on independence, as a civil community cannot fully develop outside of a political community, the State. If today we are able to speak of the weakness of Polish civil society, then we have to cite the historical context within which the Polish society and nation took shape amongst its roots. That which is conducive within the bounds of civilisation for the development of a civil community, namely unobstructed free market mechanisms, a predominant role of a wealth accumulating middle class, national sovereignty, representative governance at all levels, a system of constitutionally guaranteed laws, pluralism of the centres of thought and public opinion forming and religious tolerance, was in short supply for a long time in the Polish reality. Thus, in the first place, civil activity in Poland was not mainly conducted by the middle class but by the intel-ligentsia, Catholic activists, and even progressive nobility. Secondly, the common ties and responsibilities (including national) were emphasised just as strongly as individual rights. Thirdly, not only own social resources were relied upon but pri-marily the involvement of the State and its instruments (even those of the invad-ers) in the solution of the burning problems of backwardness, inequality, in the act of educating on and propagating universal ideas and rights. Fourthly, Polish soci-ety was quicker to get together and integrate when resisting foreigners, enemies, invaders and occupiers than it was to unite in the name of some positive idea, for something, hence the strength of the Polish bonding capital and the shortage of Polish uniting capital. With such an amalgamation of factors, the tendency dominant across Polish soil in the 19th century of instigating and strengthening patriotic forces primarily for nationalistic purposes (and, more precisely, national freedom) and civil purposes to a lesser extent comes as no surprise; as moral rationale and primacy are due to independence movements that unite the nation. Only then should civil initiatives be undertaken. The spirit of the times in the

19th century in Europe visibly oscillated towards the propagation of national or even nationalistic ideas (opposing citizenship). In a stable political system, patriotism and civic virtue may be mutually supporting attitudes[4]; however, Poland's historical context placed the moral preponderance of feelings and patriotic attitudes over Poles' civil commitments. In the 20th century, national ideas in Europe assumed a more dangerous shape of totalitarian national-socialist and communist ideologies, which turned out to be further obstacles to the development of civil societies. Countries subject to the rule of the people were affected by this problem to a larger extent due to the extensive period of societies being subject to the demobilising power of a totalitarian regime.

Nonetheless, social upheaval inspired by solidarity and the mobilisation of opposition forces in the 1980s and 1990s changed the face of Poland; citizens' actions turned out to be effective. Poland, in a peaceful manner, managed to break free from the communist system and began a new phase of establishing a democratic, self governing, free market country governed by the rule of law and protecting civil rights. The Ossowska Manifesto could once again be read by generations of fellow countrymen. Did the aforementioned upheaval forever break with our tradition of uniting in the fight against alien, enforced rule? Did it take place on the basis of indigenous inspirations or following models borrowed from the West? Did it set in motion the unity of people around the idea of social order, stabilisation and democracy? Twenty-five years have passed since the change of the political system; a new generation of Poles has come of age that does not remember the PRL reality. What are their attitudes as they enter adulthood? Have they acquired the necessary skills and desires to become active citizens? Has the generation that still remembers the times of the people's democracy changed its adaptive attitudes?

Family culture and the level of public trust

The questions above draw us back to the main thread of these deliberations: the family environment, as the place where the basic skills and attitudes to the world, other people, culture, market, politics and sacrum are attained. Among the values, norms and attitudes passed on, the family also creates its own frame of references with respect to involvement in public affairs and spheres of citizenship; as life practice, the family teaches household members to express themselves by types of activities that stem from the preferred worldview options. Certain trains

---

4   See e.g. E. Shils, *Co to jest społeczeństwo obywatelskie?*, [in:] *Europa i społeczeństwo obywatelskie. Rozmowy w Castel Gandolfo*, trans. B. Janicka *et al.*, Znak – Fundacja imienia S. Batorego, Cracow – Warsaw 1994, pp. 29–31.

of thought from this sphere of family existence and personal development, which until recently were to a large extent of interest only to family sociologists and pedagogists, were presented in the 1990s in a new perspective of relations and correlations with economic development and the economic standing of a country by F. Fukuyama in his work entitled *Zaufanie. Kapitał społeczny a droga do dobrobytu* (*Trust. The Social Virtues and the Creation of Prosperity*). As the author demonstrated, in the entirety of the preconditions for shaping social capital or a network of interpersonal relations and mutual cooperation instigated for the performance of common goals and improvement to the level of public trust,[5] an important role is played by inner family factors as well as the family status in the social structure. As such, Fukuyama was an inspiration for posing new questions and new research with reference to the family.

In places where we are dealing with family-oriented culture, i.e., a type of loyalty limited predominantly to a circle of relatives and an attitude of distrust with respect to others (strangers), in a free market setup, as Fukuyama demonstrates, a small-scale economy is dominant, based on small, family businesses, with a lack of openness to managerial staff from outside of the family circle.[6] An extreme form of familism takes on the shape of amoral familism, as described by E. Banfield and subsequently more extensively researched and confirmed by R. Putnam, characterised by the type of social and moral connections that are effective solely with respect to family members, whilst with respect to others: neighbours, local residents, members of the church community or society they remain in a distrustful relation and with no sense of responsibility for their fates.[7] A society with such culture is characterised by low public trust. It lacks social ties built on the basis of spontaneous, bottom-up initiatives. Loyalty and identification are limited to the family and to the State/nation, possibly the Church. As such, just as with a hierarchical society, patron-client relationships are dominant. Taking a closer look at such descriptions, one may notice that the elevated position of the family is a value in and of itself. In some contexts (historical and political), the family may be coupled with tendencies which are not conducive to development, or even stifle it. The self-defence and other functions of the family,[8] which for various reasons

---

5   See F. Fukuyama, *Zaufanie. Kapitał społeczny a droga do dobrobytu*, trans. from English A. and L. Śliwa, Polish Scientific Publishers PWN, Warsaw – Breslau 1997, pp. 13–23, *cf.* R. Putnam, *Samotna gra w kręgle. Upadek i odrodzenie wspólnot lokalnych w Stanach Zjednoczonych*, trans. from English P. Sadura, S. Szymański, WAiP, Warsaw 2008, pp. 33–42.

6   See F. Fukuyama, *Zaufanie...*, *op. cit.* pp. 36–47.

7   See E.C. Banfield, *The Moral Basis of a Backward Society*, Free Press, Glencoe, Ill. 1958, and for a broader view, see R. Putnam, *Demokracja w działaniu. Tradycje obywatelskie we współczesnych Włoszech*, trans. from English J. Szacki, Znak – Fundacja im. S. Batorego, Cracow – Warsaw 1995, pp. 208–225.

8   See A. Potocki, *Wychowanie religijne w polskich przemianach*, UKSW Press, Warsaw 2007, pp. 41–42.

it had to fulfil in the past, have been inscribed in its culture and the culture of the community; the culture which remains preserved, even though the external factors which have made an impact on it are long gone. Thus, it may be that in certain situations the family will appear as a suppressant of national transformations and the creation of an open society due to the type of behaviours and attitudes passes on from generation to generation that are characterised by distrust in relation to others, social apathy or even an attitude of anger towards the authorities.

For Fukuyama the dividing line between countries with low social capital versus countries with high social capital is the line running along or across familism. Is it correct to say then that pro-family attitudes do not go hand in hand with civil attitudes? Perhaps this would be a biased conclusion. As we are assuming that the family – on the scale of moral communities – is to fulfil a required role on account of building an environment for living and educating as well as supporting social cohesion and national identity. Thus, it would not be sensible to limit the family's role for the benefit of the development of networks of voluntary organisations and spontaneous social behaviours. The family as the guardian of moral and social virtues is the best guarantor of social and political order, economic growth and heydays of civil society. Without the family on board as the primary and principal model consistent with the rules of life, it would not be possible to instil moral virtues such as fairness, reliability, loyalty, moderation, diligence and responsibility, and social virtues such as solidarity, trust, tolerance and cooperation. The problem lies more with how to ensure that the family learns to apply this set of virtues in a broader social circle, and not only in its own close circle. The benefits that cooperation, solidarity and public trust bring to the lives of individuals and communities, including political and economic communities, have been recognised for a long time now. The classic interpretation is presented by A. de Tocqueville, who in citing the doctrine of enlightened self-interest, indicated the advantage of actions that take into account the interests of other individuals.[9] Fukuyama expresses this thought in words.

Law, agreement and economic rationalism are a solid but insufficient footing for post-industrial society prosperity and stability; they should be reinforced by a general approval for reciprocity of interests, moral duty, service to the society and trust – qualities rather based on habit than cold calculations, which in a contemporary society are a *sine qua non* condition for it to function'.[10] Both the liberal and republican methods for presenting arguments for social involvement and its consolidation in the moral culture of individuals and the society are evident in

---

9 And even in broadening the application of this doctrine to religious issues, see A. de Tocqueville, *O demokracji w Ameryce*, trans. from English B. Janicka, M. Król, Fundacja 'Aletheia', Warsaw 2005, pp. 500–504.

10 F. Fukuyama, *Zaufanie...*, op. cit., p. 21.

the two interpretations. Shifting now to the Polish backdrop, one may ask which of them more closely matches our native thought and practice. While it is difficult to judge, it seems that due to the significant effects and reach of the teachings of the Church, which are predominantly directed at the family, the republican set of values is more pronounced, referring to the duty to serve others, the common good, rather than the liberal with a category of interest or benefit stemming from cooperation with others. Both emphasise the significance of trust as a general attitude in relationships with others as conducive to dialogue and cooperation.

Trust and cooperation mutually support each other. Thus, in a society with a high participation culture, trusting others is still supported by a practice of common actions. Reciprocation standards do well and become established through habits proliferating across societies. The habits entice people to come together in associations, societies, meet in clubs, support groups, churches and other places natural for the given local community. Trust is mandatory for these types of places; as such, it is difficult to say if it is a result or cause for undertaking mutual initiatives. Putnam seems to present such a take on the matter in his research on the fates of American society, once very civil and today experiencing a crisis in involvement symbolised by the figure of a lone tenpin bowler. However, Polish reality is not similar to American society. We are definitely short of similar traditions of associations, crafting bottom-up initiatives, and mutual actions without looking around for suzerainty and authority. We know the historical context, which explains this phenomenon to a large extent and clarifies the source of the extensive resources of distrust, passed on from generation to generation and even today nurtured in many environments and families. In general, our children do not have the opportunity to see their parents as active members of the local community. If they are learning social involvement, the impulse is not originated by the family, but is primarily generated by educational institutions. Is it the lack of participation culture that causes low levels of public trust? Or instead, does the absence of trust bring about consequences in the form of social apathy? There is no simple answer to this question. In Poland's culture, both deficits simply fuel and strengthen each other. Even the last 25 years have not been free from new threats to the creation of a civil community.[11] My personal inclination is to favour the position to care for participation culture by various means, primarily with respect to the younger generation, which should translate into an improvement in public trust.

Polish families, in my opinion, constitute a rich stock of virtues, attitudes, habits and behaviours that have done well over the centuries in protecting the strength of the Polish nation. Today, this reservoir, strong on patriotism and

---

11   See P. Sztompka, *Trauma IV RP*, 'Europa. Tygodnik idei' 2007, 12, 155, pp. 12–13.

Catholicism[12] but also supported by other ideological traditions, should be able to excite civil Self in Polish society and invigorate it both as a civil community and as a solidarity-based society. The key to the above is – once again borrowing from Putnam's terminology – using various means to facilitate the crossing of the bonding capital threshold towards more openness to the virtues of bridging capital.[13] We require impulses which would nurse our tested communal ties – ties that integrate from the inside, provide a feeling of security and support the assurance of one's own identity – and at the same time would broaden our activity horizon by new, more extensive identities due to the perspective of cooperation and openness to others, of entering into relations which exhibit weaker bonds of loyalty but equally satisfying, bonds of loyalty that permit the attainment of various goals. In addition to the scope of the individual benefits stemming from bridging capital, we are also dealing with benefits for the entire society, which strengthened by a network of mutual relationships gains effective protection against the state's paternalism.

Both dimensions of social capital – bonding and bridging – are neither disjointed nor interchangeable. This is clearly seen using the family as an example. It would be difficult to imagine a functioning family without bonding capital. The primal trust has a symbolic role, described by E. Erikson;[14] it is born within a child in response to love, acceptance, care, reliability and parental responsibility, and constitutes a real building block for the construction of the future personality of the developing child. The next of kin, in giving themselves to the child, teach that trust and its *a priori* offering to others is possible. By ensuring compliance, consistency, continuity and repeatability of experiences, as well as delineating the sphere of prohibitions and permissions, allow for the child to find its feet in the world and to feel its reality. If strong bonding ties inside the family are optimal for the development of children,[15] the question arises concerning the possibility of its marriage with bridging capital and whether – if at all – this is in the interest of the family. It turns out that the answer is yes. Putnam documents this well through indicating large areas of social involvement opening up for the parents. These include activities oscillating around supporting or controlling educational institutions their children attend, increased interest in religious practices, again often motivated by the well-being of the children and an image of a functioning family as well as newly etched out social relationships between parents of the children who play or learn together. The social capital evident in the attitudes and behaviours of the parents (trusting others, participation in organisations, in

---

12 See *id.*, *Nie ufaj nikomu*, 'Gazeta Wyborcza', 1–2.12.2007, p. 20.
13 See R. Putnam, *Samotna gra w kręgle...*, *op. cit.*, pp. 40–42.
14 See E. Erikson, *Dzieciństwo i społeczeństwo*, trans. from English P. Hejmej, Rebis, Poznań 2000, pp. 257–261.
15 See R. Putnam, *Samotna gra w kręgle...*, *op. cit.*, p. 592.

the life of the parish, voluntary work, voting during elections, and informal social relationships with friends) turns out to be positively correlated with schooling as well as general developmental successes of their children.[16] However, this requires a social climate clearly supportive of such attitudes and behaviours. National economic and political stabilisation is clearly conducive both to the above and to effectively functioning public service institutions (public trust), respect by authorities at all levels for the citizen, institutions obeying the law, primacy of public reason (common good) in the actions of the ruling party and opposition, and related factors comprising the whole: a stable and just democracy. Otherwise, familism, in as much as it becomes a culturally enshrined social tendency in response to a general instability and changeability or uncertainty pertaining to the rules of a society, may even turn out to be the best possible solution from the point of view of the household members.

One will be able to speak of a change in mentality – which will possibly craft or reinstate the social network, trust and reciprocity standards – only when, apart from the changes in the individual approach to citizenship and social involvement in public institutions, remedial actions will appear. Due to the young age of democracy in Poland, this dimension – namely, the improvement of the structure of the state itself as well as the functions of governance from the local government level all the way to institutions of central authority – seems to be of key importance. The picture painted thus far would, however, be incomplete if at the current level of analysis references were not made to the role of the Catholic Church in awakening social awareness on the map of institutions having national reach. So far, little has been said about the role of the Church here. It does require a searching look due to the dominant position of the Catholic religion in the process of shaping the worldviews and attitudes of Poles. This in ensured by the weekly Sunday preaching in churches, which is actively made use of by half of the believers, the omnipresent catechesis in schools, as well as the presence of the voice of the Church in media and the public debate.

The Polish family and the Church

The trials which the Church has been subject to in the history of this nation, and for which, when it did represent the voice of the people, it was highly recognised, play an important role in the trust afforded to clergy in many circles of the society. Such an image became set in stone when assessing the contribution of the Church to the survival of the nation during the Partitions, then was further confirmed by the sacrifice during the two world wars. The people's democracy era,

---

16   See R. Putnam, *Samotna gra w kręgu...*, *op. cit.*, pp. 485–501.

more akin to us, is a period which is particularly vivid in the memory of Poles. The list of achievements starts with an avant-garde letter by Polish bishops to their German counterparts with the words 'we are sorry and ask for forgiveness' and is expanded upon by a message of spiritual contents in homilies, which took the load off and allowed for a somewhat easier experience of the difficulties of daily life characterised by shortages, dependence on the authorities and the omnipresence of Marxists ideology, supporting the spirit of a community contrary to the drab reality. Support for budding opposition movements was also the clergy's contribution, which took the form of providing shelter to opposition activists and organising events to help the repressed and their families. The fight with the Church, carried on by the system that had no social legitimacy, only served to strengthen this institution. Through the clergy's cooperation, it became possible to reach the faithful with appeals and the ideological messages of the secular opposition. Clergy also passed on the works of artists and news from the world of science, elaborated and presented within the confines of the church walls and often representing a point of view other than the religious. The culmination of the positive effect of the Church on the Polish postwar reality was Cardinal Karol Wojtyła becoming Pope. John Paul II gave Polish people's morale a boost during his pilgrimages to Poland, postulated a new style of Catholicism, supported the efforts of his countrymen to take over the running of the country peacefully and to create a democratic government, and supported our accession to the European Union. These and many other achievements of the Church lie at the foot of the socially established positive image of its contributions.

Today in the postmodern world, with open borders, the free flow of capital, ideas, a pluralisation of opinions and the secularisation of many aspects of life, most Poles maintain their relationship with the Church and its messages and faith. Christian thought, recently reinvigorated by the new style and message of Pope Francis, has been given the opportunity to continue to constitute an important source of meaningfulness, to be a source of answers to existential questions pertaining to a good and fulfilling life, as well as to build communities with others.[17] To an observer, parish communities are closely knit groups of participants of religious services who are united by the belief in one God. However, does that common belief interconnect them? Is it conducive to conscious participation? Does it become a source for the parish built up on the strength of mutual actions? An attentive observer will notice significant if not glaring shortages here: whereas the statistic for declaring faith and participation in services is high (even amongst teenagers), the percentage involvement of the faithful in parish life is at the same time terribly low. Religious sociologists admit that Polish religiousness

---

17 See J. Mariański, *Kościół katolicki w Polsce a życie społeczne. Studium socjologiczno-pastoralne*, Gaudium, Lublin 2005, pp. 252–263.

is manly characterised by rituality in cult practices satisfying individual (and not communal) religious needs.[18] Why is it that a common faith does not release positive energy to build bonds around other common goals? What are the reasons?

To begin with, we should delve into our difficult, suffering-marred history. The Church often stepped in to fulfil the role attributed to the state and secular institutions by protecting against the invader, occupier or regime, thus awakening the spirit of resistance in the name of grand ideas. Today, the Church sometimes still clings to that interpretation of a fight. But now it is against an enemy lurking at the gates of the modern world in the guise of the market and large capital that are blind to the needs of the poor and that reduce people to the level of consumers, the state as a soulless bureaucracy apparatus, or the media, cynical and feeding on cheap sensation, etc. The criticism of today's reality, devoid of references to God and preached from the pulpits, places many believers in a position of distrustfulness and withdrawal into the safe privacy of their homes, families. Families are thus far from the uncertain, invasive, godless world. This possibly keeps in a circle of exclusive religious communities that oppose many phenomena of modernity reminiscent of 'cultural ghettos' with the 'mental state of a bunker'.[19] Yet a hierarchical Church, which can find its feet well enough by itself in a world of global capital, fathoms its mechanisms for the good of its institution that serves for the endurance of the divine eternal truths. Such a strategy of teaching activity and entrepreneurship and not maintaining fear, distrust or even resentment can be applied equally well in our parishes. Whereas the opposition of the rich and the poor (similar to the broader category 'us' and 'them') is still a live source of antagonisms that has not been extinguished in the Church, the virtue of resourcefulness belongs to the ranks of virtual or suspicious virtues. A Catholic in Poland is associated with a friendly person who often exhibit the attitude of distrust and unwillingness at different levels of intensity that are not put out by the clergy and sometimes even fuelled and intended for the not-so-small group of 'enemies of the Church'.

Outside of the historical baggage weighing on today's state of apathy and withdrawal from the community life of the parish, I would indicate three other reasons of underdevelopment in Poland's Christian civil society.[20] Firstly, the inflexible structures of organisations and authority in the whole Church as a strictly hierarchical institution are often unyielding to any signs of democratisation. The dominance of the authoritarian style of running a parish by issuing orders, the

---

18 See J. Mariański, *Kościół katolicki w społeczeństwie obywatelskim. Refleksje socjologiczne*, Catholic University of Lublin Press, Lublin 1998, pp. 118, 138.

19 *Ibid.*, p. 142.

20 See J. Gowin, *Sześć tez na temat wolności i religii. Chrześcijanin i obywatel*, 'Europa. Tygodnik idei' 2008, 22(165), pp. 12–13.

lack or weakness of Ministry Parish Councils, and the predetermined roles for the particular 'states' in the life of a parish, including those for teenagers, are all examples of the institutional barriers put up by the Church. This is not conducive to bottom-up initiatives, meeting others on account of religious inspiration, or just because one wants to do something with others at a local church. Thus, the young meet outside of the Church, as this institution, which has extensive infrastructure (Catechesis rooms, church facilities), is scared of spontaneous teenager activity and is not forthcoming with any initiatives for enticing young people with new forms of organising free time. Instead, the Church remains within the safe, tried and tested patronising position as an agency used for the provision of individual and familial religious services. Secondly, transferring Catechesis to schools and making it a graded, scholastic subject. Apart from the measurable benefits, this decision also brought with it losses,[21] simply in distancing children and teenagers, constituting the groups most willing and susceptible to stimuli encouraging them to act with others from the parish, in which such actions might have been crafted. The result of such distancing has been the loss of mental, emotional and moral feelings of a bond with the parish. The young people, not being real subjects in the life of the local church, do not feel responsible. Thirdly, a lack of adequate social and philosophical knowledge in the moulding of new priests, accustoming them and teaching them to understand the ever-faster changes taking place in the life of modern societies and to understand the ideas voiced by secular elites who reach the social masses via media channels. This state of distrust, misunderstanding and nonacceptance of today's secular world results in the entire energy of the clergy focusing on criticism dressed up in a moralising tone and teaching the truths of the faith completely disjointed from the contested reality, in a perpetual void between 'heaven and earth'.[22] An invitation for cooperation at the parish from its stewards requires knowledge (at the least basic management, social communication, and social animation) and a dialogue with modernity and thus a change in attitude and more openness.

Just some of the causes described above that act in unison multiply the apathy effect. As such, the 'participation revolution' of the faithful still remains the Church's project in progress and perhaps remains in the pipelines of the majority of clergy. It is even more surprising that at the same time, the primary moral principle with which most Poles identify is the 'Love thy neighbour' commandment. The presence of 'participation oases' in honourable examples of parish life, and perhaps even more so from the missionary activity of some orders for the reactivation of the community centred on certain initiatives (in addition to those strictly religious, charitable, sporting, educational, artistic, recreational and civil)

---

21 For a broader perspective, see A. Potocki, *Wychowanie religijne...*, *op. cit.*, pp. 255–258.
22 *Ibid.*, pp. 258–272.

which await popularisation, do not change the diagnosis spelled out above. Such initiatives, whereas not addressed to entire families, still strengthen them, activating its particular members (children, teenagers, parents and grandparents).

'Modern' barriers to the development of local communities

All of the barriers to the development of a civil society in Poland discussed thus far, particular to our cultural context, should also be supplemented by risk factors, which run independently, but are related to the transformation of modern societies and may overlap with the previous. Following in the footsteps of Putnam, who investigated the reasons for the collapse of local communities in the United States over the last decades, the following phenomena may be mentioned: intensity of efforts associated with professional work and its preservation, or 'chasing after money', worry as to one's material standing, professional career of both parents, pressure of time, uncontrolled growth of cities (suburbanisation, including closed and monitored estates), commuting to work, popularisation of mass communication and entertainment, predominantly the television and the Internet, deteriorating (from generation to generation) residential, religious and organisational ties associated with a feeling of belonging to one's own surroundings, church and groups and organisations as a result of increased social mobility.[23] From our point of view, the author's statement on the insufficient presence of event the 'second civil generation' (for the United States, this pertains to those born in the 1920s and after who remember the times of World War II mobilising the populace to common action) in order to prevent a dispersion of social forces in the society seems particularly important. Rapidly occurring social changes in the second half of the 20th century meant that from generation to generation the ability to pass on the attitude of socialisation to children and grandchildren was lost. It is difficult not to compare this situation with post-war Poland, where the civil spirit of the prewar generation of Poles was rapidly if not violently, quashed by repression, creating a social void between the family and nation. Today, this space is starting to show signs of being cultivated, but it clearly can be seen, at the very least when compared with the United States, that this task cannot be confined to families, and perhaps it has come down to them to only a small degree. These, in the role of repository of virtues, constitute the best foundation for the creation of a civil society. Invigorating for social involvement is a task assigned to many entities, including the State, local authorities,[24] schools and other

---

23 See R. Putnam, *Samotna gra w kręgle...*, *op. cit.*, pp. 307–469.
24 See T. Talaczyński, *Samorząd uczniowski: raczej szansa niż kłopot*, 'Wychowawca' 2007, 11.

educational institutions,[25] NGO's, work places, academic centres, media and the Church. Again, following in the footsteps of Putnam, one can only repeat his just appeal to build a multi-pronged programme of 'social capitalists' with reference to all entities in the public life.[26] However, I would like to focus attention on and emphasise the role of one of these entities, whose effect on Polish families is still very significant, namely the Catholic Church. I consider that on account of the religious beliefs of most Polish families, without the contribution by the clergy to this task, and as such without the involvement of individual priests in the network of parishes[27] and monastic orders, the shaping of social virtues and awakening of the civil spirit in our society will remain shelved for a long time. It will just be an idea, possibly a niche form of spontaneous self-fulfilment for the few. All other valuable and needed attempts and efforts in this scope, starting with the state and ending with the media, may turn out essentially ineffective (as witnessed thus far) unless the Church joins the fray.

Conclusion: Parish as the community of communities

A parish brought to life by the activity of the faithful is at the moment just an idea, interestingly referred to by Catholic journalists as 'the community of communities'.[28] In my opinion, this key to building a civil society in Poland is in the hands of the clergy and active Catholic activists, without whom Polish familism with its cultivated distrust shall become the suppressant for positive social change. However, a change in conviction is necessary, namely that active parishioners do not constitute a burden for the Church; to the contrary, they are a benefit. Their involvement means enrichment of the substance Christian life and, what is more, that which is postulated in the fifth commandment of the Church ('You shall help to provide for the needs of the Church'). Putman's appeal to the American clergy, lay leaders, theologians and common believers stated:

> Let's bring forth new, pluralistic, socially responsible 'great awakening', so that in 2010 Americans were more involved than they are today, in that or the other spiritual community of meanings, at the same time trying to be more tolerant with respect to faith and practices of other Americans.[29]

---

25 See K. Wrońska, *Wartości obywatelskie w życiu szkoły*, 'Hejnał Oświatowy' 2008, 3(77), pp. 13–17.

26 See R. Putnam, *Samotna gra w kręgle...*, op. cit., pp. 653–674.

27 See J. Mariański, *Udział katolików świeckich w życiu parafii (założenia i rzeczywistość)*, Płocki Instytut Wydawniczy, Płock 2008, pp. 97–112.

28 See e.g. A. Potocki, *Jakiej potrzebujemy parafii?*, 'Teofil' 2008, 1(27), pp. 125–141.

29 R. Putnam, *Samotna gra w kręgle...*, op. cit., p. 665.

In Poland, a call for a broader opening of churches to its parishioners could take on the same form, so that they felt as lay brothers: the subject and not like today the object of the mission. To that end, an incentive is needed to craft small groups within parishes that would combine various forms of common interests. This would establish new horizontal bonds between people, not necessarily tightly bound to the Church, but drawn to it due to the openness and friendliness of the representatives of that environment. As the Dominican priest A. Potocki writes, whose reflection I would like to use as support, as one which fully reflects my point of view on the matter, a counterweight to the fossilisation of parish life,

> [...] one would like to see a democratic style – style which is in tune with the times and the Polish conditions, which corresponds well to the postulates of a civil society. It is a necessity, if we wish to move from a Church of the Clergy to a Church of the People of God.[30]

In the new structure, full of small groups, there would be a place for every parishioner as long as they wanted it. They would present an opportunity to fulfil oneself across various spheres of activity with others, in accordance with one's own preferences and to build a space for mutual trust, friendliness, cooperation and foundation of a civil community.

> Thanks to such skills – writes Potocki – the parish, without waiting for 'customers', who will either turn up or not, shall exist outside the sphere of the temple.[31]

It is here that the elites may be formed

> [...] able to cross the boundaries of the parish and knowing how to be present in public affairs. This is a new task for the parish: be the foundation for lay brothers acting around the world. Taking responsibility of its actions. Acting not under the protective umbrella of the Church, but nonetheless well rooted in it – and through none other than the parish.[32]

The new formula for the parish as a community of communities, and openness to bottom-up participation and activities of lay brothers (children, teenagers, parents and grandparents) present an opportunity for a wider social subjectification of our kinsmen and removing the barriers to more ways of building an open society without losing the foundation in the form of family assets.

---

30 A. Potocki, *Jakiej potrzebujemy parafii?*, op. cit., p. 136.
31 *Ibid.*, p. 140.
32 *Ibid.*, p. 141.

Bibliography

Banfield E.C., *The Moral Basis of a Backward Society*, Free Press, Glencoe, Ill. 1958.

Erikson E., *Dzieciństwo i społeczeństwo*, trans. from English P. Hejmej, Rebis, Poznań 2000.

Fukuyama F., *Zaufanie. Kapitał społeczny a droga do dobrobytu*, trans. from English A. and L. Śliwa, Polish Scientific Publishers PWN, Warsaw – Breslau 1997.

Gowin J., *Sześć tez na temat wolności i religii. Chrześcijanin i obywatel*, 'Europa. Tygodnik idei' 2008, 22(165).

Janowski M., *Polska myśl liberalna do 1918 roku*, Znak – Fundacja imienia S. Batorego, Cracow – Warsaw 1998.

Mariański J., *Kościół katolicki w Polsce a życie społeczne. Studium socjologiczno-pastoralne*, Gaudium, Lublin 2005.

Mariański J., *Kościół katolicki w społeczeństwie obywatelskim. Refleksje socjologiczne*, Catholic University of Lublin Press, Lublin 1998.

Mariański J., *Udział katolików świeckich w życiu parafii (założenia i rzeczywistość)*, Płocki Instytut Wydawniczy, Płock 2008.

Mencwel A., *Etos lewicy. Esej o narodzinach kulturalizmu polskiego*, PIW, Warsaw 1990.

Potocki A., *Jakiej potrzebujemy parafii?*, 'Teofil' 2008, 1(27).

Potocki A., *Wychowanie religijne w polskich przemianach*, UKSW Press, Warsaw 2007.

Putnam R., *Demokracja w działaniu. Tradycje obywatelskie we współczesnych Włoszech*, trans. from English J. Szacki, Znak – Fundacja imienia S. Batorego, Cracow – Warsaw 1995.

Putnam R., *Samotna gra w kręgle. Upadek i odrodzenie wspólnot lokalnych w Stanach Zjednoczonych*, trans. from English P. Sadura, S. Szymański, WAiP, Warsaw 2008.

Shils E., *Co to jest społeczeństwo obywatelskie?*, [in:] *Europa i społeczeństwo obywatelskie. Rozmowy w Castel Gandolfo*, trans. B. Janicka *et al.*, Znak – Fundacja imienia S. Batorego, Cracow – Warsaw 1994.

Sztompka P., *Nie ufaj nikomu*, 'Gazeta Wyborcza', 1–2.12.2007.

Sztompka P., *Trauma IV RP*, 'Europa. Tygodnik idei' 2007, 12(155).

Talaczyński T., *Samorząd uczniowski: raczej szansa niż kłopot*, 'Wychowawca' 2007, 11.

Tocqueville A. de, *O demokracji w Ameryce*, trans. from English B. Janicka, M. Król, Fundacja 'Aletheia', Warsaw 2005.

Wołoszyn S., *Nauki o wychowaniu w Polsce w XX wieku*, Strzelec, Kielce 1998.

Wrońska K., *Wartości obywatelskie w życiu szkoły*, 'Hejnał Oświatowy' 2008, 3(77).

Contributors

DARIUSZ GÓRA-SZOPIŃSKI – Ph.D., associate professor at the Faculty of Political Science and International Studies, Nicolaus Copernicus University in Toruń, Poland; political scientist. He is a member of Polish and American Political Science Associations, and a visiting Fulbright scholar in Washington, DC. He is the author of monographs: *Eglise catholique et transactions politiques* (2001), *Złoty środek. Kościół wobec współczesnych wizji państwa* (2007), and *Zakorzenianie wolności. myśl polityczna Michaela Novaka* (2013). His research interests focus on contemporary political thought and sociology of religion.

NAZILA ISGANDAROVA – D.Min. in pastoral counselling, marriage and family studies from Wilfrid Laurier University in Waterloo, Canada; Spiritual and Religious Care Coordinator at Ontario Multifaith Council and Spiritual Care Provider at the Centre for Addiction and Mental Health. She has authored several articles that appeared in different academic books and journals. She specialises in spiritual care and counselling. As an internationally published researcher, she focuses on Islamic thought and spirituality, counselling, spiritual and religious care in a healthcare setting, counselling in a multifaith context, and Muslim identity in the West. She has a strong desire and an awareness of the importance of, and willingness to be involved in educating the general public about Islamic spiritual care and counselling and diversity of Muslims.

TOSHIKO ITO – Ph.D., professor of pedagogy. Main publications: *Die Kategorie der Anschauung in der Pädagogik Pestalozzis. Theorie und Rezeption im Japan des 19. Jahrhunderts* (1995), *Übergänge und Kontinuität. Studien zur Rezeptionsgeschichte westlicher Pädagogik in Japan* (2007). Main research interests: Western and Japanese theories of education in correlation, history of ideas in education (especially Enlightenment and New Education), value education.

UTO J. MEIER – Th.D., professor of religious education at Catholic University of Eichstätt – Ingolstadt's Faculty of Religious Education and Ecclesiastical Educational Work in Eichstätt, Germany.

ANDRZEJ MURZYN – Ph.D., associate professor, director of the Department of History and Theory of Education in the Faculty of Ethnology and Sciences of Education of University of Silesia in Cieszyn. He is the founder and the editor-in-chief of a book series: *Filozofia i Pedagogika*, co-founder and co-editor of a book series *Dialog bez Granic* and co-founder and co-editor of a book series *Pedagogika i Sztuka*. Main works: *Simone de Beauvoir. Filozofia a płeć* (1999), *Filozofia edukacji u schyłku XX wieku* (2001), *Johann Friedrich Herbart i jego miejsce w kontekście pokantowskiej myśli idealistycznej* (2004), *Community college – humanizacja kulturowo-edukacyjnej przestrzeni* (2007), *Filozofia nauczania wychowującego J.F. Herbarta* (2010), *Wokół Kena Robinsona kreatywnego myślenia o edukacji* (2013). Areas of interest: dilemmas of contemporary philosophy of education, education for a civil society, contemporary British philosophy.

Mirosław Patalon – Ph.D., associate professor, he is the chair of the Faculty of Sociology and Social Work at Pomeranian University in Słupsk, Poland. His main research interest is the relation between theology and social work theory.

Eugeniusz Sakowicz – Ph.D., full professor, theologian, specialist in religious studies, encyclopaedist and lexicographer; head of the Department of the Pedagogy of Culture and Intercultural Education at the Faculty of Educational Sciences of Cardinal Stefan Wyszyński University in Warsaw, Poland; consultor of the Polish Episcopate's Council for Religious Dialogue and member of the Council's Committee for Dialogue with Non-Christian Religions. He is an author of more than 300 publications and over 1,600 entries and articles in encyclopaedias and dictionaries published by Polish Scientific Publishers PWN in Warsaw, in *Encyklopedia katolicka* (*The Catholic Encyclopaedia*) of John Paul II Catholic University of Lublin, and in other encyclopaedias. He has published numerous books. He specialises in intercultural and interreligious dialogue, education in the cultures and religions of the world, as well as comparative religion.

Dariusz Stępkowski – Ph.D., associate professor and head of the Department of the General Pedagogy in the Faculty of Educational Sciences of Cardinal Stefan Wyszyński University in Warsaw, Poland. Main publications: *Pedagogika ogólna i religia* (2010), *Wychowanie i kształcenie w systemach politycznych* (co-editor, 2012), *Bildung und Erziehung in politischen Systemen* (co-editor, 2012). Research interests: philosophy of education / general pedagogy, high school teaching theory, moral education.

Zuzana Svobodová – Ph.D., lecturer at Charles University, Prague, Third Faculty of Medicine, Department of Ethics; at the University of South Bohemia in České Budějovice, Faculty of Theology; and at the Department of Theology and Philosophy at the Jabok College of Social Pedagogy and Theology, Prague, Czech Republic. She deals with the philosophy of education, ethics, the history of education, and studies relationships of religious and cultural erudition.

Mariusz Sztaba – Ph.D., The John Paul II Catholic University of Lublin, Institute of Pedagogy, Department of Social Pedagogy. Fields of activity: social education, education process social values, John Paul II and Benedict XVI social educational thought, Christian educational theory and practice inspiration.

Ewa Teodorowicz-Hellman – Ph.D., professor of Polish philology at Department of Slavic Languages and Literatures, Stockholm University. Selected books: *Svensk--polska litterära möten* (1997), *'Pan Tadeusz' w szwedzkich przekładach* (2001); co-author of: *Polonika w bibliotece katedralnej w Strängnäs* (2011), *Między językami, kulturami, literaturami* (2013), *A Unique Polish Collection from the Skokloster Castle Library* (2011). Editor of series *Stockholm Slavic Papers*. Author of many texts in scientific journals and joint publications.

Katarzyna Wrońska – Ph.D., habilitated adjunct academic in the Institute of Education, Faculty of Philosophy, Jagiellonian University in Cracow, Poland. Publications: *Osoba i wychowanie. Wokół personalistycznej filozofii wychowania Karola Wojtyły – Jana Pawła II* (2000), *Pedagogika klasycznego liberalizmu w dwugłosie: John Locke i John Stuart Mill* (2012). Research interests: philosophy of education, history of educational thought, liberal education, civic education, moral education, culture education.

www.ingramcontent.com/pod-product-compliance
Lightning Source LLC
Chambersburg PA
CBHW072127270326
41931CB00010B/1698